Care Act
2014

by the same author

Safeguarding Adults and the Law
ISBN 978 1 84905 300 6
eISBN 978 0 85700 626 4

How We Treat the Sick
Neglect and Abuse in Our Health Services
ISBN 978 1 84905 160 6
eISBN 978 0 85700 355 3

Quick Guide to Community Care Practice and the Law
ISBN 978 1 84905 083 8
eISBN 978 0 85700 373 7

Community Care Practice and the Law
Fourth Edition
ISBN 978 1 84310 691 3
eISBN 978 1 84642 859 3

Betraying the NHS
Health Abandoned
ISBN 978 1 84310 482 7
eISBN 978 1 84642 569 1

Care Act 2014

An A-Z of Law and Practice

Michael Mandelstam

Jessica Kingsley *Publishers*
London and Philadelphia

First published in 2017
by Jessica Kingsley Publishers
73 Collier Street
London N1 9BE, UK
and
400 Market Street, Suite 400
Philadelphia, PA 19106, USA

www.jkp.com

Library of Congress Cataloging in Publication Data
A CIP catalog record for this book is available from the Library of Congress

British Library Cataloguing in Publication Data
A CIP catalogue record for this book is available from the British Library

ISBN 978 1 84905 559 8
eISBN 978 0 85700 991 3

Printed and bound in Great Britain

MIX
Paper from
responsible sources
FSC® C013604

I would like to thank Jessica Kingsley for all her support, encouragement and patience, together with Alexandra Holmes and her colleagues at JKP for their efficiency, courtesy and tolerance.

Disclaimer

In a book of this nature and complexity, there are likely to be mistakes. These are down to the author, who would be grateful for observations or comments by email (michael@mandelstam.co.uk). It should be noted that the law is constantly evolving through additional regulations and guidance and interpretation by the law courts. The book is up to date to early March 2017.

Contents

Introduction

Primarily, this book explains and analyses concisely how the Care Act 2014 underpins the provision of adult social care in England. Adult social care is, in law, distinct from health care, which comes under the National Health Service Act 2006. However, social care and health care are intertwined in real life. People need both. Secondarily, therefore, the book considers selected aspects of health care, underpinned by the NHS Act 2006.

Scope of the book

The Care Act 2014 applies to social care in England. And to adults only, except when a child, or a young carer, is approaching the age of 18. Likewise, the NHS Act 2006 applies to England only. The book notes, in passing, comparable legal provisions for social care and health care in Wales, Scotland and Northern Ireland.

Approach of the book

They say the best is sometimes the enemy of the good. With this in mind, the book is selective, striking a balance between brevity and length. The many references point the reader to more detail.

Complexity of the Care Act 2014

The Care Act simplifies adult social care law but is not straightforward. The Act itself runs to 167 pages, the regulations to over 100 pages and the statutory guidance exceeds 500 pages. The rules are by no means intuitively easy to understand – either on their legal face, or in their practical application.

Complexity of NHS legislation

The NHS Act 2006 comes in, currently, at 711 pages. The Health and Social Care Act 2012, which amended the 2006 Act, is 728 pages in length, not to mention all the subsidiary regulations and extensive guidance applying to the NHS.

Balancing accessibility, length and detail

Such volume and complexity of legislation are arguably not healthy. The original NHS Act 1946, one of the great pillars of the welfare state, required a mere 93 pages. Hence this book's attempt to make this legislation accessible, whilst providing sufficient substance.

Legal cases and ombudsman investigations

Reference is made to recent case law – but also to older case law, where this is, or is likely to be, relevant to an understanding of the Care Act. The relevance of previous case law is at least twofold. First, some of the Care Act wording is very similar, or identical, to that of previous legislation. Second, some of the case law is essentially decided on common law principles of fair and lawful decision-making (the courts) – or of good administration (the local ombudsman and health service ombudsman). These principles remain constant, whatever the legislation.

Third, a significant number of local government ombudsman cases has been included since (a) these are a useful litmus test of what is going on under the Care Act, and (b) to date, legal cases heard under the Care Act have been few. Recommendations by the ombudsman, in relation to maladministration causing injustice (or failure in service), are not legal judgements and do not establish legal precedent. Nonetheless, a complaint to the ombudsman can be an effective route for remedying faulty decision-making under the Care Act.

Care Act: positives and pitfalls

In April 2015, the Care Act replaced a large amount of piecemeal adult social care legislation. The earliest Act dated back to 1948.[1] Few knew what all this legislation was, fewer still all its content – and perhaps none how it all fitted together.

Positive notes

The Care Act has unified adult social care legislation. It contains what many would regard as principles and rules relating to good practice – such as people's well-being, outcomes people want to achieve, prevention, integration of services, etc.

Cautionary notes

There are, however, cautionary notes to be sounded:

- **Increasing demand but limited resources**. The Care Act boasts various ambitious and aspirational duties, both general and specific. Yet local authorities are short of resources at a time of growing social care need.

- **Bricks from straw**. The mismatch between ambitious legislation and resources is nothing new. In 1988, the Griffiths report laid the foundation for law reform and the NHS and Community Care Act 1990, predecessor to the Care Act. It noted that many local authorities felt that 'the Israelites faced with the requirement to make bricks without straw had a comparatively routine and possible task' – compared to delivering adult social care. It warned that it would not 'be acceptable…to allow ambitious policies to be embarked upon without the appropriate funds'.[2]

---

1   Repealed legislation includes: ss.21 and 29 of the National Assistance Act 1948, s.45 of the Health Services and Public Health Act 1968, s.2 of the Chronically Sick and Disabled Persons Act 1970 (as it applies to adults, s.47 of the NHS and Community Care Act 1990 (for the most part), schedule 20 of the NHS Act 2006, the Carers (Recognition and Services) Act 1995, the Carers and Disabled Children Act 2000, the Carers (Equal Opportunities) Act 2004, s.21 of the Health and Social Services and Social Security Adjudications Act 1983, the Community Care B (Delayed Discharges) Act 2003.

2   Griffiths, R. *Community care: Agenda for action, a report to the Secretary of State for Social Services by Sir Roy Griffiths*. London: HMSO, 1988, pp.iii, ix.

- **Noble aspiration and fine words**. The Griffiths report's warning was prescient. Nearly ten years later, in 1997, the House of Lords heard a major legal case in which battle lines were drawn between people's needs and the resources available to meet them. Lord Lloyd noted that the local authority – Gloucestershire County Council – was in an 'impossible position; truly impossible, because even if the Council wished to raise the money themselves to meet the need by increasing council tax, they would be unable to do so by reason of the government-imposed rate capping'. It was the government's departure from its 'fine words' in the community care White Paper that had brought about the situation. The 'passing of the Chronically Sick and Disabled Persons 1970 Act was a noble aspiration. Having willed the end, Parliament must be asked to provide the means.'[1]

- **All about money**. As a judge put it, much more recently, in a children's case, it 'is, inevitably, money. Making financial provision for children being looked after by local authorities under the Children Act 1989 (the Act) is expensive. Not surprisingly, local authorities are keen to trim their obligations to the minimum possible.'[2] As for children, so for adults.

Two main planks of the Care Act

Given the mismatch between the Care Act's apparent aspirations, the resources available and the degree of need, two things remain prominent when one steps back far enough from the legislation. First is the emphasis on prevention. Second is the focus on, and entitlement of, informal carers. These two planks represent, for both central and local government, a way of making limited resources go further.

It is no accident that the Health Secretary has stated that families need to care for each other more, and lamented the fact that we live in England (with merely 16% of inter-generational households), compared to Italy (with 39%).[3] However, under the Care Act, a carer must be able and willing to provide the care, before that care can legally be relied upon. There is not, currently in English law, the equivalent of the old 'liable relatives' rule under

1   *R v Gloucestershire County Council, ex p Barry* [1997] 2 All ER 1, House of Lords.

2   *R(SA) v A Local Authority* [2011] EWCA Civ 1303, para 1.

3   Wright, O. 'Jeremy Hunt calls for national debate about caring for the elderly.' *The Independent*, 1 July 2015.

section 42 of the original National Assistance Act 1948 and, before that, in section 14 of the Poor Law Act 1930.

Shortcuts and escape routes

Place enough pressure on local authorities (or the NHS), with too few resources to cope, and exploration of shortcuts and escape routes is inevitable. Something akin to a law of physics, so to speak. Under the Care Act these attempted escape routes or shortcuts will be many and various. Some will be clearly lawful, others equally clearly not. Others still will sail so close to the wind that, until or unless examined by a court, their lawfulness or otherwise will be unknown: they will occupy a legal no-man's land.

The following are some of the obvious escape routes to saving expenditure envisaged by the Care Act and the guidance, and thus, in principle at least, likely to be lawful if applied carefully:

- **universal services**: diverting people to greater use of 'universal' (open access) and preventative services in the community

- **proportionate assessments**: providing more 'proportionate' assessments requiring less staff input (e.g. telephone assessments or self-assessments)

- **qualified staff**: less reliance on qualified staff (e.g. social workers or occupational therapists)

- **eligibility**: scrutinising eligibility decisions to reduce the number of people eligible (and so reduce expenditure)

- **bare minimum of provision**: attempting to meet eligible needs 'just about' adequately – no more – though still consistent with human rights

- **carers**: greater reliance on informal carers (family and friends) to look after people – and providing those carers with just sufficient support to keep them going in their caring role.

However, reckless or excessive pursuit of these escape routes and shortcuts risks unlawfulness or maladministration. For instance:

- **universal services, wishful thinking**: when local authorities indulge in wishful thinking and pretend that people's eligible needs are going to be met by universal, preventative services which either do not exist or have insufficient capacity

- **proportionate assessments: screening people out**: when local authorities fail to give people adequate and lawful assessments, wrongly 'screen' them out from assessment (and services) – or force people to do a self-assessment (or go without), contrary to Care Act rules

- **too few qualified staff**: when local authorities rely excessively on non-qualified staff who are not competent to identify and to assess more complex needs

- **eligibility misapplied**: when local authorities fail to apply the legal eligibility criteria to their full extent, or more actively alter or mutilate them

- **reviews**: misuse of reviews to reduce or remove people's care and support

- **panels**: when local authorities make excessive use of panels, causing unacceptable delays in both care and support plans and personal budgets – sometimes meaning that people's needs are not being met either adequately or at all

- **bare minimum of provision – inadequate personal budgets**: when local authorities allocate individual personal budgets incapable of meeting assessed, eligible needs

- **unlawful reviews**: using reviews to reduce people's care and support arbitrarily, without following Care Act rules

- **care homes and topping up**: when local authorities continue to misapply – as some have done since 1992 – the rules about choosing a care home and demanding 'top-up' fees from families

- **carers not being supported**: when local authorities fail to apply the rules about carers, in terms of their ability and willingness to care, assessments, identification of need and use of arbitrarily fixed personal budgets.[1]

Some of the consequences of pushing such approaches too far will create not just legal risk for local authorities but also practical risks, including potentially poor care and neglect – always assuming people receive any care

---

1   For which there is already evidence: Bennett, B. *Care Act for carers one year on: Lessons learned, next steps*. London: Carers Trust, 2016.

at all, not just in care homes but in people's own homes – where such care, or its absence, can be truly out of sight and mind.[1]

Care Act: main points

The following represent the key parts of the Care Act covering adult social care, roughly in order as set out in the Act, with highlighted words representing entries in the main text of this book.

- **Well-being**: definition; and its promotion

- **Prevention**: preventative services for adults and carers

- **Advice and information**

- **Integration**: of adult social care with health care

- **Market shaping**: of the local social care market

- **Cooperation**: with other statutory bodies

- **Assessment**: duty to assess adults and carers, and refusal of assessment

- **Eligibility**: make eligibility decisions, giving rise to duty, eligibility criteria

- **Charging**: power but no duty to means test people, subject to exceptions

- **Divide between social care and health care**

- **Divide between social care and housing**

- **Care and support (or support) plans**

- **Personal budgets**

- **Direct payments**

- **Care cap**: rules about limits to paying for care (deferred until at least 2020)

- **Ordinary residence**: rules

- **Continuity of social care**: person moving from one local authority to another

---

1   Alzheimer's Society *Shocking reality of dementia homecare hidden behind closed doors* (survey of 1220 people with dementia), November 2016. Available at www.alzheimers.org.uk/site/scripts/news_article.php?newsID=2694, accessed on 24 November 2016.

- **Choice of accommodation** and paying extra (topping up)

- **Deferred payments**: of care home fees

- **Enquiries into abuse or neglect** (safeguarding)

- **Safeguarding adults boards**: duty of local authority to establish such a board

- **Safeguarding adults reviews**: reviews into abuse or neglect suffered by individuals

- **Business failure**: meeting people's needs if a care provider fails, and the Care Quality Commission's oversight of the market

- **Advocacy**: independent advocacy for people struggling to understand and without family or friends to help the person

- **Appeals system** (deferred until at least 2020)

- **Prisons**: meeting social care needs of prisoners and those in bail and probation hostels

- **Hospital discharge**: rules about hospital discharge from acute beds

- **Delegation of functions** to other organisations.

The 'care cap' system and the appeals procedure have both been deferred until at least 2020. The detail remains unknown (they will be subject to regulations not yet issued). Therefore, the book does not discuss these, other than in passing.

Care Act 2014: other provisions not related to social care

The Care Act contains other provisions not specific to adult social care. These are not covered in this book, but they include:

- duty of candour for health and social care providers (being honest with people when something goes wrong)

- criminal offence for the NHS if it provides false or misleading information of certain types

- provisions affecting the Care Quality Commission

- health education

- health research.

NHS Act 2006: main points

The main points concerning the NHS outlined in this book include:

- **National Health Service**: legal basis for health care provision generally, and the implications in terms of duties and entitlements, including direct payments, commissioning responsibilities and rules about overseas visitors

- **continuing health care**: funded and arranged solely by the NHS in hospitals, care homes and people's own homes

- **integration**: implications of integration of health and social care.

Other relevant legislation

The Care Act 2014 and the NHS Act 2006 do not sit in isolation. Other laws are sometimes relevant to decisions made under both Acts. It is beyond the scope of this book to cover these, although some are referred to. The core legal framework relevant to social care and health care includes the following:

- **Care Act 2014** (adult social care)

- **Children Act 1989** (children's social care)

- **Chronically Sick and Disabled Persons Act 1970** (children's social care)

- **Children and Families Act 2014** (special education including education, health and care plans, sometimes up to the age of 25)

- **National Health Service Act 2006** (health care)

- **Housing Grants, Construction and Regeneration Act 1996** (home adaptations: disabled facilities grants)

- **Health and Social Care Act (Regulated Activities) Regulations 2014** (regulatory legislation, meant to be enforced by the Care Quality Commission)

- **Mental Capacity Act 2005**

- **Inherent jurisdiction of the High Court** (residual power of court to intervene in some circumstances to protect vulnerable adults)

- **Mental Health Act 1983**

- **Human Rights Act 1998 and European Convention on Human Rights**

- **Equality Act 2010** (discrimination)

- **Health and Safety at Work Act 1974** (and derivative regulations, including, for example, the Manual Handling Operations Regulations 1992)

- **Common law of negligence** (common law duty of care and potential liability for harm)

- **Data Protection Act 1998** (access to, and protection of, personal information)

- **Freedom of Information Act 2000** (public bodies only: access to non-personal information, or information about third parties).

A–Z List: note on terminology

Carer: signifies an informal carer, as opposed to a paid care worker.

LGO (footnotes): this stands for: 'Local Government Ombudsman *Report (or Statement) on a complaint against…*'

Statutory guidance (footnotes): this stands for: 'Department of Health *Care and support statutory guidance.* London: DH, 2016' (including updates to December 2016).

A–Z List

A

Abuse, see Neglect and abuse

Adaptations, see Home adaptations

Adult protection, see Safeguarding and Neglect and abuse

Advice and information

The terms *advice* and *information* feature significantly in the Care Act.

ADVICE AND INFORMATION: GENERAL DUTY. Section 4 of the Care Act places a duty on the local authority to establish and maintain an information and advice service. This must cover, in particular, how the care and support (and support for carers) system works, how to access independent financial advice and how to raise concerns about people's well-being and safety.

It is a general duty owed to the local population rather than to each individual person. This would probably make the duty – important though it is – difficult to enforce as long as the authority is doing at least something – roughly along the lines of what the statutory guidance states.[1] Even so, the local ombudsman has referred to this general duty in a finding of maladministration

---

1   Statutory guidance, 2016, Chapter 3.

when a local authority failed to give information to a person's attorney about choosing and paying for a care home.[1]

This duty contrasts with more specific duties to provide advice and information in connection with individual assessment (see below). A failure to provide it on an individual basis could give rise to a finding of maladministration – for example, poor advice about benefits[2] or failure to tell a person about the possibility of home adaptations to meet their needs.[3]

ADVICE AND INFORMATION: SPECIFIC WAY OF MEETING NEED. Under section 8, advice and information are listed as one way of meeting the assessed needs of an adult or a carer.

ADVICE AND INFORMATION: NON-ELIGIBILITY. If an adult is assessed as not having an eligible need, the local authority must provide written advice and information to the person about how to meet, reduce, prevent or delay need. This is under section 13 of the Act.

ADVICE AND INFORMATION: ELIGIBILITY. Under section 25, in case of eligibility, a person's care and support plan must contain advice and information about meeting, preventing, delaying and reducing needs – likewise, a carer's support plan.

Advocacy

The Care Act places a duty on local authorities to appoint independent advocates, if certain conditions are met. The two conditions are that the person would struggle to understand things like assessment, care planning, review and safeguarding – *and* does not have an appropriate family member

---

1   LGO, *Dudley Metropolitan Borough Council*, 2016 (15 010 311), paras 7–8, 54–55.

2   LGO, *East Sussex County Council*, 1995 (93/A/3738).

3   LGO, *Leicester City Council and Leicestershire County Council*, 1992 (91/B/0254 and 91/B/0380).

or friend to represent and support them. These independent advocacy rules under the Care Act, summarised below, are distinct from advocacy rules under other legislation.

ADVOCACY: CARE ACT FUNCTIONS COVERED BY INDEPENDENT ADVOCACY. Section 67 of the Care Act covers the following:

- a needs assessment

- a carer's assessment

- preparing a care and support plan

- preparing a support plan

- revising a care and support plan

- revising a support plan

- carrying out a child's needs assessment

- carrying out a child's carer's assessment

- carrying out a young carer's assessment.

Section 68 covers safeguarding enquiries taking place under section 42 of the Act – or safeguarding adults reviews, conducted by safeguarding adults boards, under section 44 of the Act. The purpose of an independent advocate, under both sections 67 and 68, is to facilitate the individual's involvement in the relevant process, through representation and support.

ADVOCACY: FIRST CONDITION, SUBSTANTIAL DIFFICULTY IN UNDERSTANDING. The local authority must consider that, were an independent advocate not available, the person would experience substantial difficulty in doing any one of the following:

- understanding the relevant information

- retaining that information

- using or weighing that information as part of the process of being involved

- communicating the individual's views, wishes or feelings (whether by talking, using sign language or any other means).[1]

These four abilities are based on section 3 of the Mental Capacity Act 2005. However, that Act is concerned with an *inability* to do any of these, whereas the Care Act refers instead to *substantial difficulty*, therefore encompassing lack of mental capacity but extending more widely – namely, to those with mental capacity but nonetheless experiencing substantial difficulty, for whatever reason.

Guidance gives examples of why substantial difficulty might arise: dementia, learning disabilities, brain injury, mental ill health, somebody with Asperger's syndrome, a confused older person, a person who is nearing the end of their life and disengaged from the process.[2]

In terms of carers' assessments, it could be relevant for local authorities to consider also, for instance, exhaustion, sleep deprivation, pain and depression – all of which might prevent the carer engaging in, and understanding, an assessment.

ADVOCACY: SECOND CONDITION, FAMILY MEMBER OR FRIEND AVAILABLE. The duty to appoint an independent advocate does not arise if the local authority is satisfied that there is instead somebody else appropriate to represent and support the person, so as to facilitate the latter's involvement. The appropriate person cannot be anybody who is providing care and support for the person, either professionally or for payment.[3] Therefore, the appropriate person would need typically to be a family member or friend.

ADVOCACY: CONSENT. A family member or friend cannot in any event be appropriate to represent and support the person, unless the person consents. Or, if the person lacks capacity to take this decision, the local authority

---

1   Care Act 2014, ss.67, 68.

2   Statutory guidance, 2016, para 7.16.

3   Care Act 2014, ss.67, 68.

believes it is in their best interests that the family member fulfil that role.[1] In contrast, the appointment of an independent advocate does not rely on the person's consent. However, were such consent withheld, and non-engagement or non-cooperation to be the result, the advocate's effectiveness would be reduced.

ADVOCACY: INAPPROPRIATENESS OF FAMILY MEMBER OR FRIEND. The local authority might sometimes not be satisfied about the appropriateness of a family member or friend – for instance, if the family member or friend is opposed or impervious to what the person wants, or because there is evidence of some other clear conflict of interest.[2]

ADVOCACY: APPOINTMENT OF ADVOCATE DESPITE APPROPRIATE FAMILY MEMBER OR FRIEND. There are exceptions to the rule about not appointing an advocate, if there is an appropriate family member or friend to hand. In the following circumstances, an advocate must anyway be appointed:

- **Deprivation of liberty**: the person might be deprived of their liberty (through a decision taken under the Mental Capacity Act 2005)

- **Lacking capacity and care or hospital placement**: the person may be placed by the NHS in a hospital for more than four weeks, or a care home for more than eight – and the local authority believes it is in the person's best interests that an advocate be appointed

- **Disagreement**: there is disagreement on something 'material', between the local authority and the family member or friend, and both agree that it would be in the person's best interests for an advocate to be appointed.[3]

---

1   Care Act 2014, ss.67, 68.

2   Statutory guidance, 2016, para 7.36. For instance, this sort of point was made in a different context, under the Mental Capacity Act 2005. The judge pointed out that the role of a person's relevant representative was to maintain contact with, support and represent the person lacking capacity, under para 140 of schedule A1 of the 2005 Act. The representative, a family member, could not do this if his view of the person's best interests was contrary to the wishes and feelings of the person lacking capacity. She didn't want to be deprived of her liberty in the care home, yet he thought it was in her best interests: *AJ v A Local Authority* [2015] EWCOP 5, para 84.

3   SI 2014/2824. Care and Support (Independent Advocacy Support) Regulations 2014, r.4.

ADVOCACY: CHARACTERISTICS OF INDEPENDENT ADVOCATE. Regulations state that the local authority must be satisfied that the advocate has appropriate experience, has appropriate training, is competent to represent and support the person, has integrity and is of good character – and has appropriate supervision arrangements in place.[1]

ADVOCACY: ROLE OF INDEPENDENT ADVOCATE. Regulations further outline the role of the independent advocate, including for instance:

- **well-being**: at all times promoting the well-being of the individual

- **meeting**: meeting in private with the individual, as far as appropriate and practicable

- **records**: examining and taking copies of relevant records

- **challenge**: assisting the individual to challenge the local authority, and directly challenging the authority, if the individual lacks the capacity or competence to do so, in relation to assessment or planning – and if the advocate believes the authority is acting inconsistently with its well-being duty under section 1 of the Act.[2]

Local authorities must take account of what the independent advocate says and take reasonable steps to help the advocate represent the person.[3]

ADVOCACY: STRENGTH OF DUTY. An early legal judgement under the Care Act held that a failure to appoint an advocate when the triggering conditions were met – simply because the local authority had not commissioned sufficient numbers of advocates locally – was unlawful. Nor was it acceptable for the local authority to argue that the appointment of an advocate would have made no difference to the final decision, because how could the local authority possibly know this if the person was unable to participate in the process?[4]

---

1   SI 2014/2824. Care and Support (Independent Advocacy Support) Regulations 2014, r.2.

2   SI 2014/2824. Care and Support (Independent Advocacy Support) Regulations 2014, r.5.

3   SI 2014/2824. Care and Support (Independent Advocacy Support) Regulations 2014, r.6.

4   *R(SG) v Haringey LBC* [2015] EWHC 2579 (Admin), paras 53–56.

ADVOCACY: UNDER OTHER LEGISLATION. The appointment of an advocate under the Care Act is distinct from independent advocacy under sections 130A–130D of the Mental Health Act 1983 and under sections 35 to 39 of the Mental Capacity Act 2005 (MCA). The MCA and Care Act rules about advocacy are distinct. Differences include:

- **Mental capacity**. Under the MCA, the person must lack mental capacity to understand (etc.). Under the Care Act, it is merely substantial difficulty.

- **Circumstances triggering the duty**. The role of the independent mental capacity advocate (IMCA) under the MCA is limited to certain decisions only: a stay in hospital for four weeks or more, a stay in a care home for more than eight weeks or serious medical treatment. It is a duty to appoint an IMCA, but only if there is no appropriate family member or friend to represent and support the person.[1] Whereas, the circumstances triggering the advocacy provisions in the Care Act are wider.

- **Circumstances triggering power to appoint an IMCA**. In the case of reviewing care home or hospital accommodation (in excess of 12 weeks) – or of adult protection cases – there is under the MCA a power only but no duty to appoint an IMCA. However, confusingly, in the case of adult protection, the power can be exercised, whether or not there is an appropriate family member or friend.[2] Whereas under the Care Act, if the triggering conditions are met in case of adult protection, it is a duty, not just a power, to appoint an advocate.

- **Deprivation of liberty**. There are further, special rules about the appointment of IMCAs, under ss.39A–39D of the MCA, concerning deprivation of liberty of a person under that Act. The duty to appoint an advocate in such circumstances arises also under the Care Act.

Statutory guidance states that, in some circumstances, both a Care Act advocate and an IMCA would fall to be appointed, in which case it would be better for the same advocate to perform both statutory roles.[3]

---

1   Mental Capacity Act 2005, ss.37–39.

2   SI 2006/2883. Mental Capacity Act 2005 (Independent Mental Capacity Advocates) (Expansion of Role) Regulations 2006.

3   Statutory guidance, 2016, para 7.65.

After-care services, see *Mental Health Act 1983*

Aids, see *Community equipment*

Appeals system

The Care Act, section 72, provides for a statutory appeals system to be set up through the passing of regulations. This would be in addition to existing remedies of complaints, the local government ombudsman or judicial review in the law courts. A consultation was held by the Department of Health with a view to implementation in April 2016. Introduction was then postponed in July 2015, at least until 2020.[1]

Assessment

Under the Care Act, assessment under sections 9 and 10 is pivotal for both adults in need and carers. It is the only gateway under the Act to eligibility and to legal entitlement. Help can be provided under other sections of the Act without statutory assessment – for example, through universal, preventative help under section 2 of the Act or, if a need is urgent, under section 19, but such provision would not be enforceable (except, perhaps, to avoid a breach of human rights).

Some of the rules about assessment are common to both adults and carers. Others are specific to one or the other. The rules are detailed and put local authorities at additional risk of challenge if they are not followed.

For assessments relating to children approaching the age of 18, to their carers and to young carers approaching 18, see **Children and transition**.

---

1   House of Commons Library. Briefing Paper, CBP7265, 22 July 2015. *Social care: Delayed introduction of funding reform, including the cap, and other changes until April 2020.* London: HC, 2015.

ASSESSMENT: TRIGGER FOR ADULT. The duty of a local authority to assess an adult is triggered, under section 9 of the Care Act, if it appears to the authority that the adult may have needs for care and support. The authority must assess (a) whether the adult does have needs for care and support, and (b) if so, what those needs are. In comparison with the duty to assess carers, the duty refers to present, not future, needs.[1]

ASSESSMENT: TRIGGER FOR CARER. The duty to assess a carer is triggered, under section 10 of the Care Act, if it appears to the authority that the carer may have needs for support. The authority must assess (a) whether the carer does have needs for support (or is likely to do so in the future), and (b) if so, what those needs are (or are likely to be in the future).

The duty in the Act to assess carers refers explicitly to future issues; not so the duty to assess adults.

ASSESSMENT: DUTY IRRESPECTIVE OF LEVEL OF NEED OR FINANCIAL RESOURCES. The duty to assess either adult or carer is irrespective of the local authority's view of (a) the level of the person's needs, or (b) the level of the person's resources.[2] So, low-level need must still be assessed.[3] The duty is therefore irrespective also of the type of service a person might require.

> **Failure to assess 'low-level' needs**. A local authority failed to assess the shopping and cleaning needs of a woman with severe health problems: sarcoidosis, extensive fibrosis of the lungs, chronic obstructive airways disease, atrial fibrillation, epilepsy and a learning disability and a heart problem, pointing her instead towards a private provider. This was maladministration.[4]

---

1   *R(Davey) v Oxfordshire County Council* [2017] EWHC 354 (Admin), para 57.

2   Care Act 2014, ss.9–10.

3   *R v Bristol City Council, ex p Penfold* [1998] 1 CCLR 315, High Court.

4   *LGO, Salford City Council*, 2003 (01/C/17519).

ASSESSMENT: NOT SIMPLY ON REQUEST. The duty is not on request but, as already stated, is nonetheless triggered at a low threshold.[1] The question of whether somebody appears to 'maybe' have needs could be rephrased as 'might possibly have a need'. For instance, probability or likelihood of there being a need is not required. A request might in itself – unless obviously specious or inappropriate – constitute an appearance of need. A local authority might have a duty to assess, following a third party referral, a person who has not asked for it.

> **Failure to offer assessment**. Failure to offer an assessment – for example, to a carer known to the local authority who appears to have a possible need – would risk a finding of maladministration,[2] as would a failure to provide information about carers' assessments, so that carers would be able to request them.[3]

ASSESSMENT: NOT DEPENDENT ON ORDINARY RESIDENCE. The duty to assess is not dependent on the person being ordinarily resident in the local authority's area (unlike, normally, the duty to meet an eligible need). Nor will it depend on whether services the person might need to meet their care and support needs are available in the authority's area.[4]

ASSESSMENT: REFUSAL OF ADULT. Under section 11 of the Care Act, if an adult refuses an assessment, the local authority is not required to assess – unless any one of the following applies:

- the adult lacks capacity to refuse the assessment and the local authority is satisfied that an assessment would be in the person's best interests

- the adult is experiencing, or at risk of, abuse or neglect, or

- the adult subsequently changes his or her mind.

---

1   *R v Bristol City Council, ex p Penfold* [1998] 1 CCLR 315, High Court.

2   *LGO, Worcestershire County Council*, 2011 (09R004 363).

3   *LGO, North Yorkshire County Council*, 2002 (01/C/03521).

4   *R v Berkshire County Council, ex p Parker* [1996] 95 LGR 449, High Court.

If the adult's circumstances change, the local authority must re-offer an assessment. Implications include the following.

First, a straightforward refusal under section 11 removes the duty to assess (unless there is lack of capacity or abuse or neglect concern). Second, the wording relating to abuse and neglect suggests some sort of certainty – rather than mere reasonable cause to suspect these things (compare this with section 42 of the Care Act and the duty to make safeguarding enquiries). Third, a local authority could therefore be obliged, despite a refusal, to assess an adult (possessing the mental capacity to refuse) who is experiencing – or is at risk of – abuse or neglect. But nothing in section 11 gives a coercive legal power to enter the adult's home without consent.

Non-engagement resulting in partial assessment. Faced with non-engagement by a person with behavioural and personality disorder, the local authority had to do its best. The assessment might not be as complete as normally expected but it could still satisfy the assessment duty, as long as the local authority could demonstrate the attempts it had made.[1]

Non-engagement: failure to assess. A man with autism failed to engage with a local authority when it offered a Care Act assessment. It offered him advocacy services, which were also refused. The assessment therefore stalled: this was not maladministration.[2]

ASSESSMENT: REFUSAL OF CARER. Under section 11, if a carer refuses a carer's assessment, the local authority is not obliged to assess unless the carer changes his or her mind or the carer's circumstances change, in which case the local authority is obliged to re-offer an assessment.

ASSESSMENT: REQUIREMENTS IN ASSESSING ADULT. Under section 9 of the Act, the local authority must assess the impact of needs on well-being, outcomes the adult wishes to achieve in daily life, and whether care and support could contribute to these. A failure to consider these requirements will be a breach of statutory duty. However, the duty on the local authority

---

1   *R(WG) v Leicester City Council* [2011] EWHC 189 (Admin), para 11.

2   *LGO, Telford & Wrekin Council*, 2016 (15 015 684), paras 38–40.

in terms of outcomes is not to ensure they are achieved but only whether care and support might contribute to them.[1] The local authority must also involve the adult, any carer the adult has, anybody the adult asks to be involved, or (if the person lacks capacity) anybody who appears to be interested in the adult's welfare. Even without such explicit rules in previous legislation, the courts have held assessment to be unlawful if there is insufficient involvement of others.

Hospital discharge: failure to involve woman's daughter. A woman, with dementia and in her nineties, was discharged from hospital without her daughter (her main carer) being involved in her mother's Care Act assessment. Nor did the daughter receive a carer's assessment in her own right. This was maladministration.[2]

Not consulting with parents. A decision taken to move a severely disabled man from one supported living arrangement to another, without properly consulting his parents, was unlawful. The failure was in relation to concerns about the existing placement, and to just how far plans had advanced for an alternative placement before any consultation took place.[3]

Not involving the adult. Not making reasonable efforts to involve the adult themselves, and to ascertain their preferences, because of an obstructive relative, was unlawful.[4]

This duty to involve other people must, presumably and by implication, be subject to the common law of confidentiality, to the Data Protection Act 1998 and to article 8 of the European Convention on Human Rights (right to respect for private life). The adult might not want the carer involved or to know certain things. In which case, the local ombudsman might not find fault with the local authority for not involving other people.[5]

---

1   *R(Davey) v Oxfordshire County Council* [2017] EWHC 354 (Admin), para 21.

2   *LGO, Surrey County Council*, 2016 (16 003 456), paras 9, 28–30.

3   *R(W) v London Borough of Croydon* [2011] EWHC 696 (Admin), paras 38–41.

4   *R v North Yorkshire County Council, ex p Hargreaves* [1994] 26 BMLR 121, High Court.

5   See e.g. *LGO, Wirral Metropolitan Borough Council*, 2016 (16 004 407), para 16. See also: *LGO, Dorset County Council*, 2016 (15 014 480), para 23.

ASSESSMENT: REQUIREMENTS IN ASSESSING THE CARER. A carer's assessment, under section 10 of the Act, must include:

- whether the carer is able, and is likely to continue to be able, to provide care for the adult needing care

- whether the carer is willing, and is likely to continue to be willing, to do so

- the impact of the carer's needs for support on well-being

- the outcomes the carer wishes to achieve in daily life, and

- whether support could contribute to these outcomes.

The authority must also consider (a) whether the carer works or wishes to do so, and (b) whether the carer is participating in, or wishes to participate in, education, training or recreation. The authority must involve the carer and any person whom the carer asks the authority to involve. It must consider whether things other than support could contribute to the achievement of outcomes – and whether the carer would benefit from preventative services under section 2 of the Act, or advice and information under section 4.

Panel decision not considering willingness and ability. A social worker gathered evidence to support a request for an additional week's respite support for a carer. The panel rejected the request without this being discussed or agreed with the carer and adult in need, without knowing whether the carer was able and willing to provide night time care, and based on assumptions about the carer – all contrary to the Care Act. All this was maladministration.[1]

Failure to assess carer's needs: unwarranted assumption. A failure to offer the carer an assessment – on grounds that the services provided to the adult in need would also meet the carer's needs – was criticised by the ombudsman. Since, without a carer's assessment, the local authority could not know what the needs were.[2]

---

1   *LGO, London Borough of Bromley*, 2016 (15 020 384), paras 40–41.
2   *LGO, Kirklees Metropolitan Borough Council*, 2016 (15 017 848), para 32.

> **Sharing information without consent.** Sharing information about the carer – for example, with other family members – might be maladministration, where the carer gave consent only for other professionals to be told.[1]

ASSESSMENT: APPROPRIATENESS AND PROPORTIONALITY. Regulations state that assessment of an adult or carer must be appropriate and proportionate and that the local authority must ensure that the person being assessed can participate as effectively as possible. Appropriateness and proportionality require the local authority to consider wishes and preferences, outcomes the person wants to achieve, and the severity and overall extent of the needs. In addition, if there are fluctuating needs, the assessment must take place over a period, which the local authority considers necessary, to establish the need. Information about the assessment must be provided in an accessible format and, if practicable, before the assessment.[2]

Guidance states that telephone or online assessments could sometimes be appropriate and proportionate but that local authorities would have to consider the ramifications of such assessments, including duties relating to safeguarding, independent advocacy and mental capacity. The guidance notes that mental impairment – such as dementia, acquired brain injury, learning disabilities or mental health – should mean face-to-face assessment, and warns against local authorities disengaging from people too hastily.[3]

> **Failure to consider fluctuating needs in assessment and care and support plan.** A failure properly to consider fluctuating needs for care and support, as a result of complex medical needs – causing significant pain and fatigue and affecting joints, mobility and memory – was maladministration.[4]

ASSESSMENT: IMPACT ON OTHER PEOPLE. The impact of the needs of the person being assessed must be considered – on any person involved in caring for the individual and anybody else the local authority considers

---

1   *LGO, London Borough of Lewisham*, 2016 (15 020 251), para 41.

2   SI 2014/2827. Care and Support (Assessment) Regulations 2014, r.3.

3   Statutory guidance, 2016, paras 6.28, 6.25.

4   *LGO, Kent County Council*, 2016 (15 015 067), paras 12, 37.

relevant, on any child involved in caring for the individual, and whether any of the caring tasks are inappropriate for the child.[1]

ASSESSMENT: KNOWLEDGE, COMPETENCE, SKILLS, TRAINING. The assessor – of an adult in need or of a carer – must have the skills, knowledge and competence to carry out the assessment in question, and must be appropriately trained unless it is a supported self-assessment and the person is therefore assessing himself or herself.[2] Local authorities therefore have some discretion in determining exactly when qualified professionals are required. Guidance states, for example, that 'registered social workers and occupational therapists can provide important support and may be involved in complex assessments which indicate a wide range of needs, risks'.[3] The local authority also needs to be clear about who is authorised to carry out different types of assessment. Otherwise, purported assessments might have no legal standing.

> **Failure to conduct a manual handling assessment.** Following a reassessment of a person's needs, a manager was unsure of whether the person needed one or two carers to transfer him physically. This created an uncertainty as to what his needs were. The failure to carry out a manual handling assessment, to determine the response to this question, was maladministration.[4]
>
> **Understanding of autism.** An assessment constituted maladministration when carried out by staff with little understanding of a person's autistic condition – for example, by a social worker who had received no training in autism.[5]
>
> **Understanding of deafness.** An assessment of a profoundly deaf person, with serious sleep apnoea and mental health needs, fell short of being an appropriate and competent assessment: contradictory information taken into account, no input from the person's parents regarding their role and

---

1   SI 2014/2827. Care and Support (Assessment) Regulations 2014, r.4.

2   SI 2014/2827. Care and Support (Assessment) Regulations 2014, r.5.

3   Statutory guidance, 2016, para 6.7.

4   *LGO, Kirklees Metropolitan Borough Council*, 2016 (15 011 660), para 20.

5   *LGO, Solihull Metropolitan Borough Council*, 2016 (15 005 128), paras 71–72.

the impact on them, a lack of understanding around the person's deafness and unnecessary delays in carrying out the assessments.[1]

Assessment of deaf person: appropriate training. A woman was to be assessed by a specialist company on behalf of the local authority. It was proposed that the assessor be a trainee, who had almost completed her British Sign Language Level 2 qualification and was working towards Level 3. This was regarded as adequate training by the company, and the ombudsman found no fault. However, when the woman stated that she needed an assessor at Level 6, the company responded by saying that such an assessor would be provided, with the trainee in attendance for support. The woman then refused the assessment. The ombudsman found no maladministration.[2]

Unauthorised assessment. An NHS therapist carried out an assessment about a stairlift and made a recommendation but was not authorised and did not have delegated power to make that decision on behalf of the local authority. As a result, the failure to provide the stairlift meant the local authority was not in breach of its duty to meet assessed need.[3]

ASSESSMENT: DUAL SENSORY IMPAIRMENT. If a person is deaf–blind, the assessment must be carried out by a person with specific training and expertise. A person is defined as deaf–blind if he or she has combined sight and hearing impairment causing difficulties with communication, access to information and mobility. The local authority must provide the assessor with relevant information about the person or, in the case of a carer's assessment, about the adult needing care; in the case of a child's carer's assessment, about the child needing care; and in the case of a young carer's assessment, about the adult needing care.[4]

ASSESSMENT: CONSULTATION WITH EXPERT. The local authority must consult an expert (in the condition or other circumstances of the person), if

---

1   *LGO, Northamptonshire County Council*, 2016 (15 013 379), paras 18, 41.

2   *LGO, Surrey County Council*, 2016 (15 019 237), paras 37–44.

3   *R v Kirklees Metropolitan Borough Council, ex p Daykin* [1996] 3 CL 565, High Court.

4   SI 2014/2827. Care and Support (Assessment) Regulations 2014, r.6.

it considers this is required. The consultation can take place before or during the assessment.[1] The local authority remains the ultimate decision-maker, but must pay attention to the advice it receives and give reasons for disregarding it.

Considering expert advice. When trying to reduce a care package, a local authority disregarded, without reasons, the 'wealth of evidence' from an epilepsy nurse and doctor – about how to manage regular, nocturnal, life-threatening fits. The revised care package would have removed expert, waking night cover for all but three nights a month, thereby putting his life at risk on the remaining nights. This was unlawful.[2]

Not mentioning expert recommendations. A social worker assessed a man with attention deficit hyperactive disorder, Asperger's syndrome, dyslexia and dyspraxia. A neuropsychologist attended also and produced a report with recommendations. The recommendations were not mentioned in the social worker's assessment – nor at the subsequent panel which approved the social worker's recommendations. This was maladministration; it meant the man was without support for seven months until the error was corrected.[3]

Consulting an alternative expert, with different views, might give the local authority the reasons it needs.[4] Not consulting an expert at all, when such consultation is obviously required, also risks unlawfulness or maladministration.

Failing to consult. For reasons of expedition, a local authority failed to consult a medical doctor about a woman with multiple sclerosis, blindness, epileptic fits and incontinence, even though the social worker recognised in principle the necessity of doing so.[5]

---

1   SI 2014/2827. Care and Support (Assessment) Regulations 2014, r.5.

2   *R(Clarke) v London Borough of Sutton* [2015] EWHC 1081 (Admin).

3   *LGO, London Borough of Hackney*, 2016 (15 018 618), paras 6, 8, 15.

4   *R(Rodriguez-Bannister) v Somerset Partnership NHS and Social Care Trust* [2003] EWHC 2184 (Admin), para 47.

5   *R v Birmingham City Council, ex parte Killigrew* [1999] EWHC Admin 611, paras 34, 54.

Not waiting for a GP report about a person's well-being. A local authority needed to assess whether it could lawfully offer an alternative, cheaper care home placement to a woman, whose daughter felt unable to continue pay the top-up fee in the current care home. It sought a general practitioner's view about risks the move might pose to the woman's mental, emotional and physical well-being. However, the social worker concerned did not wait for the GP's report and sent the case to panel without it. This was fault.[1]

Not consulting specialist services to help communication. A man had physical and mental disabilities causing significant difficulties with mobility, communication and behaviour, as well as pain, for which he had to use powerful painkillers affecting his mood and communication. As a result of these communication and behaviour difficulties, the local authority had been unable to meet his assessed eligible needs, including for equipment. The ombudsman found maladministration because the local authority had not fully explored communication techniques or consulted specialist services about the issue.[2]

Similarly, informal reliance on a partial assessment by a professional from another organisation does not alleviate the duty of assessment on the local authority:

Over-reliance on hospital therapist's assessment of a dying man. A man was discharged from hospital. In gauging his needs, the local authority relied on the assessment of an NHS occupational therapist who had not done a home visit and had not been able to complete a functional assessment. As a result, the local authority underestimated the man's needs and he did not receive the support he needed at home in the last few days of his life. This was maladministration.[3]

1   *LGO, London Borough of Bromley*, 2016 (14 020 565), para 20.

2   *LGO, Suffolk County Council*, 2016 (15 008 589), paras 43–44.

3   *LGO, Royal Borough of Kingston upon Thames*, 2016 (15 020 782), paras 20–23.

ASSESSMENT: SUPPORTED SELF-ASSESSMENT. A supported self-assessment is an assessment completed jointly by the local authority and the person. The rules are as follows:

- **Wish and capacity to self-assess**. The local authority must ask the person whether they want a supported self-assessment. If the person does, and has the requisite mental capacity, then the local authority must enable such an assessment, and provide the person with any relevant information it has about them.

- **Child under 18**. In the case of a child under 18, the supported self-assessment is a power but not a duty.

- **Carers' assessments**. With relevant consent (or in best interests, if the person lacks capacity), the local authority must provide information (a) in a carer's assessment, to the carer about the adult, (b) in a child carer's assessment, to the carer about the child, or (c) if appropriate, in a young carer's assessment, to the young carer about the adult.[1]

- **Final decision**. The final decision about a person's needs remains that of the local authority. Guidance states that the authority needs to ensure that the self-assessment is accurate and a reflection of the person's needs. It needs to assure itself of this without repeating the assessment from scratch.[2] A failure to do this could be unlawful if it means that the person's needs and situation have not been properly considered.[3]

Supported self-assessment requires that the person wants it and, of course, is told about the options in the first place. This precludes a local authority forcing the issue[4] – for instance, by giving people no other option than to self-assess, by post or online (exacerbated by closing the case were no reply forthcoming). Comparably, the courts have held in the past that sending letters (offering a review or reassessment) to vulnerable people, and treating silence as a meaningful and definitive response (with a view to withdrawing

---

1   SI 2014/2827. Care and Support (Assessment) Regulations 2014, r.2.

2   Statutory guidance, 2016, para 6.46.

3   *R(B) v Cornwall County Council* [2010] EWCA Civ 55, para 68.

4   Statutory guidance, 2016, para 6.44.

services), was unlawful.[1] Over-reliance on a self-assessment, despite concerns being raised by the person that the resulting care and support plan is inadequate, will need to be guarded against – since subsequent assessment might reveal unidentified and unmet need.[2] Conversely, a supported self-assessment may be of considerable benefit:

> **Injustice caused by failure to offer self-assessment.** A carer received an assessment from the local authority. However, the assessment contained several mistakes, and she was told that she would not be eligible for help with housework even before the assessment was completed. She was not told about, and therefore not offered, the option of supported self-assessment – a means by which the mistakes could have been avoided. This was maladministration.[3]

ASSESSMENT: COMBINED. Under section 12 of the Act, a combined assessment can be carried out (for example, of an adult, child or carer) with requisite consent.

ASSESSMENT: REFERRAL TO THE NHS. When carrying out an assessment, the local authority must refer a person (adult, or child in a transition assessment) to the NHS clinical commissioning group if it appears to the local authority that the person may be eligible for NHS continuing health care. The local authority must have regard to the National Framework for NHS Continuing Health Care and NHS-funded Nursing Care guidance published by the Department of Health in November 2012.[4] Failure to comply with this duty would risk unlawfulness and could also result in findings of maladministration against the local authority. Not least because the local authority might end up providing services before it has been

---

1   *R v Gloucestershire County Council, ex parte RADAR* [1995] WL 1082300, p.5.

2   *LGO, Norfolk County Council,* 2016 (15 017 557), para 14.

3   *LGO, Kirklees Metropolitan Borough Council,* 2016 (15 017 848), paras 26–29.

4   SI 2014/2827. Care and Support (Assessment) Regulations 2014, r.7.

established whether they are within its legal remit, and financially charging people for care that should have been provided free by the NHS.[1]

> **Competent referral to NHS**. The referral process to the NHS may involve the filling out of an NHS continuing health care 'checklist'. If local authority staff do this, they need to understand how to complete it: the ombudsman found maladministration when staff didn't understand, simply recorded what a carer had told them and exercised no judgement themselves.[2]

ASSESSMENT: JOINT ASSESSMENT. If another organisation is assessing the adult or carer, the local authority can agree to assess on behalf of, or jointly with, that other body.[3]

ASSESSMENT: CONSIDERING WHETHER OTHER THINGS COULD HELP. During the assessment of an adult or carer, the local authority must consider whether things other than care and support (or just support) could help with achieving outcomes and whether preventative services, information or advice would be of benefit.[4] Guidance states that things other than care and support might include the person's own strengths or support that might be available within the local community, including mutual support or cultural support or networks. Crucially, local authority suggestions about support from family or friends should be based on appropriateness, willingness and ability, and the agreement of the adult or carer.[5]

> **Wishful thinking about neighbours and confusion about needs**. A local authority reassessed a man and concluded that he had no eligible care needs, but also that he had needs but these could be met by his friends

---

1   *LGO, Hertfordshire County Council*, 2003 (00/B/16833). And *LGO, Shropshire County Council*, 2013 (12 007 311), para 45. And *LGO, Northamptonshire County Council*, 2016 (14 007 296), para 31. And *LGO, Staffordshire County Council*, 2016 (14 017 173), paras 3–54.

2   *LGO, Kirklees Metropolitan Borough Council*, 2016 (15 017 848), paras 34–35.

3   Care Act 2014, s.12(7).

4   Care Act 2014, ss.9, 10.

5   Statutory guidance, 2016, paras 6.63–6.64.

and neighbours. First, the ombudsman noted that either he had needs or he didn't. Second, the local authority had not spoken to and checked with the informal carers – that they were indeed able and willing to continue to help – particularly because he had used his direct payment (which was now being withdrawn) previously to pay them.[1]

Meeting needs other than through care and support. A local authority reassessed a woman under the Care Act and concluded she did not have eligible needs. The reablement team concluded that she could meet her own needs for help with fastening her bra and applying cream to her back – by buying front-fastening bras and a long-handled sponge. This decision was not maladministration.[2]

ASSESSMENT: IN WRITING. The local authority must, under section 12 of the Act, provide a written record of the assessment of an adult to:

- the adult to whom the assessment relates

- any carer that the adult has, if the adult asks the authority to do so, and

- any other person to whom the adult asks the authority to give a copy.

The authority must also give a written record of a carer's assessment to:

- the carer to whom the assessment relates

- the adult needing care, if the carer asks the authority to do so, and

- any other person to whom the carer asks the authority to give a copy.

This is yet one more burden for local authorities. Yet proper recording and sharing of assessments might, in principle at least, reduce the risk of assessments of people with mental health needs – over a two-year period – which were 'shambolic', poorly executed, contrary to policy, led to inexplicable decisions and represented maladministration.[3]

---

1   *LGO, London Borough of Hounslow*, 2016 (15 016 338), paras 72–73.

2   *LGO, Southend-on-Sea Borough Council*, 2016 (15 020 090), para 9.

3   *LGO, Birmingham City Council*, 2013 (08 017 525).

No assessment in writing: delay and anxiety. A failure automatically to provide the record of the assessment in writing, meaning the person had to ask for it (thereby contributing to delay and anxiety), was maladministration.[1]

No record of carer's assessment part of poor care. Following a hospital discharge to a care home, inadequate care commissioned in a care home and a dubious refusal to allow the grandson to take his grandfather home, the local authority failed to give the grandson a copy of his carer's assessment, and could not even find the assessment in its own records. This was maladministration (as was the inadequate care provided).[2]

ASSESSMENT: ESTABLISHING ELIGIBILITY. Under section 13 of the Care Act, if a person is being assessed, and the local authority is satisfied that the adult has care and support needs – or a carer has support needs – then the authority must go on to make an eligibility decision. If at least some of the adult's needs meet the eligibility criteria, the local authority must:

- consider what could be done to meet those needs

- ascertain whether the adult wants to have those needs met by the local authority, and

- establish whether the adult is ordinarily resident in the local authority's area.

Similarly, in relation to a carer, the local authority must:

- consider what could be done to meet those needs that do, and

- establish whether the adult needing care is ordinarily resident in the local authority's area.

See **Eligibility**.

Asylum seekers, see *Immigration*

---

1   *LGO, Kirklees Metropolitan Borough Council,* 2016 (15 017 848), para 31.
2   *LGO, Leeds City Council,* 2016 (16 002 508), paras 38–42.

Autism Act 2009

The Autism Act 2009 focuses on a particular condition. The Act itself says little other than stipulating the publication of a strategy and guidance, aimed at meeting the health and social care needs of adults with autism. The statutory guidance, duly issued, refers, amongst other things, to the adequate training of staff, assessment and eligibility decisions (consistent with legislation) relating to people with autism.[1]

For instance, a failure by a local authority to implement an autism strategy and to train staff, who are assessing people with autism, was maladministration.[2] Similarly, a failure by an NHS mental health trust to enable a person with Asperger's syndrome to access an appropriate support service, and of the local authority to adhere to an agreed method of communication with the person, was maladministration.[3]

---

1   Department of Health *Implementing 'Fulfilling and rewarding lives': Statutory guidance for local authorities and NHS organisations to support implementation of the autism strategy.* London: DH, 2010, pp.14–15.

2   *LGO, Solihull Metropolitan Borough Council,* 2016 (15 005 128), paras 71–72.

3   *LGO, Lancashire County Council,* 2016 (15 004 008), paras 26, 33.

B

Bail hostels, see *Prisons*

Better Care Fund

The NHS Act 2006 makes provision for the creation of an integration fund, a pooling of money in each local area to be used to improve health and social care services in the community.[1] This is known as the Better Care Fund. At heart, its primary and overall purpose is to keep older people out of hospital.[2] It does not alter or modify duties in the Care Act 2014 and the NHS Act 2006.

Blanket policies

The consequences of blanket policies can be at least threefold: breach of statutory duty, unlawful fettering of discretion and wasting money.

BLANKET POLICIES: BREACH OF STATUTORY DUTY. If, under the Care Act, a local authority refuses to meet an eligible need because of a blanket policy, it risks breach of its statutory duty or maladministration. (In some circumstances, an NHS body might also be in breach of NHS Act obligations.)

---

1   NHS Act 2006, ss.223B, 223GA.

2   Department of Health. Department of Communities and Local Government. *2016/17 Better Care Fund: Policy framework*. London: DH, 2016, p.5.

Residential placement ceiling. A local authority unlawfully applied a cost ceiling to placement of a person with learning disabilities, thus refusing to fund the placement in question, but with no cheaper, suitable alternative yet identified, meaning his needs would not be met.[1]

Blanket policy on respite care. A local authority introduced a blanket policy on the amount of respite care a person could have each year: four weeks. The person in question, with learning disabilities and autism, had been assessed as needing eight weeks. Without any reassessment, the respite was reduced to four weeks. This was maladministration, since the duty was to meet the assessed, eligible need for eight weeks.[2]

Ceiling on home care packages. A policy of limiting home care packages to the amount a care home placement would cost might be lawful but only if (a) exceptions to the rule could be made, and (b) more cost-effective ways of meeting people's needs at home were found within the guideline amount.[3]

Blanket ban on drug for multiple sclerosis. A health authority's blanket ban on providing Beta-Interferon treatment meant it was totally disregarding Department of Health guidance which stated that health authorities should prescribe it for those most likely to benefit.[4]

Blanket reduction, under the Care Act, of respite available to carers. A local authority, under the Care Act, introduced a new policy, limiting the amount of respite available to 14 nights other than in exceptional circumstances. This meant that for the main carers (his parents) of a man with physical and learning disabilities, the previous respite of 50 days per year was now cut down to 14 nights. The assessor recorded the strains this would lead to and the risk to sustainability of the caring situation.

Nonetheless, the local authority decided in June 2015 that the reduction would take place in April 2016 (when it could not know what the needs would be), but it gave no explanation as to how it had reached this decision, and why it believed the need for respite had reduced. The offer of additional emergency respite was not an answer, since the 'need for

---

1   *R(Alloway) v Bromley London Borough Council* [2004] EWHC 2108 (Admin), para 71.

2   *LGO, Knowsley Metropolitan Borough Council*, 2016 (15 008 823).

3   *R(D) v Worcestershire County Council* [2013] EWHC 2490 (Admin).

4   *R v North Derbyshire Health Authority, ex p Fisher* (1998) 10 Admin. L.R. 27.

weekends away and a little social life are not emergencies but part of a planned sustainable support regime. The Council's assessment does not address these sustainability issues and the guidance says the impact on the carers' daily lives and non-caring activities must be included.' All this was maladministration.[1]

BLANKET POLICIES: FETTERING OF DISCRETION. A public body, such as a local authority or NHS body, must not apply a policy so rigidly as to exclude individual consideration and the making of exceptions. If it does so, it risks unlawfully 'fettering its discretion'. This principle applies to the discharge not just of duties but also of powers. In other words, a public body should not put itself in chains. One such example has already been given immediately above.[2] Other examples considered by the courts or ombudsman include the following.

Rent arrears policy. A rigid policy on rent arrears meant a local authority, by penalising the parents, failed to meet the housing needs of a severely disabled boy.[3]

Home care ceiling. A ceiling existed on the cost of care packages for older people in their own home. A panel sat to consider exceptions but never made any.[4]

NHS wheelchair provision. An NHS wheelchair service applied national guidance over-restrictively to the provision of powered indoor/outdoor wheelchairs. It failed to consider the person's individual situation and whether the need was exceptional.[5]

---

1   *LGO, Sefton Metropolitan Borough Council*, 2016 (15 013 201), paras 34–35. See similarly: *LGO, Sefton Metropolitan Borough Council*, 2016 (15 019 498), paras 19–22.

2   *R(Alloway) v Bromley London Borough Council* [2004] EWHC 2108 (Admin).

3   *LGO, Bristol City Council*, 1998 (96/B/4035 and 96/B/4143).

4   *LGO, Liverpool City Council*, 1998 (96/C/4315).

5   Health Service Ombudsman investigation into Epsom and St Helier NHS Trust, 2001 (E.559/99–00) in Health Service Ombudsman HC 278–I. *Selected investigations completed August–November 2000*. London: TSO.

NHS cancer treatment. A local NHS policy for cancer treatment (Herceptin) did allow for exceptions. But the policy gave no indication as to how they might be identified, other than arbitrarily: this was unlawful.[1] In another case, a policy allowed for exceptions and the patient's needs obviously were exceptional (no other treatments were available, and the drug in question could significantly prolong life) – but she was refused. This, too, was unlawful.[2]

Exceptionality and uniqueness. Sometimes the NHS states that an exception must be refused, unless the patient is unique (i.e. not part of a possible group of patients with similar needs). Logically, nobody could be unique, since another similar patient might always appear, so exceptions would never be made. This would be an unlawful policy, since it would be a contradiction in terms.[3]

Exercising a power – sometimes. A public body may have a mere power, rather than a duty, in legislation to do something. Even then, it should not fetter its discretion so as to preclude exercise of the power altogether.[4] For instance, a policy by a local authority never to award discretionary housing grants would have been a fettering of discretion.[5]

BLANKET POLICIES: WASTING PUBLIC MONEY. Most blanket policies in social care and health care are with a view to saving money. Yet the outcome might, sometimes and perversely, result in the opposite.

Blanket policy on home adaptations. A local authority had a blanket policy of not using its discretion to 'top up' disabled facilities grants by adding an extra amount to the mandatory maximum grant of £30,000. This resulted in the local authority funding a care home place, pending resolution of the dispute, without considering the potentially greater expense of doing this.[6]

1   *R(Rogers) v Swindon NHS Primary Care Trust* [2006] EWCA Civ 392.

2   *R(Otley) v Barking and Dagenham Primary Care Trust* [2007] EWHC Admin 1927.

3   *R(Ross) v West Sussex Primary Care Trust* [2008] EWHC 2252 (Admin), para 79.

4   *British Oxygen v Board of Trade* [1971] AC 610, House of Lords.

5   *R v Bristol City Council, ex p Bailey* [1995] 27 HLR 307, High Court.

6   *LGO, Walsall Metropolitan Borough Council*, 2008 (07/B/07346).

Box ticking

The Care Act contains much detail about how assessments should proceed and decisions be taken. For local authorities, the Act thus creates what could be viewed as many boxes which need to be ticked. However, the courts will not necessarily penalise an assessment if they believe that the local authority has in substance, if not in form, asked the right questions.[1] The situation is similar if not all the 'boxes' have been filled out but it is clear that essential needs have been assessed.[2] On the other hand, if something material or substantial has not been considered, the assessment may be held to be unlawful – for instance, failing to consider a person's condition of osteoporosis in a manual handling assessment.[3]

Business failure

If a registered care provider suffers a business failure, a local authority must step in to ensure that the needs of service users are met – that is, of both adults in need and carers. A registered provider means one registered with the Care Quality Commission under the Health and Social Care Act 2008.[4] The demise in 2011 of Southern Cross, owner of 752 care homes, underlined on a large scale the risk of just such business failure.[5]

BUSINESS FAILURE: MEANING. Business failure means that the provider is unable to carry on providing services. Failure includes the appointment of an administrator or receiver, a voluntary winding up order or bankruptcy.[6] The duty on a local authority is not triggered simply by the failure of one or more local outlets of a provider, but by the failure of the provider as a whole.

---

1   *R v Sheffield City Council, ex p Low* (2000) unreported, Court of Appeal.

2   *R(Khana) v Southwark London Borough Council* (2000) unreported, High Court, para 46.

3   *R(Clegg) v Salford City Council* [2007] EWHC 3276 (Admin), para 24.

4   Care Act 2014, s.48.

5   Wearden, G. 'The rise and fall of Southern Cross.' *The Guardian*, 1 June 2011.

6   SI 2015/301. Care and Support (Business Failure) Regulations 2015.

BUSINESS FAILURE: LOCAL AUTHORITY INTERVENTION. The local authority must step in for as long as it thinks necessary, assuming it does not anyway have a separate legal obligation to do so. The duty is to meet a person's need for care and support (or just support) irrespective of:

- the person's ordinary residence

- whether a needs or carer's assessment has been carried out

- whether the person's needs meet the eligibility criteria.

The local authority is permitted financially to charge the person, although not for information and advice. If a person, present in the local authority's area, is (legally) ordinarily resident in the area of another local authority, a cross charge can be made to that local authority.[1]

BUSINESS FAILURE: CQC OVERSIGHT OF MARKET. The Care Quality Commission (CQC) has a duty, under section 54 of the Care Act, to maintain a market oversight of larger social care providers:

- **Larger providers covered by oversight.** Only larger providers are covered, prescribed by criteria. These relate to either the number of hours of regulated care provided each week by a provider, or to the number of people provided with that care, or to both.[2]

- **Purpose of oversight.** The overall purpose is to consider the financial sustainability of the provider. If the CQC believes there is a significant risk, it can require the provider to plan how to mitigate or reduce the risk, and arrange – or require the provider to arrange – an independent review.

- **Warning to local authorities of pending business failure.** If the CQC believes that the provider is likely to be unable to continue to carry on providing care, it must inform the local authorities which it thinks will have to step in – under section 48 of the Act – to meet people's needs.[3]

---

1   Care Act 2014, s.48.

2   SI 2015/314. Care and Support (Market Oversight Criteria) Regulations 2015.

3   Care Act 2014, s.56.

C

Care and support (or support)

The Care Act hinges on the term 'care and support'. In effect, a need for adult social care is now legally termed a need for care and support. Likewise, a carer's need for help is legally termed, under the Act, a need for 'support'.

Section 8 states that the following are examples of how care and support – or just support – needs can be met under sections 18 to 20 of the Act:

- accommodation in a care home or in premises of some other type
- care and support at home or in the community
- counselling and other types of social work
- goods and facilities
- information, advice and advocacy.

These are examples not of care and support (or support) themselves, but of how needs for care and support (or support) can be met.[1]

CARE AND SUPPORT (OR SUPPORT): DEFINITION. There is no definition of care and support in the Act. It is almost a cipher, a label meant to cover a wide range of need. The nearest term in previous legislation – section 21 of the National Assistance Act 1948 – was 'care and attention'. The courts understood this term, in its natural and ordinary meaning, to be about 'looking after' but to be wider than nursing personal care:[2]

---

1   *R(GS) v London Borough of Camden* [2016] EWHC 1762, para 28.

2   *R(M) v Slough Borough Council* [2008] UKHL 52, para 32.

Looking after means doing something for the person being cared for which he cannot or should not be expected to do for himself: it might be household tasks which an old person can no longer perform or can only perform with great difficulty; it might be protection from risks which a mentally disabled person cannot perceive; it might be personal care, such as feeding, washing or toileting. This is not an exhaustive list. The provision of medical care is expressly excluded.[1]

The courts have already accepted a similarly broad approach, under the Care Act, as to what care and support needs might be beyond personal care or nursing.[2]

CARE AND SUPPORT (OR SUPPORT): BREADTH OF PROVISION. Examples are given in section 8 of how a person's care and support needs could be met. The listed services are merely the 'most common' ways of meeting need and do not preclude meeting need by other methods.[3] There are some explicit limits on provision, in sections 22 and 23 of the Care Act, placed on a local authority's ability to provide health services or housing. See **Divide between social care and health care**.

Examples of the potential breadth of provision are given in guidance – for instance, a laptop computer to enable a long-term carer to stay in contact with his family, by Skype, in the United States, or a direct payment enabling a woman caring for her father to place her four school-age children in a summer play scheme.[4]

Guidance states that local authorities should be flexible. For example, in the case of direct payments, there should not be a list of allowable purchases, and the range of options should be 'very wide'.[5]

---

1 *R(M) v Slough Borough Council* [2008] UKHL 52, para 33.

2 *R(SG) v Haringey London Borough Council* [2015] EWHC 2579 (Admin), para 71.

3 Statutory guidance, 2016, para 10.14.

4 Statutory guidance, 2016, para 11.38.

5 Statutory guidance, 2016, para 10.48.

CARE AND SUPPORT (OR SUPPORT): PROVISION OF ACCOMMODA-TION. The courts have, to date, stated that a duty to provide accommodation can arise under the Care Act only if the services required (to meet the person's care and support needs) are accommodation related – that is, they could not be provided, or would be 'effectively useless', if the person were to be without the accommodation.[1] So the ordinary meaning of care and support cannot be 'accommodation on its own'.[2]

In one case, the following were required to meet a person's need for care and support. But only two (in italic) could be regarded as accommodation related:

- assistance to improve her resilience

- assistance in learning by rote certain journeys to and from her home

- accompanied to appointments when she did not know the journey

- *visited at home to check home environment*

- is given nutritional and shopping advice

- is assisted by a local shopkeeper with using money in the shop

- is given counselling as well as practical advice and other support by Freedom from Torture

- assistance with general matters, including arranging and attending appointments, booking translators, learning English

- *assistance with domestic and practical tasks in the home*

- taken to a day centre by other women in the house.[3]

Care and support (or support) plans

Once an adult has been assessed as having a need which the local authority is going to meet, a care and support plan must be produced under section 25

---

1   *R(SG) v Haringey London Borough Council* [2015] EWHC 2579 (Admin).

2   *R(GS) v London Borough of Camden* [2016] EWHC 1762, para 28.

3   *R(SG) v Haringey London Borough Council* [2015] EWHC 2579 (Admin).

of the Care Act, likewise a support plan, if a carer has been assessed as having a need the local authority is going to meet:

Indication of breach of duty. A failure to implement such a plan could indicate breach of statutory duty[1] since the plan represents how the local authority is going to perform its duty to meet a person's needs. For example, a care and support plan specifying a sitting service which was then not provided on a number of occasions.[2]

Plan and contracted out service. The duty remains in relation to the plan even if the local authority has contracted out service provision. For instance, it was maladministration to fail to ensure that a care home implemented communication strategies and approaches – for a man with autism – as set out in his care and support plan.[3]

Minor departure from the plan. Departing from the plan might not be unlawful. For instance, if the local authority had given clear notice about the possible interruptions to the service, basically provided what they had undertaken to provide, not withdrawn the service and not interrupted a service intolerably – a day's missed cleaning might be acceptable, not a missing meal.[4]

Care and support plans in care homes. The duty to produce a care and support plan is irrespective of the care and support setting; so, a failure to create care and support plans for people entering care homes is maladministration.[5]

Substance makes up for lack of formality. A failure to produce formally a care and support plan is fault – but may be mitigated by other documentation, such as an email setting out the information of substance about service provision for the person.[6]

---

1   *R v Islington London Borough Council, ex p Rixon* [1997] 1 ELR 477.

2   *LGO, City Of Bradford Metropolitan District Council*, 2016 (15 015 462), paras 20–21.

3   *LGO, Herefordshire County Council*, 2016 (15 019 902), para 37.

4   *R v Islington London Borough Council, ex p McMillan* [1995] 160 LGRevR 321, High Court.

5   *LGO, London Borough of Bromley*, 2016 (15 016 292), para 42.

6   *LGO, Gateshead Metropolitan Borough Council*, 2016 (16 001 123), paras 19–20.

Inadequacy of plan through lack of cooperation of person. A care and support plan, inadequate because of lack of cooperation (refusing contact with local authority staff) of the adult in need, is not maladministration.[1]

CARE AND SUPPORT (OR SUPPORT) PLANS: MAIN CONTENT. The plan must address:

- **needs**: specify the needs identified by the needs assessment or carer's assessment

- **eligible needs**: specify whether, and if so to what extent, the needs meet the eligibility criteria

- **needs to be met**: specify the needs that the local authority is going to meet and how

- **provision**: specify how the provision of care and support, or support, could be relevant to the impact on the person's needs, or to achieving outcomes the person wants to achieve, etc.

- **personal budget**: include the personal budget for the person concerned

- **direct payments**: specify the amount and frequency of any direct payment, and

- **advice and information**: include advice and information about meeting, reducing, preventing or delaying needs.[2]

CARE AND SUPPORT (OR SUPPORT) PLANS: PREPARATION. When preparing a care and support plan, the local authority must involve the adult, the carer and anybody else the adult requests to be involved – or in case of mental incapacity, anyone appearing to the local authority to be interested in the adult's welfare.[3] The apparently absolute duty to involve the carer must, presumably, be subject to the adult's consent in order for confidentiality, data protection and human rights rules to be observed. Similarly, in preparing

---

1   *LGO, Buckinghamshire County Council,* 2016 (15 017 865), para 27.

2   Care Act 2014, s.25.

3   Care Act 2014, s.25.

a support plan for a carer, the local authority must involve the carer, the adult needing care (if the carer asks for this) and any other person whom the carer asks the authority to involve.[1]

CARE AND SUPPORT (OR SUPPORT) PLANS: REACHING AGREEMENT. The local authority must take all reasonable steps to reach agreement with the adult or carer for whom the plan is being prepared about how the authority should meet the needs in question.[2] This means that the local authority, ultimately, does not have to reach agreement as long as it has made reasonable efforts to do so.

Disagreement but no gross omission in plan. In the absence of a gross omission in the plan, in relation to meeting need, the courts might be reluctant to intervene in detailed matters of judgement, suggesting instead that the complaints procedure is more appropriate.[3]

No agreement through lack of cooperation. Failure to reach agreement – and to arrive at a care and support plan compliant with the Care Act – will not be maladministration if the person has not cooperated and the local authority has made all reasonable efforts.[4]

CARE AND SUPPORT (OR SUPPORT) PLANS: COPY. The local authority must give a copy of a care and support plan to the adult, to the adult's carer if the adult requests this and to any other person the adult requests. Similarly, the authority must give a copy of a support plan to the carer, to the adult needing care (if the carer requests this) and to anybody else the carer requests.[5]

---

1   Care Act 2014, s.25.

2   Care Act 2014, s.25.

3   *R(L) v London Borough of Barking and Dagenham* [2001] EWCA Civ 533, paras 26–27.

4   *LGO, Buckinghamshire County Council*, 2016 (15 017 865), para 27.

5   Care Act 2014, s.25.

CARE AND SUPPORT (OR SUPPORT) PLANS: SPEED. Guidance states that there is no defined timescale for completion of care and support (or support) plans, but that they should be completed in a timely fashion, proportionate to the needs to be met.[1]

> **Four-month delay until mother's death**. A four-month delay between assessment and a support plan for a carer – in a case in which assessment and funding was straightforward – meant that the carer received no support up to the point at which his mother died. This was maladministration and injustice.[2]

Care cap

The Care Act contains provisions for a system of capping the amount of money anybody must pay in their lifetime for meeting their eligible, assessed needs for care and support. This system was originally due to come into force in April 2016 but has been delayed until at least 2020.[3] Although the Act gives an outline, the crucial detail will be in regulations which have not yet been passed.

Care home accommodation

For the purposes of the Care Act, care home accommodation is defined in terms of section 3 of the Care Standards Act 2000[4] as an establishment (other than an NHS hospital or children's home) providing accommodation,

---

1   Statutory guidance, 2016, para 10.84.

2   *LGO, Sefton Metropolitan Borough Council*, 2016 (16 001 488), paras 22–23.

3   Department of Health *The Care Act 2014. Consultation on draft regulations and guidance to implement the cap on care costs and policy proposals for a new appeals system for care and support.* London: DH, February 2015. And for summary: House of Commons Library *Social care: Delayed introduction of funding reform, including the cap, and other changes until April 2020. Briefing Paper, 22 July 2015.* London: HCL, 2015.

4   SI 2014/2828. Care and Support (Ordinary Residence) (Specified Accommodation) Regulations 2014. And SI 2014/2670. Care and Support and After-care (Choice of Accommodation) Regulations 2014.

together with nursing or personal care, for people who are or have been ill, people who have or have had a mental disorder, people who are disabled or infirm, and people who are or have been dependent on alcohol or drugs.

Questions about regulatory and contractual requirements – and provision beyond these requirements by social services or the NHS – sometimes arise, for instance in relation to the daily living and nursing equipment that a resident might need, but also in relation to other services, such as physiotherapy, chiropody and incontinence pads:

- **Regulatory requirements**. Care homes have a duty to adhere to the Health and Social Care Act (Regulated Activities) Regulations 2014, covering a wide range of aspects of care, including safety, dignity and safeguarding.

- **Contractual requirements**. In addition, contractual obligations might go over and above what is required under the regulations. The contracting parties with the care home might be a local authority, an NHS body or a self-funding resident.

- **Over-and-above requirements**. If an individual resident has a need over and above the regulatory and contractual requirements placed on the care home, then a local authority or NHS body should consider whether the need is one which they are obliged, or have a discretion, to meet. An example of this principle, in relation for instance to equipment provision in care homes, is explained in guidance about NHS continuing health care.[1]

- **Breach of requirements and position of resident**. If a care home is apparently in breach of contract or of its regulatory duty, a local authority or NHS body should clearly not abandon a resident of a care home (even a self-funding one) who is in need, and should consider whether it is necessary to meet the need ('without prejudice' perhaps), and take up the contractual or regulatory (through the Care Quality Commission) issue separately.

Care home fees

Local authorities are sometimes challenged about the level of fee they are prepared to pay care homes. Sometimes such challenges are made by service

---

1   Department of Health *National framework for NHS continuing healthcare and NHS-funded nursing care.* London: DH, 2012, para 172, page 47.

users and relate to the rules about choice of care home and topping up (see **Choice of accommodation**).

Other challenges are made by care homes, usually by a local care home association, about the adequacy of fee levels. Some of these cases have succeeded, in relation to the following for example:

- the process of setting fees has been judged unfair or irrational[1]

- a freeze on fees with no prior consultation[2]

- non-response by a local authority to the care home's concerns[3]

- feeding inaccurate figures into the mathematical model used[4]

- benchmarked fee level, referring to neighbouring areas, but not own area[5]

- arithmetical model used, misapplied, and local authority had not relied on its own judgement and experience.[6]

Nonetheless, the Court of Appeal has more recently indicated that the courts should generally be slow to become involved in these disputes,[7] meaning that judicial interference is now less likely.[8]

Care Programme Approach

The Care Programme Approach (CPA) is an NHS policy setting out how to manage the needs of people with severe and enduring mental illness. It is an approach embedded specifically in guidance, not legislation, and

---

1   *R(Forest Care Homes) v Pembrokeshire County Council* [2010] EWHC 3514 (Admin).

2   *R(Sefton Care Association and others) v Sefton Council* [2011] EWHC 2676 (Admin).

3   *R(EMCARE) v Leicestershire County Council* [2011] EWHC 3096 (Admin).

4   *R(Care North East Newcastle) v Newcastle City Council* [2012] EWHC 2566 (Admin).

5   *R(Redcar & Cleveland Independent Providers Association and others) v Redcar & Cleveland Borough Council* [2013] EWHC 4 (Admin).

6   *R(South Tyneside Care Home Owners Association and others) v South Tyneside Council* [2013] EWHC 1827 (Admin).

7   *R(Members of the Committee of Care North East Northumberland) v Northumberland County Council* [2013] EWCA Civ 1740.

8   *Mayfield Care Ltd. v St Helen's Metropolitan Borough Council* [2015] EWHC 1057.

comes, overall, under the general duty to provide services under sections 1 and 3 of the NHS Act 2006.[1] Integrated mental health and social care teams sometimes collapse decision-making under the Care Act into the CPA approach, forgetting that the former contains separate legal obligations with different rules. CPA guidance draws attention to this pitfall.[2] Thus, a failure to offer, in addition to consideration of CPA, a Care Act assessment – carried out either by the mental health team itself or by another team in the local authority – can result in an 'error of law' or maladministration.[3]

Care providers

Much of adult social care is now provided by independent, registered care providers in the form of home care agencies or care homes contracted either by local authorities, or by self-funding service users or their families. In recent years, the local government ombudsman's remit has been extended to investigate complaints against independent providers, as well as against local authorities. See **Local Government Ombudsman**.

> **EXAMPLES OF INVESTIGATIONS INVOLVING INDEPENDENT CARE PROVIDERS**
> These include:
>
> - **missed visits**: not investigating missed or short home care visits to a self-funding person at home, and charging for missed visits
>
> - **poor or non-existent care**: providing poor, inconsistent or non-existent care to a self-funding person at home
>
> - **not monitoring care home residents**: not monitoring care home residents sufficiently to keep them safe

---

1   *K v Central and North West London Mental Health NHS Trust, and Kensington and Chelsea Royal London Borough Council* [2008] EWHC 1217 QB, paras 35, 37.

2   Department of Health *Refocusing the Care Programme Approach: Policy and positive practice guidance*. London: DH, 2009, p.13.

3   *R(HP) v London Borough of Islington* [2004] EWHC Admin 07, para 37. And *LGO, Shropshire County Council*, 2013 (12 007 311), paras 19–21, 45.

- **charging for extra services**: without clear agreement with the service user, charging him for extra services (e.g. shopping and cleaning) not covered by the care agency's contract with a local authority

- **double charging**: including in the charge for a self-funding care home resident a sum of £108, which the care home was already receiving from the NHS to cover the 'funded nursing care' element of the person's care[1]

- **retrospective double charging**: a care home trying to charge a now self-funding resident retrospectively for a previous period, when he had been placed by the local authority at a lower rate (lower, that is, than the self-funding rate). The care home now tried to claw back the difference for that previous period. The ombudsman found fault and injustice. The care provider refused to comply with the ombudsman's recommendations for reimbursement to the resident. The ombudsman therefore published an adverse findings notice and passed on details to the Care Quality Commission.[2]

Care Quality Commission (CQC)

Under the Health and Social Care Act 2008, the Care Quality Commission (CQC) regulates and inspects registered care providers in England, including care homes, care agencies, hospitals and general medical practices (GPs).

CQC: REGULATED ACTIVITIES, LEGAL REQUIREMENTS. The CQC applies the 'regulated activities' regulations, which, amongst other things, refer to matters such as person-centred care, dignity and respect, autonomy and independence, need for consent, safe care and treatment, safeguarding from abuse and improper treatment, meeting nutrition and hydration needs, and suitable premises and equipment.[3] There is nothing to stop a local

---

1   Local Government Ombudsman *Focus report: Learning the lessons from complaints about adult social care providers registered with the Care Quality Commission.* London: LGO, 2012, pp.5–8.

2   Local Government Ombudsman *Adverse Findings Notice of the Local Government Ombudsman about Cherry Acre Residential Home*, 2015.

3   SI 2014/2936. Health and Social Care Act 2008 (Regulated Activities) Regulations 2014.

authority stipulating in its contracts standards that exceed what is required by these regulations.[1]

Carers

Carers have stronger legal rights under the Care Act than under previous community care legislation.

CARERS: DEFINITION. A carer is defined so as to exclude somebody providing care under a contract or through voluntary work. Local authorities have discretion to waive this rule if the relationship between the adult and the person providing the care is such that it would be appropriate to regard the latter as a carer under the Act[2] – for instance, if that same paid carer were also providing informal care outside of the paid hours.[3] This might be so in the case of a family member receiving a direct payment for those paid hours.

CARERS: RIGHT TO ASSESSMENT. Under section 10 of the Care Act, the right to assessment for a carer is triggered if it appears to the local authority that the carer might need support now, or is likely to in the future. It doesn't matter what the level of that need is likely to be (e.g. it might be low). Under previous legislation, entitlement to assessment arose only if the carer was providing substantial care on a regular basis.[4] For the rules about assessment of carers, see **Assessment**.

CARERS: ELIGIBILITY AND ENTITLEMENT TO SUPPORT. Eligibility criteria under the Care Act apply to carers.[5] If a carer's needs are assessed

---

1   *R v Cleveland County Council, ex p Cleveland Care Homes Association* [1993] 158 LGRevR 641, High Court.

2   Care Act 2014, s.10.

3   Statutory guidance, 2016, para 6.17.

4   See previous legislation: Carers and Disabled Children Act 2000.

5   Care and Support (Eligibility Criteria) Regulations 2015.

to meet the eligibility criteria, then the local authority has a duty to meet those needs.[1]

Under previous legislation, there was no clear duty, following assessment, to meet the needs of carers, which is why many local authorities used what was effectively a discretion to make one-off annual payments to carers, irrespective of their needs. Now, personal budgets must be calculated on an individual basis and be commensurate with the carer's assessed need. See **Personal budgets**.

Flat rate, one-off payments are inconsistent with the law because one carer's needs might call for a very different level of personal budget than another's. Despite this, early evidence suggests that local authorities are continuing with flat-rate payments, despite the change in the law.[2] For the detailed rules about carers' eligibility, see **Eligibility**.

Carers with eligible needs are entitled to support plans, personal budgets and direct payments. See **Care and support (or support) plans**; **Personal budgets**; **Direct payments**.

Challenging decisions

Options for challenging decisions include asking for a second view or opinion, complaining to a local authority or NHS body, taking the complaint subsequently to the local government ombudsman or health service ombudsman, taking a judicial review legal case, raising the matter with a local councillor or Member of Parliament, or sometimes going to the press. (The latter can bear fruit, but is also an unpredictable option.)

Changes and closures

The courts have held that – even in the absence of a statutory duty on local authorities to consult about major changes to services (including closures) – service users might have a procedural, common law, 'legitimate expectation'

---

1   Care Act 2014, s.20.

2   Bennett, B. *Care Act for carers one year on: Lessons learned, next steps.* London: Carers Trust, 2016.

to be consulted fairly.[1] There are four key requirements. First, the consultation must be at a time when proposals are still at a formative stage. Second, any proposal must be explained with sufficient reasons, in order to permit intelligent consideration and response. Third, adequate time must be given for that consideration and response. Fourth, the product of consultation must be conscientiously taken into account when a final decision is being reached.[2]

In adult social care, challenges have typically been made about closure of care homes or day centres. Many have failed – for instance when a local authority has been able to demonstrate:

- **an open mind**: keeping, in principle, an open mind during the consultation[3] despite the suggestion that the local authority had already made up its mind since the budget set was consistent only with the closures going ahead[4]

- **it is rectifying the process**: rectifying a process that was initially unfair (because of too limited a consultation)[5]

- **that it had consulted**: even though the consultation was minimal and the way in which day centre users were informed was insensitive – since this was not the same as illegality or irrationality.[6]

On the other hand, challenges sometimes succeed – for instance because of:

- **a non-specific consultation**: consulting on the closure of day centres generally but not in respect of a particular day centre[7]

- **a short timeframe**: too short a consultation period for residents of a care home (five days)[8]

---

1   *R v Devon County Council, ex parte Baker* [1995] 1 All E.R. 75. And *R(Moseley) v London Borough of Haringey* [2014] UKSC 56.

2   *R(Moseley) v London Borough of Haringey* [2014] UKSC 56. And *R v London Borough of Brent, ex p Gunning* (1985) 84 LGR 168.

3   *Barwick v Bridgend County Borough Council* [2009] EWHC 1723 (Admin).

4   *R(Hide) v Staffordshire County Council* [2007] EWCA Civ 860.

5   *Barwick v Bridgend County Borough Council* [2009] EWHC 1723 (Admin).

6   *R(Bishop) v Bromley London Borough Council* [2006] EWHC 2148 (Admin), para 30.

7   *R(LH) v Shropshire County Council* [2014] EWCA Civ 404, para 25.

8   *R v Devon County Council, ex parte Baker* [1995] 1 All E.R. 75.

- **misleading information**: using misleading and wrong information in the consultation – for example, arguing that there were health and safety concerns about the physical structure of a council care home, contrary to the evidence of the survey report and barely giving the true reasons: a policy of reducing residential care services and saving money.[1]

CHANGES AND CLOSURES: SUBSTANTIVE LEGITIMATE EXPECTATION.

Occasionally, legitimate expectation might extend beyond the procedural to the substantive, meaning not only a right to a fair consultation process but to continuation of the actual service itself:

> **Breach of promise: an abuse of power.** A woman had been promised a home for life in an NHS unit free of charge before being told by the NHS that she would have to move to a nursing home. There being no overriding public interest to justify breach of the promise, the Court of Appeal held that the decision to close the unit was unlawful and an abuse of power.[2]

CHANGES AND CLOSURES: INDIVIDUAL ASSESSMENT OF HOW NEED WILL BE MET ALTERNATIVELY.

If a local authority changes significantly or closes a service, it remains under a duty to meet people's eligible needs. The courts have ruled that local authorities can lawfully adopt a two-stage decision-making process. First, decide in principle to close a care home, and only then – at the required time – carry out individual assessments to determine a precise alternative placement.[3]

CHANGES AND CLOSURES: HUMAN RIGHTS.

The courts have sometimes been prepared to accept application of articles 2 (right to life) and 8 (right to respect for home, private and family life) of the European Convention on Human Rights. For example, when a person has to move to a different care home. Diligent assessments – and carefully planned and managed moves –

---

1   *R(Madden) v Bury Metropolitan Borough Council* [2002] EWHC Admin 1882.

2   *R v North and East Devon Health Authority, ex p Coughlan* (1999) 2 CCLR 285, Court of Appeal.

3   *R(Cowl) v Plymouth District Council* [2001] EWCA Civ 1935 ([2002] 1 WLR 803), para 24. And *R(Grabham) v Northamptonshire County Council* [2006] EWHC 3292 (Admin).

will be crucial to the lawfulness of such moves, and to possible article 2 issues.[1] However, were a resident at imminent risk of mortality from any move – no matter how well planned and managed – then total closure of the home might have to be delayed.[2]

Closure of a care home might interfere with a person's private life under article 8 – including social ties, familiarity with surroundings and proximity to friends. Nonetheless, it might be justifiable legally for the economic well-being of the country (i.e. the particular local authority).[3] The same applies to the closure of a day centre.[4]

Charging

In summary, section 14 of the Care Act gives local authorities a power, but not a duty, to charge for care and support for adults in need, or support for carers, provided under sections 18 to 20 of the Act. This power does not apply to assessments, which come under different sections of the Act. If a local authority chooses to charge, detailed regulations govern how an adult or carer's resources are to be financially assessed.[5] In addition, under section 2 of the Care Act, local authorities also have a power, but no duty, to charge for services provided to prevent, delay or reduce needs – for adults or carers.[6]

Under both sections 2 and 14, carers cannot be charged if their needs are being met through the provision of services for the adult (e.g. respite care) although the adult can be. Local authorities need to be clear about this, since otherwise confusion (leading to maladministration) may arise about who – adult or carer – is eligible for what, for whom the service is legally provided and who falls to be means tested.[7]

---

1   *R(Haggerty) v St Helens Council* [2003] EWHC 803 (6 CCLR 352).

2   See e.g. arguments in *R(Wilson) v Coventry City Council* [2008] EWHC 2300 (Admin).

3   *R(Rowe) v Walsall Metropolitan Borough Council* (2001), unreported (leave to apply for judicial review).

4   *R(Bishop) v Bromley London Borough Council* [2006] EWHC 2148 (Admin), para 43.

5   SI 2014/2672. Care and Support (Charging and Assessment of Resources) Regulations 2014, r.7.

6   Care and Support (Preventing Needs for Care and Support) Regulations 2014.

7   *LGO, Surrey County Council*, 2016 (15 020 935), para 9.

However, the following cannot in any event be charged for under sections 2 and 14: community equipment in the form of aids (equipment), a minor adaptation (costing £1000 or less) and reablement for up to six weeks. Nor can any provision for an adult with variant Creutzfeldt-Jakob disease.[1]

CHARGING: POWER BUT NO DUTY. Local authorities have a power, but no duty, to charge financially for any provision they make. It might be expected that they would exercise the power to charge to the full given financial pressures. However, there are three brakes on local authorities doing this:

- **Breaking even, not generating income**. Both sections 2 and 14 stipulate that the local authority can charge only up to the cost which it, the local authority, incurs in meeting the person's need under section 14 – or providing services, facilities, resources or anything else under section 2.

- **Not impoverishing the person**. Local authorities must not, in making a charge, reduce a person's income to below a certain specified level.[2]

- **Carers**. Guidance does not encourage the charging of carers. It states that it might be a 'false economy', and affect the carer's ability and willingness to continue to care. Systematic or excessive charging of carers would be likely to lead to the refusal of carers to accept support from the local authority, in turn leading to carer breakdown – and to the local authority having to step in to meet the needs of the adult.[3]

If the carer's needs are to be met by providing a service to the adult – such as a respite or sitting service – then it is the adult who is chargeable under the Act and not the carer.[4]

---

1   SI 2014/2672. Care and Support (Charging and Assessment of Resources) Regulations 2014, rr.3, 4. And SI 2014/2673. Care and Support (Preventing Needs for Care and Support) Regulations 2014, rr.4, 5.

2   Care Act 2014, s.14. And SI 2014/2672. Care and Support (Charging and Assessment of Resources) Regulations 2014, r.7. And SI 2014/2673. Care and Support (Preventing Needs for Care and Support) Regulations 2014.

3   Statutory guidance, 2016, paras 8.50–8.51.

4   Statutory guidance, 2016, para 8.55.

CHARGING: CLARITY. Given the discretion whether to charge, each local authority needs to have a policy as to what it will and won't charge for. Guidance states that clear information must be given to individuals and/or their representatives about chargeability of services, means testing, invoicing, etc.[1]

> **EXAMPLES OF MALADMINISTRATION OR UNLAWFULNESS**
>
> - **Failure to have a charging policy or to communicate it**. Failure to have such a policy is itself maladministration, as is failure to communicate it to staff – for example, on whether and how respite care would be charged for. In turn, if service users are not informed about the local policy and rules, then that too is maladministration.[2]
>
> - **Clear explanation of charging**. A local authority came to a view about the level of a care home resident's assets, based on her interest in four different properties. But it gave no reasons for rejecting a solicitor's explanation as to what her interest in these properties was. Both in common law and under Department of Health guidance, which called for clear explanation to be given by local authorities, there was a duty to give reasons – that is, sufficient explanation as to why the solicitor's arguments were being rejected.[3]
>
> - **Timely financial assessment and invoicing**. Invoicing should be regular, and not months in retrospect. To do otherwise is maladministration,[4] as is taking six months over financial assessment, resulting in delayed invoicing.[5]
>
> - **Late invoicing and waiving of charges**. The ombudsmen will find maladministration but will not necessarily say that the charge be waived following late invoicing, since care will still have been provided. However, they recommended, following a 10-month delay in invoicing for the top-up payable by the family for a care home placement, that

---

1   Statutory guidance, 2016, para 8.2 – and Annex D, para 7.

2   *LGO, City of London*, 2011 (09 014 026), para 32.

3   *R(Bhandari) v London Borough of Croydon* (2016), unreported.

4   *LGO, London Borough of Ealing*, 2013 (12 012 697), para 44.

5   *LGO, Royal Borough of Kingston upon Thames Council*, 2014 (11 022 473), paras 67, 75.

the money owing should be repaid through a payment plan, not all at once.[1]

When a local authority delayed its financial assessment for nearly six months – which the ombudsman found was too long a period – it was reasonable to waive a third of the money owing. The family had argued that, had they been aware sooner of the cost, they might have forgone some of the care, including a sitting service, provided.[2]

• **Explaining local authority contractual and cost responsibilities.** Following a financial assessment, if a person is contributing to their care home placement, arranged by the local authority – and paying that contribution direct to the care home – it is maladministration if the local authority does not explain that it, the authority, remains contractually and legally responsible for the care and the full, overall cost.[3]

CHARGING: PREVENTION. When a local authority provides, or arranges, services, facilities or resources under section 2 of the Act to prevent, delay or reduce the needs of adults or carers, it has discretion to charge financially. Guidance points out that, on the one hand, charging might be required to make such services viable. On the other hand, charges might put people off from taking them up, which would defeat their object.[4]

CHARGING: COMMUNITY EQUIPMENT. In any event, local authorities are prohibited, under regulations, from charging for community equipment whether under section 2 (prevention) or section 14 (meeting assessed need). Community equipment means an aid, or a minor adaptation to property, for the purpose of assisting with nursing at home or aiding daily living and, for the purposes of these Regulations, an adaptation is minor if the cost

---

1 *LGO, Trafford Council,* 2016 (15 015 337), paras 40–42.

2 *LGO, City of York Council,* 2016 (16 001 312), paras 20–26.

3 *LGO, London Borough of Bromley,* 2011 (08 019 214), para 41.

4 Statutory guidance, 2016, paras 2.55–2.57.

of making the adaptation is £1000 or less.[1] This means that all aids must be provided free of charge, whatever their cost, whereas a local authority could, if it wished, charge for an adaptation costing more than £1000.

CHARGING: INTERMEDIATE CARE AND REABLEMENT. Local authorities are prohibited from charging for intermediate care, including reablement, for up to a period of six weeks. Under section 2 of the Act (prevention, etc.), intermediate care and reablement services:

- consist of a programme of services, facilities or resources

- are for a specified period, and

- have as their purpose the provision of assistance to the adult to enable the adult to maintain or regain the skills needed to live independently in their own home.[2]

The definition, for the purpose of section 14 of the Act (charging for meeting assessed need), refers to a 'programme of care and support, or support' instead of 'services, facilities and resources'[3] (see **Reablement**). The six weeks of reablement is not necessarily confined to non-residential services, and local authorities need to be clear about when reablement commences and stops. Otherwise, mistakes will be made with financial charging:

Lack of clarity about reablement period in care home. Placed for a short period in a care home, a resident was charged for what the family had believed was intermediate care or reablement under the regulations. Up to the point at which an assessment concluded that the resident needed long-term care in the care home – and the result of that assessment had

---

1 SI 2014/2672. Care and Support (Charging and Assessment of Resources) Regulations 2014, r.3. And SI 2014/2673. Care and Support (Preventing Needs for Care and Support) Regulations 2014.

2 SI 2014/2673. Care and Support (Preventing Needs for Care and Support) Regulations 2014.

3 SI 2014/2672. Care and Support (Charging and Assessment of Resources) Regulations 2014, r.3.

been communicated to the family (some weeks later) – the financial charge represented maladministration.[1]

Confusion about reablement at a person's home in care and support plan. A woman received both chargeable care and reablement visits concurrently over a period of weeks. The time allotted to each type of visit changed, but the care and support plan was not altered to reflect this. Confusion, about what charges were payable, followed.[2]

Clarity about changeover from reablement to chargeable care. A local authority was not clear with the family about the point at which reablement at a man's home (following discharge from hospital) was to stop and financially chargeable care was to start. Which meant the family could not plan how to organise the care required, taking into account the cost involved. This was maladministration and the local authority agreed to waive charges owing for a period of four weeks.[3]

Undertaking to provide intermediate care, then not doing so. An 81-year-old woman, suffering falls at home, was told she would be provided with intermediate care, free of charge for six weeks. However, there was not sufficient capacity in the area for this to be provided; instead she was provided with care, but it was not explained clearly to her that she would have to pay. The ombudsman found maladministration, and the local authority agreed to waive the charges for the six weeks.[4]

CHARGING: MEETING NEED. Section 14 of the Care Act states that a local authority has a legal power to charge for services when meeting an adult's or carer's needs under sections 18 to 20 of the Act. If it meets the needs of an adult or carer whose resources are over the financial limit, it may make an additional charge for making the arrangements for the service. If a local authority does choose to charge, there is a duty under section 17 to assess the adult or carer financially. There are detailed rules about this. The following paragraphs outline some of these.

---

1   *LGO, Lancashire County Council*, 2016 (15 019 274), paras 11, 16, 25. See similarly: *LGO, Wirral Metropolitan Borough Council*, 2016 (15 016 910), paras 27–29.

2   *LGO, London Borough of Croydon*, 2016 (15 018 193), paras 30–32.

3   *LGO, Shropshire Council*, 2016 (16 001 218), paras 19–21.

4   *LGO, Norfolk County Council*, 2016 (15 016 559), paras 35–36.

CHARGING: PERSON'S OWN RESOURCES OVER THE FINANCIAL LIMIT. If a person is in a care home, and their capital resources exceed £23,250, the local authority is not permitted to pay towards the cost of provision of accommodation in that care home. If the person is not in a care home, but has resources exceeding £23,250, then the local authority can, but does not have to, pay towards the cost of the person's care and support. The same applies in respect of paying towards the cost of a carer's support.[1]

CHARGING: PERSONAL EXPENSES ALLOWANCE. If a person is placed by a local authority in a care home, the local authority must ensure that the person retains a minimum weekly income, known as the personal expenses allowance (PEA). This is currently set at £24.90 per week.[2] Guidance clarifies that it is not a benefit payable by the local authority, but is the amount that must be left after charges have been deducted. It is for people to spend as they wish, and neither local authority nor care home should exercise pressure on the resident. It must not be spent on aspects of care and support that have been contracted for by the local authority and/or assessed as necessary to meet the person's eligible care and support needs by the local authority or the NHS.

> **Misuse of personal expenses allowance**. Care homes should not appropriate a resident's PEA to cover running costs of the care home. For instance, it was maladministration when a local authority care home used a resident's PEA for newspapers in the home (which she couldn't read), piano tuning, aquarium maintenance and garden plants.[3]
>
> **Local authority misusing its position of trust to misuse a resident's personal expenses allowance**. The assets of a woman in a care home fell below the upper financial threshold, meaning that the local authority now took over the placement, but she didn't want to move to another (cheaper) care home. What the local authority should have done was to assess whether

---

1   SI 2014/2672. Care and Support (Charging and Assessment of Resources) Regulations 2014, r.12.

2   Care and Support (Charging and Assessment of Resources) Regulations 2014, r.7.

3   *LGO, Hampshire County Council*, 2001 (99/B/03979).

she needed to be there – in which case it would have had an obligation to pay the higher fee to the care home. Or, decide she could move to another, cheaper care home. It did neither. Instead, it permitted her to remain there but was granted appointeeship to manage her finances. It withheld her PEA from her, and sought to use her funds (including what would have been the PEA amounts) for her to pay her own top-up – something that is unlawful (the top-up must come from a third party). This was maladministration.[1]

There are some circumstances in which 'it would not be appropriate' to leave the person with only the PEA. For example, if the person had a dependent child with needs.[2]

CHARGING: LEAVING A MINIMUM INCOME. A person living other than in a care home must be left with a minimum income: at least the equivalent of the value of Income Support, or the Guaranteed Credit element of Pension Credit, plus a minimum buffer of 25 per cent.[3]

CHARGING: SHORT-TERM RESIDENT. A local authority is permitted, but not obliged, financially to assess and charge a short-term resident of a care home, but this would have to be on the same basis as it would charge a person living in their own home, meaning that the local authority could not take account of the person's home. A short-term resident is defined as a resident staying eight weeks or less.[4]

This rule is distinct from rules about charging a 'temporary resident' of a care home (see below). A temporary resident is defined as one whose stay is either unlikely to exceed 52 weeks or, exceptionally, unlikely substantially to exceed 52 weeks.[5] Guidance states that, for clarity, the local authority

---

1   *LGO, North Yorkshire County Council*, 2016 (15 012 709), paras 23–26.

2   Statutory guidance, 2016, Annex C, paras 45–46.

3   Care and Support (Charging and Assessment of Resources) Regulations 2014, r.7. Department of Health. And Statutory guidance, 2016, Annex C, paras 48–50.

4   SI 2014/2672. Care and Support (Charging and Assessment of Resources) Regulations 2014, r.8.

5   SI 2014/2672. Care and Support (Charging and Assessment of Resources) Regulations 2014, r.2.

must agree with the resident and/or their representative about their status of temporary resident.[1]

> **Lack of clarity about resident's status: maladministration**. Simply informing the person and family about permanent status, as opposed to discussion and agreement, is not enough and is maladministration,[2] as is simply changing the status from temporary to permanent status, informing the family only nine months later and demanding accumulated arrears.[3]
>
> **Charging: refusal of financial assessment**. If a person refuses to be assessed financially, or has not cooperated with the financial assessment, the local authority can legally conclude that the person's resources exceed the financial limit.[4]

CHARGING: LIGHT TOUCH FINANCIAL ASSESSMENT. A local authority can decide to do a 'light touch' financial assessment. This is when the adult consents to the local authority not carrying out a detailed financial assessment as set out in the regulations but the local authority reaches a decision on the available evidence, either to view the adult as coming over the financial threshold or coming beneath it.[5]

> **Refusal of light touch financial assessment**. A man had appointed an enduring power of attorney. He did not want to disclose his finances to the local authority, and accepted that this meant he would be a full payer for the care that the local authority was arranging. However, the local authority would not accept this and persisted in its efforts to obtain financial disclosure. The ombudsman found maladministration, because there was

1   Statutory guidance, 2016, Annex F, para 5.

2   *LGO, London Borough of Ealing*, 2013 (12 012 697), para 40.

3   *LGO, Humberside County Council*, 1992 (91/C/0774).

4   SI 2014/2672. Care and Support (Charging and Assessment of Resources) Regulations 2014, r.10.

5   Care and Support (Charging) Regulations 2014, r.10.

no evidence that the local authority had considered a 'light touch' financial assessment and acknowledged his wish to be a full payer.[1]

CHARGING: TAKING ACCOUNT OF INCOME. The regulations on charging contain further, detailed rules about the assessment of income. The following summarises some of these:[2]

- **Earnings**. Earnings must be disregarded.[3]

- **Deprivation of, and notional, income**. A person will be assessed as having 'notional income', which the person has 'deprived' themselves of, in order to decrease the amount that they may be liable to pay towards the cost of care and support, or support. (There is a similar rule in relation to deprivation of capital. See below.)[4]

- **Housing-related costs**. If the person is not permanently resident in a care home, then housing-related costs of the adult's main or only home cannot be taken into account.[5]

- **Disability-related expenditure**. If the local authority is taking account of a person's disability benefits as income, then it must disregard the person's disability-related expenditure. Disability benefits are: attendance allowance, disability living allowance, and personal independence payment. Disability-related expenditure includes but is not limited to payment for any community alarm system, costs of any privately arranged care services required including respite care, and the costs of any specialist items needed to meet the adult's disability. Examples of specialist items include:

  » **day or night care**: which is not being arranged by the local authority

  » **laundry**: specialist washing powders or laundry

---

1   *LGO, Royal Borough of Kingston upon Thames*, 2016 (15 013 797), paras 52–55.

2   Care and Support (Charging) Regulations 2014, schedule 2. And Statutory guidance, 2016, Annex C.

3   Care and Support (Charging) Regulations 2014, r.14.

4   Care and Support (Charging) Regulations 2014, rr.17, 22.

5   Care and Support (Charging) Regulations 2014, schedule 1, Part 1, applying to this bullet point and immediately following.

> » **diet**: additional costs due to illness or disability

> » **clothing or footwear**: special, or extra need from disability-related wear and tear

> » **additional costs of bedding**: for example, because of incontinence

> » **heating**: costs, or metered costs of water, above the average levels for the area and housing type needed through age, medical condition or disability

> » **garden, cleaning, etc.**: reasonable costs of basic garden maintenance, cleaning or domestic help, if necessitated by the individual's disability and not met by social services

> » **equipment**: purchase, maintenance and repair of disability-related equipment

> » **personal assistance**: costs

> » **internet**: access for example for blind and partially sighted people

> » **transport and mobility component of DLA**: other transport costs necessitated by illness or disability, including costs of transport to day centres, over and above the mobility component of DLA or PIP

> » **incontinence pads, etc.**: it may be reasonable for a council not to allow for items where a reasonable alternative is available at lesser cost. For example, a council might adopt a policy not to allow for the private purchase cost of continence pads, where these are available from the NHS.

- **Direct payment**. Any direct payment received by the adult must be disregarded.

- **Mobility component**. The mobility component of disability living allowance or personal independence payment must be disregarded.

- **Armed forces payment**. Armed forces independence payment must be disregarded.

- **Temporary care home residents: benefits**. If the adult is a temporary resident, the following must be disregarded: (a) any attendance allowance, (b) the care component of any disability living allowance, or (c) the daily living component of any personal independence payment.

- **Payments recognised in care and support – or support – plans**. Up to a certain level of disregard, any regular payment intended and used for any item which was not specified in the personal budget but was specified in the care and support plan, or support plan, must be disregarded. The payments covered are:

  » a charitable payment

  » a voluntary payment

  » a payment from a trust whose funds are derived from a payment made in consequence of any personal injury to the adult

  » as a result of personal injury, a payment under an annuity purchased – (i) under an agreement or court order to make payments to the adult, or (ii) from funds derived from a payment made, or

  » any other payment received through any agreement or court order to make payments to the resident, as a result of any personal injury to the adult.

CHARGING: DISABILITY-RELATED EXPENDITURE. Local authorities need to be clear and not overly restrictive about what constitutes disability-related expenditure (DRE; see above) – that is, outgoings that should not be considered as available to pay a charge. Explanation should be given as to why claims for disability-related expenditure are rejected and people be given a chance to appeal.[1] An overly rigid application of what could count as DRE risks unlawfulness.

> **Avoiding rigid approach to disability-related expenditure: adult paying a family member for help**. A local authority, as a matter of policy, refused to allow as DRE payments made to family members by an adult in need. A woman was paying her daughter, an experienced nurse, £45 a week for a range of assistance (laundry, ironing, correspondence, finances, some housework, toenail cutting, outings) – over and above that which the council carers provided. Her daughter had reduced her working week as a nurse in order to spend more time with her mother. It was an 80-mile round trip. To compensate her for loss of earnings, her mother paid her. The rigid policy –

---

1   LGO, *Northamptonshire County Council*, 2016 (15 016 511), para 13.

based on the idea that family members would do things free of charge – did not apply in this case; it had been unlawfully applied.[1]

Ruling out certain expenditure without explanation. A woman's costs for laundry and gardening were included as DRE. But it was maladministration to exclude the following *without explanation* as to why: transport costs to health appointments and activities, assistance with dog costs, extra costs charged by professionals to visit her at home, complementary therapist for her condition, domestic tasks such as window cleaning, delivery costs for items the person could not get out to buy.[2]

Fuel allowance: mental health as well as physical disability consideration. A local authority rejected a person's claim – that expenditure on fuel be disregarded – on the grounds that it would only consider car journeys under five miles to be disability-related (i.e. an able-bodied person could have walked or cycled, whereas the disabled person could not). Longer distances would anyway require fuel expenditure, whether or not the person had a disability. The authority allowed only £2 a week on fuel. However, the ombudsman doubted that the local authority had taken account of his mental health needs and his need to maintain a social circle, and recommended a reassessment.[3]

Ruling out, reasonably, certain expenditure. A local authority approached disability-related expenditure as follows, in the case of a brain-injured man with physical and mental disabilities. It allowed for extra expenditure on energy and food which were related to the person's disability. However, the following were not related to his disability: wear and tear around the house, housing costs (he had no outstanding mortgage and did not pay council tax), alcohol, cigarettes, cost of keeping a dog and SKY television. In addition, no extra allowance was made for transport, since his transport costs were lower than the mobility component of disability living allowance which he was receiving. This was not maladministration.[4]

---

1 *R(Stephenson) v Stockton-on-Tees Borough Council* [2004] EWHC 2228 (Admin), High Court; [2005] EWCA Civ 960, Court of Appeal.

2 *LGO, Central Bedfordshire Council*, 2016 (13 014 946), paras 47–50.

3 *LGO, East Riding of Yorkshire Council*, 2016 (14 018 693) paras 52–56.

4 *LGO, Shropshire County Council*, 2016 (15 019 410), paras 19–22.

Informal payments by mother to son disregarded. A mother lived with her son, who had made certain adaptations to his home (including a conservatory). She paid him £50 a week, but this was not reflected in any formal rental agreement. In the absence of a formal agreement, the local authority declined to accept this as DRE: this was not maladministration.[1]

CHARGING: TAKING ACCOUNT OF CAPITAL. The regulations on charging contain detailed rules about the assessment of a person's capital. The following are a selection.[2]

- **Joint beneficial entitlement**. If more than one person is beneficially entitled to a capital asset, it has to be treated as if equally shared, unless the local authority has reason to believe otherwise, in which case the adult will be treated as possessing a different proportion of the asset.[3] Therefore, for example, taking account of the whole of the joint savings account held by a man and his wife led to this rule being breached, him being overcharged and to maladministration.[4]

- **Temporary care home resident but not a prospective resident**. The value of the adult's main or only home is disregarded where (a) the adult is taking reasonable steps to dispose of the dwelling in order that they may acquire another dwelling which they intend to occupy as their main or only home, or (b) the adult intends to return to occupy that dwelling as their main or only home and the dwelling is still available to them.[5]

- **Temporary care home resident but also a prospective resident**. The value of the adult's main or only home is disregarded if the adult, when provided in fact with accommodation under the Act, is intending (a) to take reasonable steps to dispose of the dwelling in order to acquire another dwelling which they intend to occupy as their main or only home, or (b) to return to

---

1   *LGO, Derby City Council*, 2016 (16 003 970), paras 15, 20.

2   Care and Support (Charging) Regulations 2014, schedule 2. And Statutory guidance, 2016, Annex B.

3   Care and Support (Charging) Regulations 2014, r.24.

4   *LGO, Solihull Metropolitan Borough Council*, 2016 (15 000 201), para 22.

5   Care and Support (Charging) Regulations 2014, schedule 2, para 1.

occupy that dwelling as their main or only home and the dwelling to which the adult intends to return is available to them.[1]

- **Twelve-week disregard for a permanent resident**. Where the adult is a permanent resident, the value of the adult's main or only home is disregarded for a period of 12 weeks beginning with the day on which the adult first moves into accommodation in a care home.[2] The 12-week disregard can be awarded more than once, as long as two periods of permanent residency are separated by more than 52 weeks.[3]

    The purpose of this period is to enable the resident and family to decide what to do about the property – for example, rent it out in some cases. So, a failure to inform the family that the 12-week period had started, following the decision that the stay in the care would be permanent, was maladministration.[4] Local authorities also need to be clear with families – for example, that although the person's main home is disregarded during 12 weeks, a charge may still be payable based on other assets. Failure to explain that the 12 weeks are not necessarily free of charge is maladministration.[5]

- **Deprivation of, and notional, capital**. A person will be assessed as having 'notional capital', which the person has 'deprived' themselves of in order to decrease the amount that they may be liable to pay towards the cost of care and support, or support.[6] It is probable that the existence of notional income does not mean that the local authority can set aside its duty to meet a person's needs,[7] in which case it would need to pursue the 'transferee' of the assets under section 70 of the Act.

- **Relatives living in the person's home before care home entry**. The person's only or main home is disregarded if it is occupied by a 'qualifying relative' of the adult. The relative must have occupied the premises as their main or only home since before the date on which the adult was first provided with

---

1   Care and Support (Charging) Regulations 2014, schedule 2, para 1.

2   Care and Support (Charging) Regulations 2014, schedule 2, para 2.

3   Care and Support (Charging) Regulations 2014, schedule 2, para 2.

4   *LGO, Brighton & Hove City Council*, 2016 (15 018 329), paras 20–22.

5   *LGO, Suffolk County Council*, 2016 (16 000 621), para 16.

6   Care and Support (Charging) Regulations 2014, r.22.

7   *Robertson v Fife Council* [2002] S.C. (H.L.), para 53 (Scottish case).

accommodation in a care home under the Act.[1] Under previous case law, occupation of the only or main home need not necessarily be, or have been, continuous.[2]

Qualifying relative means the adult's (a) partner, or (b) another family member or relative who is aged 60 or over or who is incapacitated, or (c) a child who is under 18. In case of estrangement or divorce from their former partner, the value of the adult's interest in that dwelling where it is still occupied as the home by the former partner who is a lone parent is disregarded.[3]

- **Relatives living in the person's home after care home entry**. A local authority may – but does not have to – disregard the value of any premises occupied in whole or in part by a qualifying relative of the adult as their main or only home, if the qualifying relative occupied the premises after the date on which the adult was first provided with accommodation in a care home under the Act.[4]

    A failure to show either that this discretion has been considered at all in an individual case, or, if it was, how the decision was reached not to exercise it (e.g. the decision not being recorded in the formal minutes of the relevant meeting) – is maladministration.[5]

- **Other person occupying the premises**. The value of any premises occupied in whole or in part by any other third party can be disregarded if the local authority considers it would be reasonable to disregard the value of those premises.[6] The local authority would have to show it had considered whether to exercise its discretion. In one case, it was reasonable to decide to take account of the value of the dwelling, even though the son was living in it. One of the factors was that he had returned from Australia not specifically to look after his mother (before she went into a care home) but for employment reasons.[7] But failing to give clear information about this rule to a family,

1   Care and Support (Charging) Regulations 2014, schedule 2, para 4.

2   *R(Walford) v Worcestershire County Council.* High Court: [2014] EWHC 234 (Admin), para 36. And Court of Appeal: [2015] EWCA Civ 22, para 19.

3   Care and Support (Charging) Regulations 2014, schedule 2, para 5.

4   Care and Support (Charging) Regulations 2014, schedule 2, para 4.

5   *LGO, Torbay Council,* 2016 (15 020 436), paras 49, 51, 57.

6   Care and Support (Charging) Regulations 2014, schedule 2, para 24.

7   *R v Somerset County Council, ex p Harcombe* [1997] 96 LGR 444, High Court.

when the son might have given up his job to care for his mother at home – had they known about the rule – was maladministration.[1]

Equally, the discretion may seem harshly applied but not amount to maladministration. As when a woman, under 60 years old, had given up her own home to live with and look after her mother. The local authority considered whether to exercise its discretionary disregard but decided to take the property into account, though offering the daughter a deferred payment agreement so she would not have to sell the home yet. The local authority's reasoning included the fact that the daughter continued to work, had benefited by living rent free and had provided considerable support, but the local authority did not consider the level of care to have been substantial in terms of savings to the public purse.[2]

- **Capital below the lower financial limit**. Capital of below £14,250 is disregarded. Over that amount, but below £23,250, it is treated as generating an income of £1.00 per week for every £250 between those two figures.[3] (Somebody with capital assets less than £14,250 would be assessed to pay for care on the basis only of any other income being received, and which can be taken into account.)

- **Personal possessions**. Any personal possessions are disregarded, except those acquired by the adult with the intention of reducing their capital in order to satisfy a local authority that they were unable to pay towards the cost of their care and support or support.[4]

- **Valuation of capital**. A capital asset may have a current market value. The current market value will be the price a willing buyer would pay to a willing seller. The way the market value is obtained will depend on the type of asset held. In case of dispute, an independent valuation should be obtained.[5] In case of a shared dwelling, the question of whether there is a willing buyer, when somebody else is still living there, currently, with a share of the property,

1   *LGO, Cumbria County Council*, 2001 (98/C/4738).

2   *LGO, West Sussex County Council*, 2016 (16 003 484), paras 24–31.

3   Care and Support (Charging) Regulations 2014, schedule 2, para 25.

4   Care and Support (Charging) Regulations 2014, schedule 2, para 13.

5   Care and Support (Charging) Regulations 2014, r.20. And: Statutory guidance, 2016, Annex B, paras 15, 18.

can be a moot point. At the very least, it would be maladministration not to obtain an independent valuation.[1]

- **Personal injury trusts**. Any amount referred to which would be disregarded under certain income support regulations must be disregarded.[2] This means that where the funds of a trust are derived from a payment made as a result of personal injury to the person or person's partner, the value of the trust fund, and the value of the right to receive any payment under that trust, are disregarded.[3]

- **Personal injury payments**. Any amount which would be disregarded under paragraph 12A of schedule 10 to the Income Support Regulations must be disregarded. This means a payment made to the person or their partner as a result of personal injury. The disregard lasts for 52 weeks only from when the person first receives any payment. The disregard doesn't apply to any subsequent payment made. It stops applying when the person no longer possesses the payment. This particular rule does not apply if the payment is made from a trust set up with a personal injury payment.[4] These rules do not apply if it is a payment specifically identified by a court to deal with the cost of providing care.[5]

- **Personal injury generally**. The rules are complicated and not intuitively easy to understand. For example, a local authority is not allowed to charge for providing services, even if the personal injury amount (in trust or administered by a court) is meant to cover the private purchase of care.[6] Administration by a court includes the management by a court-appointed deputy.[7] However, local authorities are encouraged to get involved when damages are first calculated.

  For instance, the cost of private accommodation and care would be included in the damages, but on the undertaking that assistance would not

---

1 *LGO, Staffordshire County Council*, 2016 (15 016 140), paras 18–24. See also: *LGO, City Of Bradford Metropolitan District Council*, 2016 (16 002 291).

2 Care and Support (Charging) Regulations 2014, schedule 2, para 15.

3 SI 1987/1967. Income Support (General) Regulations 1987, schedule 10, para 12.

4 SI 1987/1967. Income Support (General) Regulations 1987, schedule 10, para 12A.

5 Care and Support (Charging) Regulations 2014, schedule 2, para 16.

6 *Crofton v NHS Litigation Authority* [2007] EWCA Civ 71.

7 *R(ZYN) v Walsall Metropolitan Borough Council* [2014] EWHC 1918 (Admin).

be sought by the person's court-appointed deputy from the local authority at a later date, so avoiding 'double recovery'. But once damages have been awarded, and at a later date a person with a personal injury payment in trust or administered by a court (deputy) needs care, then the local authority appears to be precluded from taking account of the payment in deciding whether to provide care and at what cost.

This rule sometimes exasperates local authorities and has led one to refuse to adopt the recommendations of the local government ombudsman to disregard the personal injury payment.[1] In general, the courts are loathe to deny the cost of private care needs being built into personal injury awards because of the uncertainty over time of the quantity and quality of possible state-funded care.[2]

CHARGING: DEPRIVATION OF ASSETS. Section 70 of the Care Act contains a rule about a person giving away assets in order to avoid paying care charges under sections 18 to 20 of the Act. The outline of the rule is as follows:

- **Intending to avoid payment**. The adult transfers an asset to somebody else 'with the intention of avoiding charges for having the adult's needs met'.

- **Given away or under value**. The asset was given away, either for nothing or under value.

- **Amount owed**. The person who now has the asset must pay the local authority the difference between what the local authority has actually charged the adult, and what it would have charged the adult had the adult still had the asset.

- **Limit to payment**. The person with the asset does not have to pay more than the benefit they got from the asset.

- **Proportionate liability**. If there is more than one person to whom the asset or assets were transferred, there is proportionate liability.

- **Definition of asset**. An asset is defined as anything that can be taken account of under the rules for financial assessment.

---

1   *LGO, St Helens Metropolitan Borough Council*, June 2016 (14 009 949). And in the same case *Further report*, November 2016.

2   *Peters v East Midlands Strategic Health Authority* [2009] EWCA Civ 145, paras 64–88.

- **Value of asset**. The value of the asset must be calculated equal to the amount which would have been realised, given a willing seller on the open market at the time the transfer of the asset took place. But there must be a deduction to reflect any encumbrance (e.g. a mortgage) on the asset, and what would have been a reasonable expense incurred in a sale.

Guidance states that, in the first instance, the local authority should try to charge the adult concerned as if the deprivation had not occurred, thus treating the adult as having 'notional' capital or income. Failing this, it is the third party that is liable to pay.[1]

CHARGING: DEPRIVATION OF ASSETS – MOTIVATION. The key question is whether the adult had the 'intention' of avoiding charges. Guidance states that the local authority needs to consider whether avoidance of charges was a 'significant motivation' and that it would be unreasonable to impute intention if, at the time of the disposal of the assets, the person was fit and healthy and could not have foreseen the need for care and support.[2] The question is about the person's actual, subjective state of mind. But this can be decided on the basis of reasonable inference from the primary facts, given that local authorities are not mind-readers.[3] Even then local authorities should not make assumptions and should give reasons:

> **Not making assumptions about a 91-year-old**. An independent 91-year-old, already with some care needs but no serious condition or illness, with no idea or wish to go into a care home, gave £3000 to his grandson who was getting married and setting up home and £2000 for medical treatment for his son-in-law who lived in Australia and had cancer. Then, when his son-in-law died, he paid £4000 for his daughter to come home for a visit and then for her to visit her sister in Australia. Six months later, following a fall, he entered a care home.

---

1   Statutory guidance, 2016, Annex E.

2   Statutory guidance, 2016, Annex E.

3   *R(Beeson) v Dorset County Council* [2001] EWHC Admin 986, High Court, paras 9, 11; [2002] EWCA Civ 1812, Court of Appeal, para 13.

> The local authority claimed the expenditure was to avoid care home fees; the ombudsman found this was maladministration because it had assumed what the man's motivation was and given no 'logical explanation or basis' for its decision.[1]
>
> **Giving reasons for treating a disposal of a share in property, put into trust, as deprivation**. A woman put into trust her share of her property in 2013, a year after she had been diagnosed with dementia. She needed to go into a care home in 2015. The local authority treated the disposal as a deprivation of resources. The trustee, the couple's son, argued that the purpose had been estate planning and possible loss of mental capacity in the future of his parents. The local authority rejected this explanation without having considered all the relevant information or having given reasons for its decision. This was maladministration.[2]

Equally, a local authority might come to a decision on defensible grounds:

> **Foreseeable needs and explanation of consequences**. A woman with deteriorating health entered extra care accommodation. She sold her own home and distributed the proceeds to her four children. Some months later she suffered further deterioration and entered a care home. The local authority argued that it was not unreasonable to assume that residential care would be likely in the near future, and that it had explained at the time the possible legal consequences of her distribution of the proceeds. This was a defensible decision and not maladministration.[3]
>
> **Care needs developing over three years**. A woman developed Alzheimer's disease in late 2012. In August 2013, she put her home into a discretionary trust for her daughter and son and made a power of attorney. Her daughter provided care for her. By October 2013, the local authority began to provide care for her at home, and in December 2015 she moved into a care home. The ombudsman found that the local authority was justified in treating the disposal of the home as motivated by the wish to avoid care

---

1   *LGO, Cornwall Council*, 2016 (15 014 558), paras 9, 18–20.

2   *LGO, Lancashire County Council*, 2016 (16 001 845), para 22.

3   *LGO, Stockport Metropolitan Borough Council*, 2016 (15 014 345), para 21.

home fees, given the woman's decisions in relation to planning for her care, as a response to her deteriorating health.[1]

CHARGING: RECOVERY OF DEBTS. Under section 69 of the Care Act, local authorities can recover money owing as a civil debt in the county court with these provisos:

- **Deferred payment**. If a deferred payment agreement could be entered into, in order to secure the money owing, then the local authority is not permitted to pursue debt recovery. If the adult refuses the offer of a deferred payment agreement, then the authority can pursue the debt.

- **Six-year rule**. The local authority needs to act within six years of the sum becoming due.

- **Misrepresentation, concealment**. If a person misrepresents or fails to disclose relevant information – whether fraudulently or for any other reason – the local authority can pursue as a debt (a) expenditure it incurs because of this, or (b) any payment it did not seek because of this.

- **Sensitive debt recovery**. Because the local authority is dealing with vulnerable people, guidance states that debt recovery should be approached sensitively and reasonably.

- **Discretion to waive**. Local authorities have the discretion to waive debt.[2]

Children

It is beyond the scope of this book to consider children's legislation in any detail. The Care Act 2014 itself covers children in relation to transition to adulthood: assessment of the child approaching 18, the carer (parent) or a young carer approaching 18. See below. But, in summary, other following children-related legislation includes the following:

---

1   *LGO, Durham County Council,* 2016 (16 006 801).

2   Statutory guidance, 2016, Annex D.

- **Children Act 1989**. Section 17 of the Children Act 1989 covers children in need generally (including disabled children). As well as provision for the child, it includes provision for their family and for assessment of the carer parents of disabled children.[1] The duty under section 17 is a general duty towards children in the local authority's area. As such, provision of services under section 17 for any one child is barely enforceable.[2] The Act sets out provisions for child protection.[3] It also contains leaving care provisions for children who have been legally looked after by a local authority under the age of 18.[4]

- **Chronically Sick and Disabled Persons Act 1970 (CSDPA)**. Section 2 of the Act contains a strong duty to meet the needs of a disabled child by providing any of the wide range of services listed in section 2. The duty is triggered if a local authority considers such provision necessary to meet the needs of a child. It is a strong, enforceable duty owed to each individual child.[5]

- **Children and Families Act 2014**. This Act contains the legal framework for children with special educational needs. Key points include:

  » **Education, health and care (EHC) plans**. For children and young people with needs that cannot be met within the normal resources of the school or college (including further, but not higher, education), the Act provides for education, health and care (EHC) plans to be made.

  » **EHC plans extending into adulthood**. Such plans can go up to the age of 25 if the person remains in education. From the person's 18th birthday onward, adult social care legislation – the Care Act – becomes relevant.

  » **EHC plans: duties**. Once provision is specified in the plan, then the local authority must make educational provision, the NHS (clinical commissioning group) health provision, and the local authority care provision.[6]

---

1   Children Act 1989, s.17 and s.17ZD.

2   *R(G) v Barnet London Borough Council* [2003] UKHL 57, House of Lords.

3   Children Act 1989, ss.47–52, etc.

4   Children Act 1989, ss.23A–23E.

5   *R(JL) v Islington London Borough Council* [2009] EWHC 458 (Admin), para 62.

6   Children and Families Act 2014, ss.37, 42.

» **EHC plans: social care**. Although the timing of the change will not be precise, the care part of the plan will shift on the young person's 18th birthday. Before that, the care part of the plan will reflect social care provision made for the child under section 2 of the CSDPA and section 17 of the Children Act 1989.

However, local authorities have discretion in the case of an EHC plan, in any event, to continue to provide services under section 17 of the Children Act (and the CSDPA) after the young person's 18th birthday.[1]

Children and transition

If it appears to a local authority that a child is likely to have needs for care and support after becoming 18, the authority must assess under the Care Act. However, for this duty to apply, the authority must be satisfied that this would be of significant benefit to the child. This is under section 58 of the Care Act.

CHILDREN AND TRANSITION: CONSENT TO ASSESSMENT. The duty depends on consent, which must either be the decision of the child – if he or she has the requisite mental capacity – or be the decision of the local authority that the assessment would be in the child's best interests. If the child refuses but is experiencing – or is at risk of – neglect or abuse, then the local authority must carry out the assessment anyway.[2]

CHILDREN AND TRANSITION: WELL-BEING AND OUTCOMES. The assessment of the child must consider impact on the child's well-being, outcomes wished for by the child, and how care and support could contribute to those outcomes. The local authority must involve the child, the child's parents and any other person the child or parent or carer of the child asks to

---

1   Children Act 1989, s.17ZG.

2   Care Act 2014, s.58.

be involved. The local authority must consider what things, other than care and support, could contribute to achieving the outcomes.[1]

CHILDREN AND TRANSITION: ELIGIBILITY. The local authority must give the child – or the child's parents (if the child lacks capacity to understand) – an indication as to whether the child will have eligible needs for care and support when he or she becomes 18. Also, it must give advice and information about what can be done to meet or reduce needs, and prevent or delay the development of need. When the child becomes 18, the local authority must decide whether to treat the assessment carried out before the age of 18 as a full Care Act assessment, bearing in mind when the assessment was carried out and whether circumstances have since changed.[2]

CHILDREN AND TRANSITION: CHILD'S CARER'S ASSESSMENT. Under section 60 of the Act, the local authority must also assess the carer, usually a parent, of a child if:

- it appears to the authority that the carer is likely to have needs for support when the child turns 18

- it is satisfied that the assessment would be of significant benefit to the carer, and

- the carer is not refusing the assessment.

Normally the definition of 'carer' excludes a person under contract or doing voluntary work. But the local authority, if it considers it appropriate, can nonetheless assess.[3] The main elements of the child's carer's assessment are as follows:

- **Core elements of assessment.** It must include whether the carer is able and willing to care when the child turns 18, impact on the carer's well-being, outcomes the carer wishes to achieve (and whether support could contribute

---

1   Care Act 2014, s.59.

2   Care Act 2014, s.59.

3   Care Act 2014, s.60.

to these), whether things other than support could contribute to these, and whether the carer is working or wishes to (or participates, or wishes to, in education, training or recreation).

- **Involvement of others, eligibility, advice and information**. It must involve the carer and anybody else the carer requests. The local authority must indicate whether the carer will have eligible needs when the child reaches 18, and give advice and information (about preventing, reducing or delaying need).

- **Status of assessment prior to 18**. When the child reaches 18, the local authority must consider whether to treat, as a Care Act assessment, the carer's assessment carried out prior to this point, bearing in mind when the assessment was carried out and whether circumstances have changed.

Whilst the child is still under 18, the local authority can meet the carer's needs as it considers appropriate, having regard to provision already being made under the Children Act.[1]

CHILDREN AND TRANSITION: YOUNG CARER'S ASSESSMENT. Under section 63 of the Act, the local authority must assess the young carer of a person – if it appears to the authority that the young carer is likely to have needs for support when he or she becomes 18 and if it is satisfied that the assessment would be of significant benefit to the young carer. The duty does not apply if the young carer refuses the assessment, unless the young carer lacks mental capacity to decide this and the local authority considers it is in the young carer's best interests.

A young carer is somebody under 18 years old and providing care for an adult. Normally the definition of 'young carer' excludes a person under contract or doing voluntary work. But the local authority, if it considers it appropriate, can nonetheless assess.[2] The main provisions of the young carer's assessment are:

- **Core elements of assessment**. It must include whether the young carer is able and willing to care when he or she turns 18, impact on the young carer's well-being, outcomes the young carer wishes to achieve (and whether

---

1 Care Act 2014, ss.61 and 62.

2 Care Act 2014, s.63.

support could contribute to these), whether things other than support could contribute to these, and whether the young carer is working or wishes to (or participates, or wishes to, in education, training or recreation).

- **Involvement of others, eligibility, advice and information**. It must involve the young carer, the young carer's parents, and anybody else the young carer or parent requests. The local authority must indicate whether the young carer will have eligible needs when they reach 18, and give advice and information (about preventing, reducing or delaying need).

- **Status of assessment prior to 18**. When the young carer reaches 18, the local authority must consider whether to treat, as a Care Act assessment, the young carer's assessment carried out prior to this point, bearing in mind when the assessment was carried out and whether circumstances have changed.[1]

CHILDREN AND TRANSITION: CONTINUITY OF CARE. The Care Act amended the Children Act to ensure that a gap in provision does not occur when a child reaches 18. The effect is that until a decision is made under the Care Act about the child's needs, then the local authority must continue to comply with section 17 of the Children Act. Until it reaches a 'conclusion in the case' means that:

- the person does not need care and support

- the person has needs, the local authority is going to meet them and has begun to do so, or

- there are needs, but the local authority is not going to meet them because they do not meet the eligibility criteria or for some other reason.[2]

Similarly, these continuity rules are replicated in section 2A of the Chronically Sick and Disabled Persons Act 1970 when the local authority has been providing services to a child under section 2 of that Act.[3]

CHILDREN AND TRANSITION: NO GAP. It should not legally be possible for services under the children's legislation to cease without Care Act

---

1   Care Act 2014, s.64.

2   Children Act 1989, s.17ZH.

3   Chronically Sick and Disabled Persons Act 1970, s.2.

services having started. (There could nonetheless be a change in provision if an eligibility decision under the Care Act does not deliver the same as was provided under the children's legislation.) The reason for the continuity rule is obvious. In the past, under previous legislation, delays and gaps did sometimes occur, leaving young people without assessment and services, as in the following.

CASES OF MALADMINISTRATION

- **One-year delay**: in making appropriate provision for a young man with learning disabilities, thereby heaping physical and emotional strain on his mother[1]

- **Two-year delay**: in assessment of a young man with learning disabilities, leaving the family to cope without practical support[2]

- **Three-year delay**: in assessment of a man with multiple disabilities, causing distress and anxiety to him and his mother[3]

- **Four years and more**: failure to have a recorded plan for transition of a woman who was deaf and had learning disabilities, a delay of two years in allocating a social worker to her, another two years in assessing – and, overall, allowing her to remain for 10 years after she became an adult with people who were only approved as foster carers for children.[4]

However, under the Care Act, there is no guarantee that gaps will still not emerge, despite the clear legal rule that they must not.

One year gap in respite care provision under the Care Act. A local authority took a year to put in place respite care for a woman, living at home with her parents. She had severe autism, learning difficulties, a number of health conditions and some behavioural problems. She had to leave the

---

1   LGO, *Knowsley Metropolitan Borough Council*, 1997 (95/C/4681).

2   LGO, *Liverpool City Council*, 1997 (96/C/0581).

3   LGO, *East Sussex County Council*, 1995 (92/A/2085).

4   LGO, *Birmingham City Council*, 2008 (05/C/18474).

respite centre at 18, but other options would not allow trials until she was 18, so this contributed to the delay. But, in finding maladministration, the ombudsman stated that the local authority should have offered an alternative in the interim – for example, night-time carers.[1]

Six-month gap under the Care Act: local authority to reimburse cost of missed care. A local authority failed for six months to put in place care and support for a person when he reached 18. The local ombudsman recommended that the local authority pay to the parents the cost of the missed respite care and other support and, in addition, £1000 for the stress, anxiety, time and trouble for the parents. The cost of the missed care and support would be based on the costs of the children's services which, under the Care Act rules, should have continued during this time.[2]

Choice of accommodation

Under the Care Act there are rules about 'choice of accommodation' concerning care homes, supported living and 'shared lives' (for definitions of these types of accommodation, see separate headings in this book).

CHOICE OF ACCOMMODATION: BASIC CONDITIONS. If a local authority is going to meet a person's needs by arranging provision of one of these types of accommodation, then – if certain conditions are met – the local authority must give effect to the person's choice:[3]

- **Care and support plan**. The care and support plan for the adult specifies that the adult's needs are going to be met by the provision of one of these types of accommodation, and the adult has now chosen particular accommodation of that type.

- **Suitability**. The preferred accommodation is suitable for the adult's needs, and is available.

---

1   *LGO, Lincolnshire County Council,* 2016 (15 020 374), paras 34–35.

2   *LGO, London Borough of Bromley,* 2016 (16 000 780).

3   Care Act 2014, s.30.

- **Agreement**. The provider of the accommodation agrees to provide the accommodation on the local authority's terms.

- **Personal budget**. The cost of the chosen accommodation falls within the person's personal budget.[1]

If a local authority refuses to arrange for the person's preferred accommodation, it must give written reasons.[2]

CHOICE OF ACCOMMODATION: TOPPING UP BY THIRD PARTIES. If the cost of the preferred accommodation exceeds the adult's personal budget, then the local authority must still give effect to the person's choice, but only if it is satisfied that a third party (not the person themselves) is able to pay the additional cost – that is, the difference between the amount of the personal budget and the actual cost (to the local authority under the Care Act) of the accommodation. The third party must enter into a written agreement with the local authority. (The person themselves is allowed to top up in limited circumstances during the 12-week property disregard period, when a permanent resident's property cannot be taken into account[3] and also in the case of a deferred payment agreement.) A local authority might not be satisfied about the reliability of the third party – for instance, if there has been a previous default by the third party, and there is now a risk of repetition. It might not then be obliged to enter into the agreement.[4]

CHOICE OF ACCOMMODATION: PRINCIPLE OF CHOICE. Topping up can apply only when the more expensive option is a matter of choice, meaning there must be a cheaper alternative within the personal budget that would meet the person's needs. Failing this, the local authority must fund the more expensive option and not request a top-up.

---

1   SI 2014/2670. Care and Support and After-care (Choice of Accommodation) Regulations 2014.

2   SI 2014/2670. Care and Support and After-care (Choice of Accommodation) Regulations 2014.

3   SI 2014/2670. Care and Support and After-care (Choice of Accommodation) Regulations 2014, r.5.

4   *R(Daniel) v Leeds City Council* [2004] EWHC 562.

Wrongly trivialising need when deciding about top-ups. In deciding whether a more distant, cheaper care home was suitable – before demanding a top-up for one closer by – the local authority should not simply have dismissed as 'trivial' an elderly woman's concerns about a round two-hour trip to the distant care home, involving two buses, in order to visit her husband there.[1]

Wrongly charging top-up to meet essential need. When a local authority had assessed that a person needed to be in a nursing home – because of the risk of moving him anywhere else – it should not have charged a top-up for the next three years. At the end of that period, it still insisted on a top-up without having reassessed and explored whether an alternative, cheaper placement was safe and available. Both decisions were maladministration.[2]

CHOICE OF ACCOMMODATION: PITFALLS. There is considerable evidence that local authorities struggle to adhere to the legal rules, which in essence have been in place since 1992. Department of Health statutory guidance highlights key points.

- **Genuine choice within the personal budget amount**. The local authority must ensure that the person has genuine choice, that at least one option is available and affordable within a person's individual budget, and that they can choose more expensive options if a third party is willing and able to pay the difference.[3]

- **Arbitrary personal budget allocation**. The local authority should not set arbitrary amounts or ceilings for particular types of accommodation that do not reflect a fair cost of care.

- **Lack of choice precludes top-up requests by local authorities**. A person must not be asked to pay a 'top-up' towards the cost of their accommodation because of market inadequacies or commissioning failures, resulting in lack of genuine choice.

---

1   *LGO, Cambridgeshire County Council*, 2015 (13 016 935), paras 4, 76–80.

2   *LGO, Solihull Metropolitan Borough Council*, 2016 (14 014 177), paras 30–31.

3   Statutory guidance, 2016, para 8.37.

- **Increase of personal budget where there is no choice**. If someone is placed in a more expensive setting solely because the local authority has been unable to make arrangements at the anticipated cost, the personal budget must reflect this amount. Top-up arrangements do not apply.

- **Local authority responsibility for the whole of placement, including top-up – and in case of breakdown**. When entering into a contract to provide care in a setting that is more expensive than the amount identified in the personal budget, the local authority remains responsible for the total cost of that placement. If there is a breakdown in the arrangement – for instance if the third party ceases to make the agreed payments – then the local authority would be liable for the fees until it has either recovered the additional costs it incurs or made alternative arrangements to meet the cared-for person's needs.

- **Increase in care home costs: effect on third party top-up amount**. The local authority must set out clearly in writing how any increased costs may be shared. This should also state that there is no guarantee that these increased costs will automatically be shared evenly should (a) the provider's costs rise more quickly than the amount the local authority would have increased the personal budget and (b) there is an alternative option that would be affordable within that budget.[1]

The Department of Health's guidance in effect identifies some of the common pitfalls, which local authorities seem regularly to fall into. A national overview report by the local ombudsman pinpointed some of these:

- **No information**: people being given no information or wrong information

- **No choice**: lack of choice, or that the only choices available to them are ones which cost more than the funding provided by the council

- **Top-ups extracted behind the local authority's back**: councils abdicating responsibility for top-ups, with care providers charging top-ups 'behind the council's back'

- **Care homes forcing top-ups without agreement**: care homes raising fees and families being forced, on an ad hoc basis and without an agreement, to pay top-up amounts

---

1   Statutory guidance, 2016, Annex A.

- **Inadequate personal budgets**: assessing finances before assessing needs, thus allocating an inadequate personal budget.[1]

EXAMPLES OF MALADMINISTRATION FOLLOWING OMBUDSMAN INVESTIGATIONS

- **Forcing a top-up in the absence of a suitable assessment**. A local authority wrongly forced a top-up to pay nursing home fees. A placement was actually available at the council's standard rate, but it had failed to assess whether it would be suitable for meeting the man's needs.[2]

- **No evidence of identification and offer of cheaper care home placement**. If a local authority is unable to provide evidence – for example, written – that it had identified and offered a cheaper home within its usual rate or the person's personal budget, the ombudsman may find fault and ask the local authority to repay the family for top-up fees paid.[3]

- **Originally self-funding resident**. A resident, originally self-funding, now came to rely on local authority support. In order for her to remain in the care home, the authority said the family would have to pay a top-up, but had neither identified any cheaper, alternative placement, nor considered the risks of moving her.[4]

- **Hospital discharge and fait accompli by way of care home placement**. Discharged from hospital (a process often involving haste), the local authority presented as a fait accompli a care home, for which the family would have to pay a top-up, without any evidence that this was a choice and that cheaper alternatives had been identified.[5] The pressures of hospital discharge, the family's concerns to find a suitable care home and a local authority's failure to make efforts to provide clear

---

1   Local Government Ombudsman *Counting the cost of care: The council's role in informing public choices about care homes*. London: LGO, 2015, pp.3–9.

2   *LGO, Solihull Metropolitan Borough Council*, 2016 (14 014 177).

3   *LGO, Wirral Metropolitan Borough Council*, 2016 (16 003 969), paras 30–32.

4   *LGO, Blackburn with Darwen Council*, 2016 (15 001 533), paras 21, 23.

5   *LGO, Lancashire County Council*, 2016 (15 019 274), paras 39–40.

information about the options and financial consequences led all too easily to breach of the rules, because a true choice of more expensive accommodation (and top-up) was not made.[1]

- **Excluding shorter-term placements in council homes from the rules**. A local authority disapplied, wrongly, the choice of accommodation rules in the case of short-term residential placements in the council's own care homes.[2]

- **Reducing the local authority contribution, effectively forcing a top-up arrangement without adequate assessment**. A local authority changed the funding arrangements for a care home placement (which originally involved no top-up) by reducing the fee it would pay. This meant that for the resident to remain in the home, a top-up would now be needed. However, the local authority did not first assess the resident's care needs to determine the impact of any change. Nor did it establish the willingness of the third party, the son, to pay the top-up. He was unable to, which meant his mother paid the top-up (which was anyway not lawful).[3]

- **Charging a top-up following an emergency move without first checking whether cheaper alternatives were suitable and available**. A woman was moved from one care home to another following an emergency incident, and a top-up was demanded from the daughter. But there was no evidence that the local authority had checked whether any residential beds at the standard cost were available.[4]

- **Charging a top-up even though a cheaper home had neglected a resident**. When a son moved his mother to a more expensive home, after the cheaper home had neglected his mother, the council charged a top-up without having acted promptly to protect the mother or given her son information about other potential homes.[5]

---

1   *LGO, Liverpool City Council*, 2016 (15 019 256), paras 15, 19.

2   *LGO, Kent County Council*, 2012 (11 001 504). And *LGO, Kent County Council*, 2012 (10 012 742), para 47.

3   *LGO, Tameside Metropolitan Borough Council*, 2015 (12 019 862). (Further report.)

4   *LGO, Walsall Metropolitan Borough Council*, 2012 (10 018 968).

5   *LGO, Bristol City Council*, 2011 (09 005 944), paras 70, 72.

> • **Local authority liable for care home extracting a discrete top-up**. A woman was placed in a care home, with the local authority responsible for the whole fee. The care home then charged a top-up separately. The ombudsman found this was illegal and held the local authority to be guilty of maladministration because it was, by default, responsible for the care home's actions.[1]

Clinical commissioning groups

Under section 3 of the NHS Act 2006, clinical commissioning groups (CCGs) are responsible for commissioning most local health services. Their predecessor bodies were called primary care trusts, and before that health authorities.

Community equipment

Under the Care Act, community equipment is defined to include aids and minor adaptations, meaning 'an aid, or a minor adaptation to property, for the purpose of assisting with nursing or aiding daily living'. Any piece of equipment, or any minor adaptation costing £1000 or less, must be provided free of charge under the Care Act.[2] This suggests that central government places considerable importance on such provision. Making it free of charge encourages uptake.

COMMUNITY EQUIPMENT: JOINT SOCIAL SERVICES AND NHS PRO-VISION. Section 3 of the Care Act states that social services must consider integration with the NHS. Guidance has long since stressed the importance of a joint social care and health care approach to equipment provision.[3] This

---

1   *LGO, London Borough of Merton*, 2013 (12 010 181), para 31.

2   SI 2014/2672. Care and Support (Charging and Assessment of Resources) Regulations 2014, r.3. And SI 2014/2673. Care and Support (Preventing Needs for Care and Support) Regulations 2014, r.4.

3   HSC 2001/008; LAC(2001)13. Department of Health *Community equipment services*. London: DH, 2001.

was issued following a highly critical Audit Commission report.[1] More recent Care Act guidance also refers to community equipment as one example of integration which local authorities and the NHS should at least consider.[2]

Some equipment – and the use to which it is put – straddles both health and social care. The scope for uncertainty and confusion – and for arguments as to who (social services or the NHS) will provide the equipment – is considerable, not least because the purpose of community equipment under the Care Act is defined as assisting with nursing, not just daily living.

The duty of cooperation imposed on social services and the NHS, in sections 6 and 7 of the Care Act, is also clearly relevant.

Complaints

Both social services and the NHS are obliged to operate complaints procedures under the 2009 regulations.[3] Once a complainant has used, or attempted to use, the local complaints procedure, the local government ombudsman can consider the complaint independently, as can the health service ombudsman in respect of the NHS. Both social services and the NHS are obliged, in their written response to a complaint, to tell complainants how to refer to one or other of the ombudsmen (or both, if the complaint relates to both health and social care).[4]

Continuing health care (CHC)

NHS continuing health care (CHC) for people aged 18 or over refers to a legal category of patient, determined by a set of assessment rules. It is a highly contentious and confusing area of law, leading to considerable tensions between the NHS, local authorities, patients and their families. At heart there

---

1 Audit Commission *Fully equipped: The provision of equipment to older or disabled people by the NHS and social services in England and Wales.* London: Audit Commission, 2000.

2 Statutory guidance, 2016, para 15.7.

3 SI 2009/309. Local Authority Social Services and National Health Service Complaints (England) Regulations 2009.

4 SI 2009/309. Local Authority Social Services and National Health Service Complaints (England) Regulations 2009, r.14.

is an artificial divide created between health care and social care, which is essentially about finance and who should pay for the care of people with high levels of need.

CHC is provided, ultimately, under the broad duties contained in sections 1 and 3 of the NHS Act 2006. There are more specific procedural legal rules contained in regulations, and in guidance issued by the Department of Health. Although the guidance is obviously not law, the use of some of it is legally stipulated in regulations.

CHC: SOLE RESPONSIBILITY OF THE NHS. CHC means a package of care funded and arranged solely by the NHS.[1] This responsibility lies with the local clinical commissioning group (CCG). The package of care must be free of charge to the person.[2] The practical implications are:

- **Nursing home residents without CHC status.** Ordinarily, if a person is in a nursing home, the NHS will contribute, at the time of writing, £156.25 per week.[3] This is called 'funded nursing care' (FNC). The rest of the fee will be paid for by social services (subject to a means test), the resident themselves, or a combination of the two.

- **Nursing home residents with CHC status.** If a person has CHC status, then the NHS will pay for the whole of care home placement (i.e. for the accommodation, board, personal care and nursing care), free of charge.

- **Person in own home without CHC status.** Ordinarily, if a person is in their own home, the NHS will provide health services only (e.g. district nursing, physiotherapy). They will be free of charge. Other, personal, care will be regarded as social care and be provided by social services (subject to a means test), by the person or their family – or a combination.

---

1   SI 2012/2996. NHS Commissioning Board and Clinical Commissioning Groups (CCGs) (Responsibilities and Standing Rules) Regulations 2012, r.20.

2   NHS Act 2006, s.1.

3   SI 2012/2996. NHS Commissioning Board and CCGs (Responsibilities and Standing Rules) Regulations 2012, r.20 (as amended). See Department of Health News item 'NHS-funded nursing care rate for 2016 to 2017', accessed on 30 September 2016 at www.gov.uk/government/news/nhs-funded-nursing-care-rate-for-2016-to-2017.

- **Person in own home with CHC status**. With CHC status, a person in their own home must have both their health and social care needs met by the NHS. Services to meet care and support needs, normally arranged by a local authority (and financially chargeable), must instead be arranged by the NHS, free of charge[1] – for example, transport to a day centre.[2] (It is doubtful whether this NHS duty can stretch to providing or paying for ordinary, private accommodation as opposed to care-related accommodation.)[3]

CHC: SIGNIFICANCE, MEETING PEOPLE'S NEEDS ADEQUATELY.

Financial implications aside, CHC status can affect the adequacy of care provided.

Cessation of CHC leading to poor care commissioned by local authority. The NHS shifted a person's status away from CHC to social care. The local authority accepted this decision (possibly erroneously?) and then, for essentially financial reasons, moved the person from a care home which was meeting his needs well to one that didn't. This led ultimately to poor care, a safeguarding investigation against the local authority itself and a finding of maladministration.[4]

CHC: KEY POINTS. The rules for determining CHC are complicated and arguably somewhat incoherent (see below). That said, the key points are as follows:

- **Local authority prohibited from providing to meet CHC needs**. Local authorities are prohibited from providing, under sections 18–20 of the Care Act, anything that the NHS is required to provide (unless doing so would be 'incidental or ancillary to doing something else to meet needs under those

---

1   Department of Health *National framework for NHS continuing healthcare and NHS-funded nursing care.* London: DH, 2012, para 2.3, p.50.

2   *R(MH) v National Health Service* [2015] EWHC 4243 (Admin), para 108.

3   *R(Whapples) v Birmingham Cross City Commissioning Group* [2015] EWCA Civ 435, paras 33, 45, 48.

4   *LGO, Worcestershire County Council,* 2014 (12 004 137).

sections' and 'would be of a nature that the local authority could be expected to provide'),[1] a point reinforced by guidance.[2]

- **CHC definition**. NHS continuing health care is defined as 'a package of care arranged and funded solely by the health service for a person aged 18 or over to meet physical or mental health needs which have arisen as a result of illness'.[3] Illness is defined so as to include any disorder or disability of the mind and any injury or disability requiring medical or dental treatment or nursing.[4]

- **Primary health need**. Regulations state that if a person has a primary health need, then he or she must be provided with CHC. Primary health need is determined by deciding whether the services needed by the person are merely incidental or ancillary, or of a nature that is beyond the responsibility of social services.

  The first condition applies if the person is in a registered care home, and the services required are 'more than incidental or ancillary to the provision of accommodation which a social services authority is, or would be but for a person's means, under a duty to provide'. (This is sometimes referred to as the 'quantity' test.)

  The second, alternative, condition (applying to any setting) is that the services are 'of a nature beyond which a social services authority whose primary responsibility is to provide social services could be expected to provide'. (This is sometimes referred to as the 'quality' test.)

  If the nursing and any other health services needed by the person, 'in their totality', fall within either of the above, then the NHS must decide that the person has a primary health need and so be provided with CHC.[5]

- **Nature, intensity, complexity or unpredictability of need**. Guidance states that in deciding the 'incidental/ancillary' (quantity of care) or 'nature'

---

1 Care Act 2014, s.22.

2 Statutory guidance, 2016, para 6.79.

3 NHS Commissioning Board and CCGs (Responsibilities and Standing Rules) Regulations 2012, r.20.

4 NHS Act 2006, s.275.

5 SI 2012/2996. NHS Commissioning Board and CCGs (Responsibilities and Standing Rules) Regulations 2012, r.21(6).

(quality of care) questions, the CCG should consider the nature, intensity, complexity or unpredictability of a person's health care needs. And that each of these characteristics, alone or in combination, might demonstrate a primary health need because of the quantity or quality of care required.[1]

- **Checklist**. If the NHS uses a screening tool for CHC purposes, then it must use the CHC checklist published by the Department of Health.[2]

- **Decision about funded nursing care must precede the CHC decision**. Regulations state that the NHS must consider whether a person might be eligible for CHC before deciding whether they will be eligible for funded nursing care (FNC) – the £156.25 weekly NHS contribution for care in a nursing home when a person does not have CHC status.[3] Failure to adhere to this rule is unlawful.[4]

- **Eligibility assessment**. An assessment for CHC must be carried out by a multi-disciplinary team. This requires, at a minimum, two health professionals from different health care professions, or one health care professional, and a person responsible for assessing a person's social care needs under section 9 of the Care Act. In making CHC decisions, the NHS must cooperate with social services, generally and in respect of arranging for social services staff to participate in the multi-disciplinary team. The duty is reciprocated, on social services, in separate regulations.[5] The decision support tool (DST) for CHC, published by the Department of Health, must be used for the assessment.[6]

- **Decision support tool (DST)**. At the core of the DST are a number of 'domains' – behaviour, cognition, psychological and emotional needs,

1   Department of Health *National framework for NHS continuing healthcare and NHS-funded nursing care*. London: DH, 2012, paras 35–36.

2   NHS Commissioning Board and CCGs (Responsibilities and Standing Rules) Regulations 2012, r.21(4). And Department of Health *Delayed discharge directions*. London: DH, 2013. And Department of Health *NHS continuing healthcare checklist*. London: DH, 2012.

3   NHS Commissioning Board and CCGs (Responsibilities and Standing Rules) Regulations 2012, r.21(3).

4   *R(Grogan) v Bexley NHS Care Trust* [2006] EWHC 44, para 49.

5   SI 2014/2821. Care and Support (Provision of Health Services) Regulations 2014, r.3.

6   NHS Commissioning Board and CCGs (Responsibilities and Standing Rules) Regulations 2012, rr.21(5), 21(13). And Department of Health *Delayed discharge directions*. London: DH, 2013. And Department of Health *Decision support tool for NHS continuing healthcare*. London: DH, 2012.

communication, mobility, nutrition, continence, skin and tissue viability, breathing, drug therapies, altered states of consciousness – and a last domain for any other needs. People are 'scored' against these domains. If they score sufficiently highly, they will normally be awarded CHC on the basis that such a score will indicate a primary health need in terms of nature, complexity, intensity or unpredictability of need (see above).

The guidance states that a clear recommendation for CHC 'would be expected' if a person scores at least one 'priority', or at least two 'severe' scores. Alternatively, the following 'may indicate' CHC – one domain recorded as severe, together with needs in a number of other domains, or, alternatively, a number of domains with high and/or moderate needs.[1]

- **Terminal illness: fast track to CHC**. The rules, about the checklist, multi-disciplinary assessment and decision support tool, do not apply if instead a 'fast track pathway' tool has been completed. This arises if an 'appropriate clinician' decides the following. First, that an individual has a primary health need arising from a rapidly deteriorating condition. And, second, that the condition may be entering a terminal phase. The clinician must have completed the fast track pathway tool published by the Department of Health, giving reasons for their decision. An appropriate clinician is defined as a registered nurse or doctor, responsible for the diagnosis, treatment or care of the person under the NHS Act 2006.[2]

- **Unilateral withdrawal by NHS or local authority**. Neither the NHS nor a local authority should unilaterally withdraw from an existing funding arrangement without a joint reassessment of the individual, consulting one another and invoking the local resolution procedure. The original funding stream should be maintained until the dispute is resolved.[3]

- **Dispute resolution process between NHS and social services**. Locally, both local authority and the CCG have a duty to agree and to use a dispute

---

1   Department of Health *Decision support tool for NHS continuing healthcare*. London: DH, 2016, para 31.

2   SI 2012/2996. NHS Commissioning Board and CCGs (Responsibilities and Standing Rules) Regulations 2012, rr.21(8), 21(13). And Department of Health *Delayed discharge directions*. London: DH, 2013. And Department of Health *Fast track pathway tool for NHS continuing healthcare*. London: DH, 2012.

3   Department of Health *National framework for NHS continuing healthcare and NHS-funded nursing care*. London: DH, 2012, para 143.

resolution process about CHC and joint funding cases.[1] It was therefore maladministration on the part of the local authority, when the NHS decided that the person involved was no longer its responsibility but the local authority had then simply done nothing (neither paid the care home fees nor invoked the dispute resolution procedure), thus leaving the care home owner out of pocket.[2] Similarly, a failure by the local authority to escalate a care package issue to the dispute procedure, which it believed to be an NHS responsibility and therefore legally outside its social care responsibilities, was maladministration).[3]

- **Independent review panel**. NHS England, a national body, has a duty to offer an independent review panel to resolve local disputes between patients (and their families) and the NHS. The dispute must be about the procedure followed, or the decision about a person's primary health need, by the CCG. The local resolution procedure must have been used first, and the matter resolved – unless NHS England believes that requiring this attempt at local resolution would cause undue delay.[4]

CHC: PITFALLS TO AVOID. Department of Health guidance on CHC is extensive. It contains key points, including the following:

- **Joint funding**. The definition of NHS CHC, as funded and arranged solely by the NHS, means that it is not possible to have joint funding for somebody with CHC status. However, absent CHC status, joint funding becomes an option.[5]

---

1   SI 2012/2996. NHS Commissioning Board and CCGs (Responsibilities and Standing Rules) Regulations 2012, r.22(2). And SI 2014/2821. Care and Support (Provision of Health Services) Regulations 2014, r.4.

2   *LGO, London Borough of Enfield*, 2016 (15 018 745), paras 13–15.

3   *LGO, Northamptonshire County Council*, 2016 (14 007 296), para 29.

4   SI 2012/2996. NHS Commissioning Board and CCGs (Responsibilities and Standing Rules) Regulations 2012, r.23.

5   Department of Health *National framework for NHS continuing healthcare and NHS-funded nursing care*. London: DH, 2012, para 108.

- **Setting**. NHS continuing health care may be provided in any setting – for example, care home, hospice or the person's own home.[1] The health service ombudsman has in the past made findings against NHS bodies that allowed continuing health care in hospital settings only,[2] or at least in NHS premises only.[3]

- **Well-managed needs are still needs**. Eligibility for CHC – including on review – should not be denied a person just because their needs are being well managed, since a successfully managed need is still a need.[4]

- **Identity of carers does not determine need**. Whether or not NHS staff are required to provide care does not determine eligibility. Nor is eligibility to be determined by whether specialist staff are required.[5] For example, despite the fact that the wife of a man with dementia was his main carer at home – and that he was not receiving regular nursing care – he nonetheless had CHC needs. She was providing expert care to a professional level.[6]

- **Role of panels and decision support tool (DST)**. If the CCG utilises a local panel or other mechanism to decide on, or authorise, eligibility in relation to the DST, the panel should reject only exceptionally the multi-disciplinary team's (MDT) assessment, DST completion and recommendations. If exceptionally it does so, it must provide reasons and refer the matter back to the MDT to look at the case again.[7] In other words, the panel itself should not rescore the DST.

- **Role of panels and fast track pathway tool**. If the CCG utilises a panel or other mechanism to decide on, or authorise, eligibility in relation to the

---

1   Department of Health *National framework for NHS continuing healthcare and NHS-funded nursing care*. London: DH, 2012, para 56.

2   HSO: *Berkshire Health Authority*, 2003 (E.814/00–01). And HSO: *North Worcestershire Health Authority*, 1995 (E.264/94–95).

3   HSO: *Dorset Health Authority*, 2003 (E.208/99–00).

4   Department of Health *National framework for NHS continuing healthcare and NHS-funded nursing care*. London: DH, 2012, para 56.

5   Department of Health *National framework for NHS continuing healthcare and NHS-funded nursing care*. London: DH, 2012, para 58.

6   HSO: *Cambridgeshire Health Authority*, 2004 (E.22/02–03).

7   Department of Health *National framework for NHS continuing healthcare and NHS-funded nursing care*. London: DH, 2012, para PG33.1, para (h).

fast track pathway, the panel should accept and action the recommendation without delay and only exceptionally query it with the appropriate clinician.[1]

- **Equipment and home adaptations**. If a person has CHC needs, then they are entitled to equipment on the same basis as they are to care – namely, that the NHS is responsible for meeting those needs.[2] In the case of home adaptations, and a person with CHC status, the guidance refers to the potential responsibilities of the NHS.[3]

- **Carers**. If a person has CHC status, the NHS will have responsibilities for informal carers – including meeting any training needs the carer might have, or arranging replacement services so the carer can have a break.[4]

- **Legal case of *Coughlan***. CCGs should be aware of relevant legal and ombudsman case law. The *Coughlan* case (see below) remains directly relevant to determining whether a person has a primary health need and should receive CHC.[5]

CHC: RELEVANT CASE LAW. Key legal or health service ombudsman (HSO) cases include:

> **Leeds case**: A man was doubly incontinent, could not eat or drink without assistance, could not communicate, and had a kidney tumour, cataracts in both eyes and occasional epileptic fits. The health authority had refused to meet his needs in a nursing home. The ombudsman found a failure in service and that he was entitled to CHC.[6]

---

1   Department of Health *National framework for NHS continuing healthcare and NHS-funded nursing care*. London: DH, 2012, paras PG50.3, PG50.4.

2   Department of Health *National framework for NHS continuing healthcare and NHS-funded nursing care*. London: DH, 2012, para 172 and para PG2.3.

3   Department of Health *National framework for NHS continuing healthcare and NHS-funded nursing care*. London: DH, 2012, paras PG79.1–PG79.6.

4   Department of Health *National framework for NHS continuing healthcare and NHS-funded nursing care*. London: DH, 2012, para PG89.1, p.110.

5   Department of Health *National framework for NHS continuing healthcare and NHS-funded nursing care*. London: DH, 2012, paras 30, 90.

6   HSO: *Leeds Health Authority*, 1994 (E.62/93–94).

Coughlan case: A woman, who had been badly injured in a road traffic accident, was now tetraplegic, doubly incontinent (requiring regular catheterisation), partially paralysed in respiratory function, and subject to problems attendant on immobility and also to recurrent headaches caused by an associated neurological condition. She required regular nursing input but not active medical treatment. Her nursing needs were held to be more than just 'incidental or ancillary' to the provision of accommodation, and were not of a nature that social services could be expected to provide.[1]

Wigan and Bolton case: A woman had suffered several strokes, had no speech or comprehension, was unable to swallow and required feeding by a PEG (percutaneous endoscopic gastrostomy) tube into the stomach, and was doubly incontinent. Her needs were more than just incidental or ancillary to the provision of nursing home accommodation or of a nature that social services could be expected to provide; they were on a par with those in the Coughlan case, and should have attracted continuing health care funding.[2]

Berkshire case: A woman had vascular dementia, confusion and challenging behaviour; she had been assessed as having multiple and complex nursing and medical problems. These required an 'intensive and complex' personal care package, well beyond the customary level of care offered by a nursing home. The ombudsman could not see how the nursing care required could be only 'incidental or ancillary' to the provision of accommodation or of a nature that social services could be expected to provide.[3]

Cambridgeshire case: A man with Alzheimer's disease was now living at home, being cared for by his wife and other personal assistants. He was totally reliant on them for his needs to be met. He was subject to epileptic seizures, muscular spasms, panic attacks and episodes of choking, visual spatial difficulties and hallucinatory experiences. He required constant supervision. The ombudsman found that he should have been assessed as having CHC needs.[4]

---

1   *R v North and East Devon Health Authority, ex p Coughlan* (1999) 2 CCLR 285, Court of Appeal.

2   HSO: *Wigan and Bolton Health Authority*, 2003 (E.420/00–01).

3   HSO: *Berkshire Health Authority*, 2003 (E.814/00–01).

4   HSO: *Cambridgeshire Health Authority*, 2004 (E.22/02–03).

Shropshire case: A woman in a nursing home was assessed as requiring full assistance with all personal care tasks including washing, dressing, feeding and toileting. She was doubly incontinent, dependent on others for her safety and could mobilise only with assistance. The health authority refused a request for an independent review. The ombudsman was advised by her (the ombudsman's) independent clinical assessor that it was debatable whether the significant nursing care required could properly be regarded as merely incidental or ancillary. The ombudsman recommended that a reassessment take place to determine the status of the woman.[1]

Shropshire case (no.2): A woman was discharged to a nursing home without continuing care funding. She was unable to manage any aspect of personal care independently, had an in-dwelling urinary catheter, suffered from occasional faecal incontinence, required a soft puréed diet, had a PEG feed, needed a hoist for all transfers because of hemiparesis and contracture, required repositioning every two hours in order to manage pressure risks, communicated by eye contact and head movement, could not speak, and was totally reliant on others for safety. The ombudsman's assessor concluded that the health authority's decision to deny continuing care status was debatable. The ombudsman recommended that the health authority re-determine the CHC decision.[2]

North Worcestershire case: A 55-year-old man had a stroke and was admitted to hospital and discharged to a nursing home. He had continuing serious medical problems for which he remained under consultant care, could not walk, was relatively young and had become chronically depressed, was incontinent of urine, had difficulty eating, had diabetes controlled with insulin, his care was coordinated by a consultant, his blood condition meant he was also under the care of a haematologist, and he had Crohn's disease and hypertension. The ombudsman found that his care should have been provided by the NHS; it was a failure in service not to.[3]

---

1   HSO: *Shropshire Health Authority*, 2003 (E.5/02–03).

2   HSO: *Shropshire Health Authority*, 2003 (E.2119/01–02).

3   HSO: *North Worcestershire Health Authority*, 1995 (E.264/94–95).

CHC: INVOLVEMENT OF PERSON AND CARERS. Guidance states that the person themselves and/or their representative should be fully involved in the assessment and decision-making process.[1]

> **Lack of information**. Failure to explain to patients and their families how a decision has been taken, and its consequences, is fault for the health service ombudsman,[2] as is failure to give information about eligibility to the family and to involve them in the hospital discharge process.[3]

CHC: CHALLENGING DECISIONS. Challenging CHC decisions can be difficult. Challenging the decision-making process – rather than the merits of professional judgement about a person's needs – is likely to bear more legal fruit.[4] People can also seek reviews through the independent review panel (see above) or go further to the health service ombudsman.

CHC: COUNTER-INTUITIVE DECISIONS. CHC decisions are sometimes counter-intuitive and confusing. Application of the decision support tool (DST) sometimes means that people who – in ordinary life and language – would be considered to have very high and severe health needs are assessed as not eligible for CHC. They, or family members, are left incredulous.[5]

The decision-making process can be very difficult to understand. There is also a view that the DST is inconsistent with the *Coughlan* case (see above) that the DST seems to set a higher threshold than the legal case law. Guidance states that local authorities and the NHS should consider arranging independent advice or advocacy in CHC-related cases because

1 Department of Health *National framework for NHS continuing healthcare and NHS-funded nursing care*. London: DH, 2012, para PG4.3, p.53.

2 Health Service Ombudsman *Investigation into a complaint against Central Manchester Primary Care Trust*, 2003 (E.629/01–02).

3 HSO: *Gloucestershire Health Authority*, 2003 (E.112/02–03).

4 *St Helens Borough Council v Manchester Primary Care Trust* [2008] EWCA Civ 931, paras 35–37.

5 Beales, M. 'Continuing healthcare: a severe stroke, yet Ted Beales still doesn't qualify.' *The Guardian*, 9 November 2013.

of the 'historical difficulty' people have in understanding and participating in the process.[1]

In 2003, the health service ombudsman published a major report on CHC, doubting that the system was fair, equitable or understandable.[2] The Department of Health's 2016 guidance does not suggest that progress has been made. The heart of the matter is that a significant amount of care that would have been provided free by the NHS in hospital settings some 30 years ago no longer is. It has become financially chargeable social care. Such fundamental change should arguably have been publicly debated and underpinned by clear policy instead of being brought about by default and by stealth.[3]

Continuity of social care: moving area

If a person is receiving care and support in one local authority area under the Care Act but is now moving to another area, there must be no gap in the care and support provided. Sometimes, this rule is referred to loosely as the 'portability of care' rule. This is somewhat misleading, since whilst there can legally be no gap, there could be a change in provision between one local authority and another, if the latter takes a different view to the former.

CONTINUITY OF SOCIAL CARE: SUMMARY. In outline, the rules apply if the adult's needs are being met by the first local authority, the adult has informed the second authority that he or she is intending to move there (into the community, not a care home or supported living), and the second authority regards the intention as genuine. (This includes the situation when a person has been placed in accommodation – for instance, a care home or supported living – by the first local authority in the area of the second

1   Statutory guidance, 2016, para 7.23.

2   Health Service Ombudsman *NHS funding for long term care*. London: TSO, 2003, paras 29, 31.

3   Henwood, M. *NHS continuing care in England*. London: King's Fund, 2006, p.13.

authority. The person then indicates their intention to move out into the local community, but still in the area of the second authority.)[1]

The following rules then apply:

- **Assessment not complete by the day of the move: second local authority must meet the needs as assessed by the first authority**. If, on the day of the move, the second authority has not concluded its assessment or has not then taken other steps required for the adult following the assessment (e.g. put services in place), the second authority must meet the person's needs for care and support – and the needs of any carer – which the first authority had been meeting.[2] In working out how to do this, regulations set out in detail what the second local authority should take account of.[3]

- **Limits to continuity duty**. The duty on the second authority to continue what the first local authority had been doing lasts only until the second local authority has concluded its own assessment and taken other necessary steps.

- **Second authority has a different view of need or personal budget**. If the second local authority takes a different view of the person's needs, or of the personal budget required to meet them, it must provide a written explanation.[4]

The basic continuity of care rule is clear. Until the new local authority has completed its own assessment, care and support plan and personal budget, it must continue with the previous package of care.

Breach of continuity of care rule by new local authority. A manager approved continuation of the previous care package in a new authority, until the latter had completed its own assessment. This approach was overruled by a panel which refused to approve the personal budget involved. The consequence was that the man's parents had to fund his care for a while, until the new authority had completed its assessment and reduced his personal budget. Up to this point the authority was guilty of

---

1   Care Act 2014, s.37.

2   Care Act 2014, s.38.

3   SI 2014/2825. Care and Support (Continuity of Care) Regulations 2014.

4   Care Act 2014, ss.37, 38.

maladministration and the ombudsman recommended reimbursement of the parents for the care they had funded.[1]

New local authority reduces direct payment. Following a move from one authority to another, a person's direct payment was reduced. In addition, the new local authority did not accept that the person's needs should be met fully by giving a direct payment to his parents (with whom he lived). This was not maladministration, since the local authority could show that it had considered the relevant issues, including the severity of the son's needs.[2]

Cooperation

The Care Act contains three key duties to cooperate between organisations. The first and second are what can be called general duties – that is, duties, but of the target or aspirational sort, difficult to pin down. The third is more specific and, therefore, in principle at least, more amenable to enforcement. Overall, cooperation must relate to, or be relevant to, adults in need and carers. The purposes of cooperation should include, but not be limited to:

- promoting the well-being of adults and carers in the area

- improving the quality of care and support for adults, or support for carers, in the area

- 'smoothing' the transition process for children when they become adults (age 18) for the purposes of the Care Act, and

- identifying lessons for the future from cases of adults who have experienced serious abuse or neglect.

COOPERATION: GENERAL DUTY ON STATUTORY PARTNERS. Section 6 of the Care Act states that statutory partners should cooperate with one another. Statutory partners are defined as local social services authorities, housing authorities, NHS bodies, police, probation service, prison service and Department of Work and Pensions.

---

1   *LGO, Isle of Wight Council*, 2016 (15 019 587), paras 11–17.

2   *LGO, Lincolnshire County Council*, 2016 (15 017 828), paras 15–19.

Section 6 is more of a general duty, compared to section 7 (see below) which applies specifically to the case of each individual person. Section 6 therefore will not be an automatic panacea for disputes and gaps in services. The courts will not be enthusiastic about legal cases being brought, one partner against another – something they have made clear in the past, when considering a similar duty of cooperation under section 27 of the Children Act 1989.[1]

Failing to agree a prisoner's needs. The duty of cooperation might require good faith discussions between partners but not extend to forcing a partner to do something it believes it has no duty to do. This became clear when the probation service and a local authority failed to agree about their respective rehabilitation duties to meet the needs of an elderly disabled prisoner being discharged to a hostel, which meant he could not be released, an impasse the judge felt unable to remedy.[2]

COOPERATION: BETWEEN A LOCAL AUTHORITY'S SEPARATE DEPART-MENTS. In addition, a local authority must make arrangements for ensuring cooperation between its social services, housing, children's services and public health departments.

COOPERATION: GENERAL DUTY TO COOPERATE WITH OTHER OR-GANISATIONS. Section 6 of the Care Act states also that local authorities must cooperate with other bodies it considers appropriate whose activities relate to adults with care and support needs or to carers. Examples of those with whom the local authority 'may' consider it appropriate to consult are:

- providers of care and support, or support services, in relation to prevention, delay or reduction of need under section 2 of the Care Act

---

1   *R v Northavon District Council, ex p Smith* [1994] 2 A.C. 402. And *R(C1 and C2) (by their mother and litigation friend) v London Borough of Hackney* [2014] EWHC 3670 (Admin).

2   *R(John Taylor) v Secretary of State for Justice, National Probation Service North West Division v Wakefield Council, The Parole Board* [2015] EWHC 3245 (Admin).

- providers of primary medical, dental, ophthalmic and pharmaceutical services (i.e. general practitioners, dentists, opticians and pharmacists)

- independent hospitals

- private registered providers of housing (e.g. housing associations).

There is no reciprocal duty on these other bodies to cooperate with the local authority.

COOPERATION: SPECIFIC DUTY. Section 7 of the Care Act places a more specific cooperation duty on statutory partners, when a request is made in relation to a particular adult in need, a carer, a child's carer or a young carer. (The duty also relates to a request made to any other local authority not defined as a statutory partner.) The requested party must comply with the request unless it gives written reasons as to why it considers that compliance (a) would be incompatible with its own duties or (b) would otherwise have an adverse effect on the exercise of its functions. The reference to incompatibility of function means that partners can't force each other to do what they are not empowered to do. The following case considered these matters under a similar duty of cooperation in section 27 of the Children Act 1989.

Incompatibility and adverse effect on functions. In a dispute about tracheostomy care for a child, the court noted that the provision of such specialist health care could not, as a matter of law, come under the Children Act – and the local authority could not in any event legally provide it. Such provision would be incompatible with their functions. Conversely, the NHS were providing a certain level of tracheostomy care, but refused to provide more. The cooperation duty did not mean that the NHS was bound by the local authority assessment of the amount of care required (and therefore under a duty to provide it). Otherwise, there could be prejudice to (i.e. adverse effect on) the discharge of NHS functions.[1]

---

1   *R(T) v London Borough of Haringey* [2005] EWHC 2235 (Admin), paras 95–101.

Cross-border placements

Section 39 and schedule 1 of the Care Act cover the situation in which an English local authority places a person in a care home in Scotland, Wales or Northern Ireland, and when these three countries make a cross-border placement into England. In such circumstances, the position broadly is that the person remains the responsibility of the first local authority – situated in whichever of the four countries – he or she was living in immediately before the placement was made.

Statutory guidance elaborates on communication between the two different local authorities concerned and on how practical arrangements could be made for the second local authority (in the new area) to discharge ongoing management of the placement on behalf of the first (placing) authority with suitably clear arrangements for reporting back to the first authority, and also for any payments from the first local authority to the second.[1]

Regulations made in relation to Scotland state that in case of business failure of a care provider in Scotland, but in relation to a person placed there by an English local authority, a Scottish local authority will have a temporary duty under the Social Work (Scotland) Act 1968 to meet the person's needs.[2]

---

1   Statutory guidance, 2016, Chapter 21.

2   SI 2014/2839. Care and Support (Cross-border Placements) (Business Failure Duties of Scottish Local Authorities) Regulations 2014.

D

Decision-making process

The courts and the local ombudsmen are mostly concerned with examining the decision-making process of assessments and other decisions under the Care Act 2014. They are averse to taking a view on the 'merits' of a decision, in terms, for example, of professional judgements. A bit like teachers of mathematics marking a school test: it is the working out that scores the bulk of the marks, not the final answer. See: **Judicial review**. Also: **Local ombudsman**.

Deferred payments

In certain circumstances, a local authority has a duty to defer payment of care home fees, under sections 34 and 35 of the Care Act. This enables a person to become a resident of a care home without having to sell their home. However, the duty arises only if certain conditions are met. The local authority must place a registered charge on the person's home so that, at the end of the deferred payment agreement, the home can be sold and the local authority paid what it is owed.

The main criteria for deferring payment are contained in regulations and, broadly, are as follows.[1]

- **Local authority meeting need in a care home**. The local authority must be meeting a person's needs under sections 18 and 19 of the Act, and have specified in the care and support plan that the needs must be met in a care home. Or, the local authority is not going to meet the needs but considers that it would have done so – by arranging care home accommodation – had it been asked.

---

1   SI 2014/2671. Care and Support (Deferred Payment) Regulations 2014, rr.2, 4.

- **Person's own home**. The local authority must be satisfied that the person has a legal or beneficial interest in the property, and that it is the adult's only or main home. In addition to the value of that interest, the adult's capital must not exceed £23,250.

- **Adequate security: mortgage**. The local authority must obtain adequate security for the deferred payment. This is a legal mortgage, for an amount which covers at least the deferred amount as well as any interest or administration costs. The local authority has a power to charge both interest and administration costs. Regulations set out how to determine both the deferred amount and the equity value to be imputed to the property.

- **Repayment**. Repayment is due when the property is sold or 90 days after the person has died, whichever is sooner.

A failure to give people not only information about the availability of deferred payments, but also details about how they work, may be maladministration.[1] Likewise, a delay of many months, in providing a settlement figure, following the death of the care home resident – thereby creating difficulties with managing probate.[2]

DEFERRED PAYMENTS: POWER. There is, in addition, a power to make deferred payments. This arises if the local authority is going to meet the person's needs in a care home or supported living, or would have done so had it been asked, there is adequate security (legal mortgage on property or some other form of security) and the person agrees to the conditions. There is no requirement that, aside from the value of the person's home, their resources do not exceed £23,250.[3]

Delay

For assessment, and the provision of care and support, the Care Act contains no timescales. In their absence, there is a general public law duty to make a

---

1   *LGO, London Borough of Lewisham*, 2016 (15 015 828), para 20.

2   *LGO, Suffolk County Council*, 2016 (16 008 736).

3   SI 2014/2671. Care and Support (Deferred Payment) Regulations 2014, r.3.

decision within a reasonable period of time – and identifying a reasonable period of time will depend upon all the circumstances of the case.[1] Waiting lists may be justifiable up to a point, but at the very least the local authority must have a system of priorities and be regularly reviewing the relative needs of those on the waiting list.[2] Guidance states that an assessment should be done within an appropriate and reasonable timescale, taking into account the urgency of needs, and that the person should be given an indicative timescale and be kept updated.[3] The local ombudsman considers, normally at least, that assessments should be carried out within four to six weeks of request.[4]

THE IMPORTANCE OF PRIORITIES AND REVIEW

- **Four-month delay in assessment about admission to care home.** A woman with learning disabilities wished to go into a care home and requested an assessment in October 2015. This was not carried out until January, when the request was turned down but respite care increased. The assessment delay, and the uncertainty it caused, was maladministration.[5]

- **Applying referral information correctly to establish urgency.** A social worker made an urgent referral to the occupational therapy service to assess and provide equipment for a woman, so she could return home from a respite care stay. The occupational therapists treated it as non-urgent, and did not visit for two weeks, when they ordered a slide sheet, commode and profiling bed. This meant the woman had to stay two weeks longer than necessary in respite care. This was maladministration, and the local authority agreed to waive the financial charge for the extra respite.[6]

---

1   *R(D) v London Borough of Brent* [2015] EWHC 3224 (Admin), para 19.

2   *MacGregor v South Lanarkshire Council* [2001] S.C. 502, para 10.

3   Statutory guidance, 2016, para 6.29.

4   Local Government Ombudsman. *Complaints about councils that conduct community care assessments.* London: LGO, 2013, p,2.

5   *LGO, Warwickshire County Council,* 2016 (15 020 544), para 1.

6   *LGO, Nottingham City Council,* 2016 (16 002 731), paras 7–13.

- **Two-year failure in assessment**. A failure for two years to assess a woman with learning disabilities, ready for discharge from NHS premises, amounted to a breach of the duty to assess.[1]

- **Six-month delay in placement acceptable**. A six-month delay in deciding on a placement in the best interests of a person after finishing college – including exploring options and talking to providers – was not a breach of duty. The local authority had offered interim provision until a final decision was made.[2]

- **Six-month delay in direct payment**. An assessment about a person's needs, and arranging a direct payment, took six months instead of the four weeks the local authority admitted it should have achieved. This was maladministration.[3]

- **Delaying 11 months to make alternative care home placement**. Having assessed the need that a person move to an alternative care home – since the existing care home was not suitable for his needs and led to increased stress and anxiety, thereby having an impact on his well-being under the Care Act – the local authority's delay was maladministration.[4]

In practice, delay is more likely to be considered by the local government ombudsman than the courts.

FACTORS THE OMBUDSMAN MIGHT LOOK AT

- **Having priorities which are not simplistic**. Being able to treat complex cases urgently, as well as emergency cases,[5] or not having 360 out of 390 people on the waiting list in one of the three priority categories.[6]

---

1   *R v Sutton London Borough Council, ex p Tucker* [1998] CCLR 251, High Court.

2   *R(D) v London Borough of Brent* [2015] EWHC 3224 (Admin), paras 23, 31–32.

3   *LGO, Cheshire East Council*, 2015 (14 005 078), paras 79–80.

4   *LGO, Herefordshire County Council*, 2016 (15 019 902).

5   *LGO, Rochdale Metropolitan Borough Council*, 1995 (93/C/3660).

6   *LGO, Halton Borough Council*, 2002 (01/C/09625).

- **Priority criteria, applied properly**. Having well-defined priority criteria applied properly and the person reappraised in the light of new information; service users informed about their priority and waiting time, and about alternative suppliers.[1]

- **Adequate referral information**. Having adequate referral information so that priorities can be made for assessment – for example, a newly blind woman was judged lower priority despite risks of burning, scalding and other injuries because of poor referral information and failure to follow up and find out more.[2]

- **Long delay**. Avoiding excessive delay in assessment, even in lower priority cases – for example, in excess of six months may be too long.[3]

- **Adhering to own policy**. Not exceeding the local authority's own policy on assessment waiting times (whatever times the local authority has itself set).[4]

Undue delay is therefore dependent up to a point on the individual person concerned. What is undue delay for one person might not be for another.

- **Ten-day wait following hospital discharge**. A ten-day wait for a visit – to a man discharged from hospital after a major operation, and with poor mobility – was maladministration (he did in fact just about survive on tinned food and shopping with considerable difficulty).[5]

Delegation of functions

Up to April 2015, local authorities were not permitted, under community care legislation, to delegate wholly their own legal functions – such as assessment, eligibility decisions and care planning – to other organisations, except to

---

1   *LGO, Wakefield Metropolitan District Council*, 2004 (02/C/14023).

2   *LGO, Stockport Metropolitan Borough Council*, 2003 (02/C/03831).

3   *LGO, Wakefield Metropolitan District Council*, 2004 (02/C/14023).

4   *LGO, Wakefield Metropolitan District Council*, 2004 (02/C/14023).

5   *LGO, Sheffield City Council*, 1996 (95/C/2483).

NHS bodies through arrangements made under section 75 of the NHS Act 2006. Section 79 of the Care Act 2014 changes this. It allows, but does not require, local authorities to authorise other organisations to discharge a local authority's legal functions under the Care Act on the local authority's behalf. (It also allows local authorities to do the same in respect of services under section 117 of the Mental Health Act 1983.)

DELEGATION OF FUNCTIONS: EXCLUDED FUNCTIONS. Certain functions must be discharged by the local authority itself. These are integration, cooperation with other statutory bodies, exercising the power to charge financially, and the overall duty about making enquiries into abuse or neglect (safeguarding) in sections 3, 6, 7, 14 and 42 of the Act respectively.

The Department of Health has stated that the rule about excluded functions does not apply to an agreement made between a local authority and an NHS body under section 75 of the NHS Act 2006 and the relevant regulations.[1] Assuming this is a correct view, it means that the local authority could still delegate, for example, its safeguarding functions to the NHS.[2]

Some things cannot, in any event, be delegated to the NHS – charging, financial assessments and debt recovery.[3]

DELEGATION OF FUNCTIONS: LEGAL RESPONSIBILITY. The local authority retains legal responsibility, under section 79 of the Care Act, for what the other organisation does (although not in relation to criminal proceedings, or to contractual issues between the local authority and the other organisation).

DELEGATION OF FUNCTIONS: NEGLIGENCE. The courts have anyway and separately ruled that, in negligence cases (in common law), local authorities remain legally liable in some circumstances, even when they have

---

1   SI 2000/617. NHS Bodies and Local Authorities Partnership Arrangements Regulations 2000.

2   Statutory guidance, 2016, para 18.5.

3   SI 2000/617. NHS Bodies and Local Authorities Partnership Arrangements Regulations 2000, r.6.

taken all reasonable care in contracting out a service, particularly in the case of vulnerable people. For example, in the case of children at school (and maybe elderly people in a care home), the courts have held that certain core functions, and therefore legal liability, is ultimately not delegable in the sense of avoiding liability.[1]

DELEGATION OF FUNCTIONS: MALADMINISTRATION. Section 25 of the Local Government Act 1974, the Act which governs the local ombudsman's work, states that the local authority remains responsible for what is done on its behalf. This means the local ombudsman might find maladministration against a local authority when a service has been contracted out – for instance, when a local authority has commissioned a care home to meet a person's needs and the care home does this inadequately.[2] Similarly, if a core legal function has been delegated out – as occurred when a local authority delegated its social care assessment and eligibility functions for people with Asperger's syndrome to an NHS Trust – the complaint and finding of maladministration lay against the local authority.[3]

Direct payments

Direct payments come under section 31 of the Care Act. They come into play as follows. First, a personal budget for an adult specifies an amount which the local authority must pay towards meeting the person's needs. Second, the adult asks the local authority to meet some or all of those needs by making payments to the adult themselves or to a person nominated by the adult.

1   *Woodland v Essex County Council* [2013] UKSC 66, para 23.

2   *LGO, Worcestershire County Council*, 2014 (12 004 137), paras 2, 45. And *LGO, London Borough of Ealing*, 2013 (12 012 697), para 42.

3   *LGO, Somerset County Council*, 2015 (13 019 566), paras 3, 35.

DIRECT PAYMENTS: CHOICE. A direct payment is effectively a choice and should not be forced on to people:

> **Choice to have a direct payment**. Local authorities need to make clear to people that they can choose whether to have a direct payment to meet all, or just some (or none), of their needs: failure to do so is maladministration.[1] So it was maladministration when a local authority told a woman that to have care at home she had to have a direct payment – otherwise she would have go into residential care, despite her previous bad experience there. The alternative, of direct care provision in her own home, would not have met the woman's needs, because the local authority had wrongly fettered its discretion by capping what it was prepared to pay care agencies.[2]
>
> **Offering a direct payment in the absence of a directly provided service**. The courts have held that local authorities can nonetheless offer direct payments to people unbidden, but that a person's consent would still be required. Sometimes, a local authority might bring pressure to bear on the person by pointing out that an alternative, directly provided service would take longer to find and set up. If the person still refuses the direct payment, the local authority could not delay a direct service indefinitely, only for a reasonable time. But what is a reasonable time might depend partly on how far the person's refusal of the direct payment were judged to be arbitrary or unreasonable.[3]

DIRECT PAYMENTS: SPEED OF DECISION. Guidance states that requests for direct payments should be dealt with in as 'timely a manner as possible'.[4]

DIRECT PAYMENTS: FOUR MAIN CONDITIONS. If four main conditions are met, the local authority must then make the direct payment, following the request:

---

1   *LGO, London Borough of Ealing*, 2008 (07/A/08746), para 27.

2   *LGO, Cambridgeshire County Council*, 2002 (01/B/00305).

3   *P(MP) v London Borough of Hackney* [2007] EWHC 1365 (Admin), para 39.

4   Statutory guidance, 2016, para 12.22.

- **Mental capacity**. First, the adult must have capacity to make the request (but see below for lack of mental capacity), and any person nominated to receive the payment must agree.

- **Prohibitions not applying**. Second, the local authority is not prohibited from making the payments, because the person comes under various criminal justice provisions relating to release on licence, or drug or alcohol treatment or rehabilitation orders.[1]

- **Ability to manage**. Third, the local authority must be satisfied that the adult or the nominated person can manage the direct payments, either by themselves or with assistance.

- **Appropriateness**. Fourth, the local authority is satisfied that making the direct payment is 'an appropriate way' to meet the needs.[2]

DIRECT PAYMENTS: PERSON LACKING MENTAL CAPACITY.

Direct payments, for a person lacking mental capacity to make the request, come under section 32 of the Care Act. They arise as follows: First, a personal budget for an adult specifies an amount which the local authority must pay towards meeting the person's needs. Second, the adult lacks capacity to request the direct payment. Third, an 'authorised person' asks the local authority to meet some or all of those needs by making payments to that authorised person.

If certain conditions are met, the local authority must make the direct payment, following the request. There are five main conditions:

- **Authority under the Mental Capacity Act**. First, the person making the request has authority under the Mental Capacity Act 2005 (MCA) to take decisions about the adult's needs for care and support.

- **A suitable person**. Second, the person to whom the payment will be made does not have authority under the MCA, but somebody who does have that authority agrees with the local authority that the person in question (the proposed authorised person) would be suitable to receive the direct payment. Alternatively, there is nobody with authority under the Mental Capacity Act,

---

1   SI 2014/2871. Care and Support (Direct Payments) Regulations 2014, schedule 1.

2   Care Act 2014, s.31.

but the local authority considers the person (the proposed authorised person) suitable to receive the direct payment.

- **Best interests**. Third, the local authority is satisfied that the authorised person receiving the direct payment will act in the person's best interests.

- **Ability to manage**. Fourth, the local authority is satisfied that the authorised person receiving the direct payments is able to manage the direct payment, either alone or with assistance.

- **Appropriate**. Lastly, the local authority is satisfied that making direct payments is an appropriate way to meet the needs.

In deciding whether it is appropriate to make the direct payment to the authorised person, the local authority must:[1]

- **consult**: undertake reasonable and practicable consultation with anybody named by the adult, anyone caring for the adult or interested in their welfare, and anybody authorised under the Mental Capacity Act to make decisions about the person's care and support needs

- **consider wishes and feelings**: consider the adult's past and present wishes and feelings (in particular, any relevant written statement made by the adult when the adult had capacity requesting a direct payment)

- **consider beliefs and values**: consider the beliefs and values that would likely influence the adult if he or she had capacity, as well as other factors the adult would be likely to consider if able to

- **obtain a criminal record**: obtain an enhanced criminal record certificate if the authorised person, to whom the direct payment will be made, is not a family member or friend, or if the payment will be made to an organisation, obtain the certificate in relation to the individual who will manage the payment day to day.

DIRECT PAYMENTS: TERMINATION OR REPAYMENT. If the key conditions for people with or without capacity (see above) are no longer met, the local authority has a duty to terminate the direct payment. If any other

---

1   SI 2014/2871. Care and Support (Direct Payments) Regulations 2014.

condition attached to the making of the direct payment has been breached, or the payment has been used on something other than the needs specified in the care and support plan (or support plan), the local authority can (but does not have to) terminate the direct payment. It can also seek repayment.[1]

Consultation before withdrawal. Natural justice and fairness demand that the person be consulted and given an opportunity to make representations before withdrawal of the direct payment takes place. Failure to do this is maladministration.[2]

Items not within care and support plan. A local authority claimed repayment of direct payment monies spent on items which did not relate to the care and support plan: wide-fit shoes, unauthorised payments to three individuals, a charitable donation, paying for respite breaks for two people, paying for a short break at a holiday camp for two people. Reclaiming the money was not maladministration – but not auditing the direct payment for two years was, and so the local authority waived the money owing. An additional overpayment was, however, justifiably repayable.[3]

Cleaning not covered by the direct payment. A care and support plan was meant to cover three visits per day. A morning call for washing and dressing, breakfast and sandwich made for lunch. A teatime call to prepare a hot meal and encourage the woman to eat. A bedtime call to help her orientate herself toward the time of day, and to help her change and get into bed. She had a private arrangement for gardening and cleaning, and her expenditure on this was excluded from the means test conducted. She then used some of the direct payment on the latter two services. The ombudsman found the local authority justified in reclaiming £1280.[4]

Surplus funds. Enforcement of a condition that surplus funds (on death of the person or otherwise) should be repaid may be quite acceptable and reasonable.[5]

---

1   Care Act 2014, s.33.

2   *LGO, London Borough of Hounslow*, 2016 (15 016 338), para 63.

3   *LGO, Lincolnshire County Council*, 2016 (15 013 234), paras 59–60

4   *LGO, Sefton Metropolitan Borough Council*, 2016 (16 006 738).

5   *LGO, North Yorkshire County Council*, 2016 (15 015 676), paras 58–59.

> **Termination of direct payment used to make ad hoc gifts**. A direct payment was made enabling a woman to have some respite from caring for her husband. Some of this respite was enabled by friends, for whom she would buy occasional gifts by way of thanks, such as flowers, chocolates or a meal out. The local authority then stated that either she should formalise such arrangements, or instead use the direct payment to buy a sitting service from an agency. The woman declined both options, so the local authority withdrew the direct payment. The ombudsman found no fault.[1]

DIRECT PAYMENTS: MUST BE USED TO MEET SPECIFIED NEED.

Direct payments can only be made if they are an appropriate way of meeting a person's needs, and must be made on condition that they be used to pay only for arrangements for meeting needs specified in the care and support, or support, plan.[2] This means that the direct payment must be reasonably capable of meeting the assessed, eligible need for which the payment is made.

> **Wrongly converting care into inadequate direct payment**. A local authority converted an amount of respite care, provided previously, into a direct payment – with the stated aim of giving choice and personalisation. The notional direct payment rate – based on this conversion – came to nearly double what was actually paid, leaving only one choice of provider and reliance on family help. This was maladministration.[3]
>
> **Wrongly placing a ceiling on direct payment**. Placing a general ceiling on the amount of a direct payment, £360 per week, for two carers to make evening visits was maladministration because that amount was not capable of meeting the woman's needs.[4]

Costs such as recruitment costs and national insurance should be included in the direct payment, where these will be incurred.[5]

---

1   LGO, *Staffordshire County Council*, 2016 (16 004 984), paras 9–12.

2   Care Act 2014, s.33.

3   LGO, *Lancashire County Council*, 2014 (13 003 902), para 60.

4   LGO, *Cambridgeshire County Council*, 2002 (01/B/00305).

5   Statutory guidance, 2016, para 12.27.

> **Higher rate bank holiday payments**. It was maladministration for a local authority not to include a supplement in the direct payment to cover bank holiday rates of care agency staff. All care agencies charged this, so there was no way that the direct payment recipient could have gone to a cheaper agency.[1]
>
> **Holiday pay**. Failure to include holiday pay for a personal assistant was maladministration.[2]

DIRECT PAYMENTS: COST-EFFECTIVENESS. Guidance states that in some circumstances it may be more appropriate to meet a person's needs through a directly arranged service rather than through a direct payment – for instance, if the same outcomes could be achieved more cheaply through the arranged service than through the direct payment.[3]

DIRECT PAYMENTS: AMOUNT. Because personal budgets are based on what the cost to the local authority would be of meeting the person's needs, issues may arise about whether the amount of the direct payment is adequate (see **Personal budgets**). This proviso aside, once a local authority has accepted a particular way of meeting a person's needs, then it must pay sufficiently such that those needs are met. For instance, having accepted that a person's needs should be met in their own home, it was maladministration to restrict the amount of the direct payment to what a care home placement would have cost.[4]

DIRECT PAYMENTS: PAYING SPOUSES, PARTNERS, CLOSE RELATIVES. Direct payments cannot be used by the recipient of the direct payment to pay certain specified family members for providing the care. These are defined as spouses, partners or close relatives living in the same household. This rule can

---

1   *LGO, Tameside Metropolitan Borough Council*, 2016 (15 016 959), para 15.

2   *LGO, Hertfordshire County Council*, 2016 (15 010 528).

3   Statutory guidance, 2016, para 11.26.

4   *LGO, London Borough of Bromley*, 2016 (15 020 580), paras 30–33.

be waived if the local authority is satisfied that using the direct payment is necessary for the following reasons:

- to meet the care needs of the adult, or

- to provide administrative and management support or services to enable the direct payment recipient to (i) comply with legal obligations arising from the direct payment or (ii) monitor the receipt and expenditure of the direct payment.[1]

If a relative is paid in this way, it counts as income for tax purposes and also social security entitlement.[2] Local authorities tend to apply an exceptionality policy to the question of whether a spouse, partner or relative in the same household can be paid, by the direct payment recipient, to provide care. Neither regulations nor the guidance refer to the question of exceptionality, but simply whether it is 'necessary'. Yet were local authorities to make such payments commonly, it would undermine one of the main purposes of the Care Act, which is to encourage and support informal (unpaid) care.

Refusal to pay relative for administration of direct payment. Just because a direct payment is large and complex, it is not necessarily maladministration for the local authority to refuse to agree to a relative undertaking, and being paid for, the administrative function – and to use an external agency instead.[3]

Refusal to pay daughter to care for her mother. A woman wanted her daughter (with a child) to live with her and that she should pay her daughter, by way of direct payment, for the care she would provide. The local authority refused, judging that her needs could be met by other means: agency care, residential or nursing care. Furthermore, the move would have resulted in overcrowding in the mother's property. This decision was not maladministration.[4]

---

1 SI 2014/2871. Care and Support (Direct Payments) Regulations 2014, r.3.

2 *Casewell v Secretary of State for Work and Pensions* [2008] EWCA Civ 524.

3 *LGO, Salford City Council*, 2016 (15 010 119), paras 33–36.

4 *LGO, West Sussex County Council*, 2016 (15 015 744), paras 10–11.

Refusal to pay relative of person with complex needs. A woman (presumably the man's partner) applied to be paid to care for a man with rare and complex needs, on grounds of exceptional circumstances. Both woman and the man were distrustful of strangers and didn't want them in the home. The local authority refused, on the grounds that the Care Act referred to prevention, delay and reduction in need – and that paying her to care would not help the man's social interaction, behaviour management and independence. The ombudsman found this was a reasoned decision the local authority was entitled to come to.[1]

Excessive payment to wife for direct payment administration. A local authority demanded the repayment of £7200 that a man had made to his wife's company, for administration of his direct payment. A local support organisation would have charged £325 for this function, a reasonable cost. Such a payment was not part of his care and support plan, and the local authority's decision was justified.[2]

Longstanding spouse payment discontinued. A woman had used her direct payment for 12 years to pay her husband to provide care. The local authority reviewed and made the decision that her needs should be met in a different way, because the situation did not fall within exceptional circumstances in terms of geographical location, severe communication, or urgent and short-term requirements for which no alternative provision existed. This was not maladministration.[3]

DIRECT PAYMENTS: CONDITIONS GENERALLY. Local authorities can impose conditions on direct payments. These can prohibit the person's need being met by a particular person, and can stipulate that the recipient provide information to the local authority. However, there are conditions which the local authority is not allowed to impose:

- that the adult's needs be met by a particular person

1   *LGO, Solihull Metropolitan Borough Council*, 2016 (16 002 332), paras 12–16.

2   *LGO, Bournemouth Borough Council*, 2016 (15 018 170), paras 31–33.

3   *LGO, Leicestershire County Council*, 2016 (16 003 086), paras 8–9.

- that information be provided to the local authority more frequently and in more detail than is reasonably required to check on the appropriateness of direct payment and compliance with conditions

- that information be provided to the local authority in a format which is not reasonably practicable for the recipient to provide.[1]

The courts might, in general, object to restrictive or onerous conditions.

> **Wrongful insistence about use of a payroll company.** A local authority had child protection concerns relating to an adult recipient of a direct payment. It demanded that the direct payment be channelled through a payroll company, so it could identify the personal assistants employed. The court rejected this as legally impermissible.[2]

But not necessarily:

> **Justifiably changing direct payment support provider, contrary to the guidance.** A court accepted that it was permissible for a local authority to enforce a change of direct payment support provider. This was because of suspicion of fraud – and even though some service users objected to the change. The court held that the restriction of choice was not consistent with Care Act statutory guidance, but that guidance could be departed from with good reason: here there were exceptional circumstances and the local authority was seeking to protect the well-being of the service users.[3]

Guidance states that if a local authority becomes aware that a direct payment recipient is not complying with tax rules – or is generally not complying with employer obligations – the direct payment should be reviewed and consideration be given to alternatives to the direct payment.[4]

---

1   SI 2014/2871. Care and Support (Direct Payments) Regulations 2014, r.4.

2   *H and L v A City Council* [2011] EWCA Civ 403.

3   *R(Collins) v Nottinghamshire County Council, Direct Payments Service* [2016] EWHC 996 (Admin).

4   Statutory guidance, 2016, para 12.49.

DIRECT PAYMENTS: RESIDENTIAL ACCOMMODATION. Direct payments cannot currently (this may change in the future) be used to fund care home accommodation, other than short breaks. The rules are that in any 12-month period, a direct payment cannot be used in this way for more than four consecutive weeks. If two periods of care home accommodation are provided, each less than four weeks long, then they are added together – but only if the two periods are separated by less than four weeks.[1] The effect of this rule is that direct payments could be used for regular short-term breaks throughout the year, if each break is less than four weeks long and is separated from any other break by more than four weeks.

DIRECT PAYMENTS: WHEN IN HOSPITAL. Guidance states that if a person is receiving a direct payment and goes into hospital, 'consideration should be given to how the direct payment may be used in hospital to meet non-health needs or to ensure employment arrangements are maintained'.[2]

DIRECT PAYMENTS: REVIEWS. A local authority must review a direct payment at least within the first six months, and then at least annually. In addition, if the payment is for somebody with mental capacity, the local authority must carry out reviews if it considers:

- the adult no longer has the mental capacity to request the direct payment

- a condition has been breached

- there is a change in mental capacity, or

- information has been received that the direct payment may not be being used to meet the needs for which it has been given.

In the case of somebody lacking capacity, the local authority must review if it considers or has been told that:

- the person no longer lacks the mental capacity to request the direct payment

---

1   SI 2014/2871. Care and Support (Direct Payments) Regulations 2014, r.6.

2   Statutory guidance, 2016, para 12.52.

- the direct payment may not have been used to meet needs

- the authorised person is not acting in the adult's best interests

- the authorised person is not able to manage the direct payment, or

- making the direct payment to the authorised person is not an appropriate way of meeting the adult's needs.

The local authority must take all reasonable steps to reach agreement as to the outcome of a review with the adult, or with the person with authority under the Mental Capacity Act to take care and support decisions or, if there is no such person, then with anybody else interested in the adult's welfare.[1]

Failure to review and getting into debt. A failure to review at least annually, with the consequence that the recipient got into debt – not because of deliberate mismanagement but of genuine difficulty in managing certain costs (in this case travel costs) – was maladministration.[2]

DIRECT PAYMENTS: CHARGING. If a person is assessed to make a financial contribution to their care and support (or support), a direct payment can be paid gross (and the person be subsequently billed) or net (the amount owing to be deducted at source).[3]

DIRECT PAYMENTS: HARMONISATION WITH NHS DIRECT PAYMENTS. Regulations state that a local authority must take reasonable steps to coordinate its direct payment systems, processes and requirements to minimise administrative or other burdens on a person also receiving a direct payment from the NHS[4] (see **NHS: direct payments**).

Discrimination, see Equality Act 2010

---

1   SI 2014/2871. Care and Support (Direct Payments) Regulations 2014, r.7.

2   *LGO, Shrophsire County Council*, 2016 (14 020 381), para 38.

3   Statutory guidance, 2016, para 12.26.

4   SI 2014/2871. Care and Support (Direct Payments) Regulations 2014, r.10.

Divide between social care and health care

Section 22 of the Care Act prohibits a local authority from meeting, under the Care Act, adults' or carers' needs by providing what the NHS is required to provide, unless what is required is in some sense peripheral and is what is expected to fall within social care. More specifically, a local authority may not meet needs under sections 18 to 20 by providing or arranging for the provision of a service or facility that is required to be provided under the National Health Service Act 2006 unless:

- doing so would be merely incidental or ancillary to doing something else to meet needs under those sections, and

- the service or facility in question would be of a nature that the local authority could be expected to provide.

This has become known as the quantity (incidental or ancillary) and quality (expected) test. The meaning and implications of all this are not that clear.

- **Required to be provided under the NHS Act 2006**. Apart from NHS continuing health care and registered nursing care (see below), there can be considerable uncertainty as to just what the NHS is required to provide. NHS legislation and policies are vague about most services, and local practices within the NHS as to what is provided can in reality vary significantly. This is because section 3 of the NHS Act 2006 gives clinical commissioning groups wide discretion as to the making of priorities and to the scope of what they will or won't provide.

  Explanatory notes to the Care Act 2014, also rather vague, refer to 'all health care services which the NHS is required to provide, for instance, primary medical, dental and ophthalmic services, by clinical commissioning groups...NHS England...or any other NHS body'. The explanatory notes go on to state that 'a local authority may provide some health care services in certain circumstances, that is, where the service provided is minor and accompanies some other care and support service which the local authority is permitted to provide and is of a nature that a local authority would be expected to provide'.[1] The problem is that what is 'expected' is somewhat circular and anyway changes over time. Local authorities now meet a range of needs which two or three decades ago tended to fall to the NHS to meet.

---

1   Care Act 2014: explanatory notes, paras 159–160.

- **Incidental or ancillary – and nature**. The meaning of the first proviso – 'unless doing so would be merely incidental or ancillary to doing something else to meet needs under those sections [of the Care Act]' – is vague.

DIVIDE BETWEEN SOCIAL CARE AND HEALTH CARE: NHS CONTINUING HEALTH CARE. A local authority is not permitted to meet a person's NHS continuing health care (CHC) needs. This is because regulations made under the NHS Act 2006 state that CHC must be arranged and funded solely by the NHS,[1] a point emphasised by Care Act guidance[2] (see **Continuing health care**). This prohibition would not prevent a local authority meeting the person's CHC needs on behalf of the NHS,[3] but provision would then be under the NHS Act 2006 and not the Care Act.

DIVIDE BETWEEN SOCIAL CARE AND HEALTH CARE: REGISTERED NURSING CARE. In addition, section 22 of the Care Act states that local authorities are not permitted to meet needs under the Care Act by providing or arranging for the provision of nursing care by a registered nurse. This means provision by a registered nurse of a service involving:

- the provision of care, or

- the planning, supervision or delegation of the provision of care, other than a service which, having regard to its nature and the circumstances in which it is provided, does not need to be provided by a registered nurse.

Notwithstanding these prohibitions, a local authority is permitted to arrange for the provision of accommodation with registered nursing care (i.e. a nursing home) in two situations – first, if it has obtained consent from the relevant NHS clinical commissioning group (CCG); second, in case of urgency and where the provision is going to be temporary, with consent sought from the CCG as soon as feasible.

---

1   NHS Commissioning Board and Clinical Commissioning Groups (Responsibilities and Standing Rules) Regulations 2012, r.20.

2   Statutory guidance, 2016, para 6.79.

3   By way of an agreement under s.75 of the NHS Act 2006.

Divide between social care and housing

Under section 23 of the Care Act, a local authority is not permitted to meet the needs of an adult in need or carer by doing anything which it or another local authority is required to do under the Housing Act 1996. This rule is designed to prevent people routinely trying to obtain ordinary housing through social services rather than housing legislation – by the back door as it were. Under previous community care legislation, the courts ruled that this prohibition did not prevent social services providing 'ordinary housing' in some cases, but as a last resort only, since otherwise Housing Act procedures and priorities would be distorted.[1] Under the Care Act, the courts have to date stated that a duty to provide accommodation can arise only if the provision, required to meet the person's care and support needs, is accommodation related – that is, the provision would be 'effectively useless' if the person were without accommodation.[2]

Duties and powers

Legislation contains duties and powers. A duty is normally detectable by either the word 'must' or the word 'shall', a power, usually, by the word 'may'. A duty is what a local authority or NHS body is obliged to do. A power is, at simplest, a discretion. Take it or leave it. But things are not quite so straightforward and there are provisos:

- **General duties**. A general duty, sometimes referred to as a target duty, is identified either by the word 'general' or wording which aims the duty at people collectively rather than at specific individuals. For example, section 17 of the Children Act contains a 'general duty' to safeguard and promote the welfare of children in need in the area. Such a duty, towards children in the area, not any particular child, is weak and barely enforceable in terms of provision of services.[3]

---

1   *R(Wahid) v Tower Hamlets London Borough Council* [2002] EWCA Civ 287.

2   *R(SG) v Haringey LBC* [2015] EWHC 2579 (Admin).

3   *R(G) v Barnet London Borough Council* [2003] UKHL 57, House of Lords.

Similarly, the duty on clinical commissioning groups to commission local health services – to meet all reasonable requirements under section 3 of the NHS Act 2006 – is so vague as to be difficult to enforce by any one particular person.[1] And the duty under section 2 of the Care Act to provide preventative services is a general duty owed to the local population, not to any particular person.

- **Individual duties**. Individual duties contrast with general duties. The duty to assess a person under section 9 of the Care Act applies to each individual who appears maybe to be in need of care and support. This is amenable to enforcement by the individual,[2] as is the duty to meet eligible need.[3]

- **Powers**. A power is a mere discretion. But public bodies must give due consideration to exercising it, at least from time to time. A blanket policy never to do so can amount to an unlawful 'fettering of discretion'.[4]

---

1   *R v Secretary of State for Social Services, ex p Hincks* [1980] 1 BMLR 93, Court of Appeal. And many other cases, including: *R v Cambridge Health Authority, ex p B* [1995] 6 MLR 250, Court of Appeal.

2   *R v Bristol City Council, ex p Penfold* [1998] 1 CCLR 315, High Court.

3   *R(McDonald) v Royal Borough of Kensington and Chelsea* [2011] UKSC 33, para 9.

4   *British Oxygen v Board of Trade* [1971] AC 610, House of Lords.

E

Education, health and care plans, see *Children*

Eligibility

Eligibility under the Care Act is pivotal for local authorities, and for adults and for carers. Eligibility triggers a legal duty for the local authority to meet a person's needs. This will often involve, though not always, expenditure. By the same token, it is eligibility which confers entitlement on adults and carers. The eligibility rules are set out in regulations.[1] As law, they must be followed.

> **Unofficial eligibility rule.** A local authority ignored relevant criteria in the case of a woman with learning disabilities, with multiple needs, living with her aged parents. Instead it applied an unofficial eligibility threshold, in a financial crisis, responding only to 'critical and inescapable' situations. This was maladministration.[2]

Tampering locally with the eligibility criteria will therefore also be unlawful.[3]

The eligibility test applies throughout English local authorities and in principle is aimed at consistency of provision. However, variations are likely from one authority to another because of different local interpretation and

---

1   SI 2015/313. Care and Support (Eligibility Criteria) Regulations 2015.

2   *LGO, Cambridgeshire County Council*, 2001 (99/B/04621).

3   *R(Heffernan) v Sheffield City Council* [2004] EWHC 1377 (Admin).

application.[1] The rules differ for adults and carers (see **Eligibility of adults in need** and **Eligibility of carers** below).

ELIGIBILITY: ENFORCEABLE DUTY AND COST-EFFECTIVENESS. Once eligibility is established, the local authority has an enforceable duty to meet it. A lack of resources would be no defence to non-performance of the duty.[2] This might, in principle, mean having to find the money from other budgets within the local authority.[3] So long as the local authority can evidence that the option on offer is capable of meeting the assessed, eligible need. The duty goes only so far as requiring the most cost-effective option to be offered.[4] This principle was explored under previous legislation and will remain the position under the Care Act.

- **Needs not wants.** It is about meeting needs, not wants.[5] Provision does not have to be 'generous', just 'adequate'[6] – for example, incontinence pads instead of a night-time carer, care home accommodation instead of support in one's own home[7] or an adapted downstairs area of a dwelling rather than a more expensive stairlift.[8]

- **Exploring different ways of meeting need.** It might be lawful to explore with the service user, within the personal budget, more flexible support, greater use of technology, training in independent travel, access to benevolent funds, use of cheaper care or of voluntary assistance.[9]

---

1   Fernandez, J-L., Snell, T., Forder, J., Wittenberg, R. *Implications of setting eligibility criteria for adult social care services in England at the moderate needs level.* London: London School of Economics and Political Science, 2013, p.5.

2   *R (Davey) v Oxfordshire County Council* [2017] EWHC 354 (Admin) para 58. And *R v Gloucestershire County Council, ex p Barry* [1997] 2 All ER 1, House of Lords. And *R(McDonald) v Royal Borough of Kensington and Chelsea* [2011] UKSC 33.

3   *R v East Sussex County Council, ex p Tandy* (1998) 1 CCLR 352, House of Lords.

4   *R(McDonald) v Royal Borough of Kensington and Chelsea* [2011] UKSC 33.

5   *R(KM) v Cambridgeshire County Council* [2012] UKSC 23, para 34.

6   *R(Heffernan) v Sheffield City Council* [2004] EWCH Admin 1377, para 21.

7   *R(McDonald) v Royal Borough of Kensington and Chelsea* [2011] UKSC 33. And *R(Khana) v Southwark London Borough Council* [2001] EWCA Civ 999.

8   *R v Kirklees Metropolitan Borough Council, ex p Daykin* [1996] 3 CL 565, High Court.

9   *R(D) v Worcestershire County Council* [2013] EWHC 2490 (Admin), para 102.

- **Cheaper option must still meet need**. The cost-effective option must be capable of meeting the need. Forcing a person to move to a cheaper care home, not checking that it could meet the person's needs – and with an assessment that the move would be detrimental – resulted, foreseeably, in deterioration and neglect. This was maladministration.[1] Likewise, putting the life of an epileptic person at risk several times a month – by removing the availability of expert, waking night cover to reduce the cost of the care package – was held to be unlawful.[2]

- **Cost-effectiveness under the Care Act: reduction of personal budget**. A 40-year-old man had severe disabilities: quadriplegic cerebral palsy, contractures of hips and knees, hip dislocation, very little trunk control, stretched bowel and hypersensitivity to touch. He was unable to bear weight or mobilise and used a wheelchair. He had severe visual impairment and was registered blind. He needed assistance with all of his intimate personal care needs, all domiciliary tasks and activities of daily living, including accessing the community. He was subject to depression, persistent low mood and anxiety. He had a team of seven personal assistants and lived in a specially adapted bungalow.

  The local authority now sought to reduce his personal budget from what had been £1651 to £950 per week. The two main savings were to be that he could spend more time alone – three periods of two hours during the day. In addition, the rate paid to the personal assistants should be reduced.

  Despite the man's objection that he would suffer undue anxiety from longer periods alone, that some of his outings would be curtailed – and that he would risk losing his personal assistants who had been with him 17 years – the court held that the local authority decision was lawful. The latter had considered relevant evidence (about his anxiety, the curtailment possibly of some longer trips and the market rate for personal assistants), had considered his wishes and made a decision in compliance with the Care Act.[3]

---

1   *LGO, Worcestershire County Council,* 2014 (12 004 137).

2   *R(Clarke) v London Borough of Sutton* [2015] EWHC 1081 (Admin).

3   *R(Davey) v Oxfordshire County Council* [2017] EWHC 354 (Admin), paras 2, 10, 142, 154, 181–183.

ELIGIBILITY: NO HIERARCHY OF NEEDS. Guidance states importantly that, in relation to both adults and carers, neither the aspects of well-being nor the different outcomes considered form a hierarchy of need.[1] For instance, local authorities could not lawfully concentrate only on personal care need, ignoring other aspects of well-being and outcomes (getting out, family relationships, contribution to society, etc.) or ignoring social, recreational and leisure needs.[2]

ELIGIBILITY: FLUCTUATING NEEDS. If the adult or carer has a fluctuating level of needs, the local authority must take into account the person's circumstances, over a period it considers necessary, to establish accurately that level.[3]

ELIGIBILITY: MINIMUM – BUT NOT THE ONLY – PROVISION. Eligibility determines the minimum that a local authority must do. However, this does not mean that a local authority is not allowed to exceed that minimum and help somebody without eligible needs. Under section 2 of the Care Act, a local authority has a general duty to provide preventative services for adults in need or carers – irrespective of eligibility. And sections 19 and 20 of the Care Act state explicitly that a local authority has a power to meet a person's (adult or carer's) non-eligible needs. In addition, section 19 provides a power to meet people's urgent needs – irrespective of whether they are ordinarily resident in the area – prior to an assessment and eligibility decision, including in the case of a person who is terminally ill.

ELIGIBILITY: WRITTEN RECORD OF ELIGIBILITY DECISION. A written record of the eligibility decision must be provided with reasons.[4] For reasons to be meaningful, they need to be more than circular. To state, for example, that somebody is ineligible because they don't meet the eligibility criteria

---

1   Statutory guidance, 2016, para 1.6.

2   *R v Haringey London Borough Council, ex p Norton* (1997–98) 1 C.C.L. Rep. 168.

3   SI 2015/313. Care and Support (Eligibility Criteria) Regulations 2015.

4   Care Act 2014, s.13.

without explaining why would be circular. As the courts have put it in a children's welfare case, 'unless the repetition of an assertion is to be regarded as a proper manifestation of a reasoning process, there was none here'.[1] Without reasons, it might appear that the local authority had failed, in law, to consider critically important factors.[2]

> **Absence of explanation due to underlying problems.** Failure by the local authority to provide written explanation overlay the fact that the assessment had only been partially completed, significant information was missing, the eligibility decision was not well expressed and the decision had not been agreed by a manager. All of which was maladministration.[3]

ELIGIBILITY: NEXT STEPS. If a local authority decides to meet an adult's or carer's needs under sections 18–20 of the Care Act, it must do certain things:

- prepare a care and support plan (adult in need) or a support plan (carer)

- tell the person which (if any) of the needs that it is going to meet may be met by direct payments, and

- help the adult with deciding how to have the needs met.[4]

See **Care and support (or support) plans**.

ELIGIBILITY: NON-ELIGIBILITY. If the local authority is not going to meet the adult's or carer's needs, it must give written reasons, and (unless it has already done so) advice and information about what can be done to meet or reduce the needs, and to prevent or delay the development of needs.[5]

---

1   *R v Ealing London Borough Council, ex p C* (2000) 3 CCLR 122, Court of Appeal.

2   *R v Birmingham City Council, ex p Killigrew* (2000) 3 CCLR 109, High Court. And *R(Goldsmith) v Wandsworth London Borough Council* [2004] EWCA Civ 1170.

3   *LGO, Dorset County Council*, 2016 (15 012 395), para 16.

4   Care Act 2014, s.24.

5   Care Act 2014, s.24.

Reasons: no explanation of impact on well-being. An assessment identified that, under the eligibility criteria, a person was unable to achieve certain outcomes. Her mental health needs meant it took her significantly longer than normally expected to do things. In addition, she suffered significant pain, distress or anxiety when accessing community facilities. Despite all this, the assessment concluded that there was not a significant impact on her well-being. This conclusion about her well-being, so at variance with the decision about outcomes, was not evidenced by any reasoning and so constituted maladministration.[1]

Eligibility of adults in need

For an adult, three questions determine eligibility:[2]

- **Impairment or illness**. Do the adult's needs arise from, or are they related to, a physical or mental impairment or illness?

- **Outcomes**. Because of those needs, is the adult unable to achieve two or more of the outcomes listed in the regulations? And

- **Well-being**. Consequently, is there, or is there likely to be, a significant impact on the adult's well-being?

The questions need to be asked in order. Eligibility depends on the answer 'yes' to all three.

Assessment of person with autism: no reference to outcomes. A person with autism was assessed twice and found not to be eligible for services. But neither assessment referred to the outcomes listed in the eligibility criteria. Although the council considered different 'issues', these did not necessarily correlate with legally prescribed outcomes. Therefore, the decision about non-eligibility could not be explained. This was maladministration.[3]

---

1   *LGO, Milton Keynes Council*, 2016 (15 001 422), paras 25–28.

2   SI 2015/313. Care and Support (Eligibility Criteria) Regulations 2015.

3   *LGO, Liverpool City Council*, 2016 (15 020 293), paras 9–10.

ELIGIBILITY OF ADULTS IN NEED: IMPAIRMENT OR ILLNESS. The first is about impairment or illness. Guidance states that the local authority should base its judgement 'on the assessment of the adult and a formal diagnosis of the condition should not be required'.[1] (By way of comparison, the equivalent Welsh regulations are more inclusive, referring as they do to physical or mental ill-health, age, disability, dependence on alcohol or drugs, or other similar circumstances.)[2]

ELIGIBILITY OF ADULTS IN NEED: OUTCOMES. The second question relates to outcomes, of which the adult must be unable to achieve at least two or more:

- managing and maintaining nutrition

- maintaining personal hygiene

- managing toilet needs

- being appropriately clothed

- being able to make use of the adult's home safely

- maintaining a habitable home environment

- developing and maintaining family or other personal relationships

- accessing and engaging in work, training, education or volunteering

- making use of necessary facilities or services in the local community, including public transport and recreational facilities or services, and

- carrying out any caring responsibilities the adult has for a child.[3]

ELIGIBILITY OF ADULTS IN NEED: LEGALLY NOT ACHIEVING AN OUTCOME. The regulations define legal (as opposed to actual) inability to achieve an outcome – that is, when the adult is:

---

1   Statutory guidance, 2016, para 6.102.

2   SI 2015/1578. Care and Support (Eligibility) (Wales) Regulations 2015, r.3.

3   SI 2015/313. Care and Support (Eligibility Criteria) Regulations 2015.

- unable to achieve it without assistance

- able to achieve it without assistance but doing so causes the adult significant pain, distress or anxiety

- able to achieve it without assistance but doing so endangers or is likely to endanger the health or safety of the adult, or of others, or

- able to achieve it without assistance but takes significantly longer than would normally be expected.[1]

Thus, for example, an adult assisted by an informal carer to get dressed and washed would not legally be achieving those two outcomes. The same would be true if the adult was achieving them but at the cost of significant pain, distress or anxiety, or with the risk of falling, or if they took the adult a long time to perform.

ELIGIBILITY OF ADULTS IN NEED: GUIDANCE ABOUT OUTCOMES.
Statutory guidance gives 'non-exhaustive' pointers to considering outcomes:

- **Managing and maintaining nutrition**: whether the adult has access to food and drink to maintain nutrition, and the adult is able to prepare and consume the food and drink

- **Maintaining personal hygiene**: the adult's ability to wash themselves and launder their clothes

- **Managing toilet needs**: the adult's ability to access and use a toilet and manage their toilet needs

- **Being appropriately clothed**: the adult's ability to dress themselves and to be appropriately dressed – for instance, in relation to the weather to maintain their health

- **Being able to make use of the home safely**: the adult's ability to move around the home safely, which could, for example, include getting up steps, using kitchen facilities or accessing the bathroom. This should also include the immediate environment around the home such as access to the property – for example, steps leading up to the home

---

1   SI 2015/313. Care and Support (Eligibility Criteria) Regulations 2015.

- **Maintaining a habitable home environment**: whether the condition of the adult's home is sufficiently clean and maintained to be safe. A habitable home is safe and has essential amenities. An adult might require support to sustain their occupancy of the home and to maintain amenities, such as water, electricity and gas

- **Developing and maintaining family or other personal relationships**: whether the adult is lonely or isolated, either because their needs prevent them from maintaining the personal relationships they have or because their needs prevent them from developing new relationships

- **Accessing and engaging in work, training, education or volunteering**: whether the adult has an opportunity to apply themselves and contribute to society through work, training, education or volunteering, subject to their own wishes in this regard. This includes the physical access to any facility and support with participation in the relevant activity

- **Making use of necessary facilities or services in the local community, including public transport and recreational facilities or services**: the adult's ability to get around in the community safely and to use facilities such as public transport, shops or recreational facilities when considering the impact on their well-being. Local authorities do not have responsibility for the provision of NHS services such as patient transport. However, they should consider needs for support when the adult is attending health care appointments

- **Carrying out any caring responsibilities the adult has for a child**: the adult's ability to carry out any parenting or other caring responsibilities the person has.[1]

The ombudsman has considered the implication of some of these outcomes.

Only one outcome, community activities: no eligibility. A man with social phobia and social anxiety wanted help with meeting his domestic and welfare needs and to enable him to participate in social activities such as going to the theatre and football matches. The assessment found only one outcome that he was unable to achieve – making use of community facilities – since it took him a long time to do so. With only one outcome, he

---

1   Statutory guidance, 2016, para 6.104.

was anyway not eligible but, in addition, the local authority justifiably took the view that there was anyway no significant impact on his well-being.[1]

Only one outcome, habitable home environment: no eligibility. A man with Asperger's syndrome and mild learning difficulties lived alone in a two-bedroom privately rented flat. His mother and step-father lived nearby. He was previously supported with a direct payment for management of his household, correspondence about benefits and socialisation. He was reassessed under the Care Act as unable to achieve one outcome only – habitable home environment – and so as being ineligible. The ombudsman found no fault, since the assessment took account of all the relevant information.[2]

Getting into the community: eligible need for care home resident? An assessment of a care home resident had identified the outcome of activities in the community, and that without these there would be detrimental impact on his psychological, social and cultural well-being, and cause him to become more institutionalised and isolated. (On its face, therefore, an eligible need.) But the local authority did not translate this clearly into the care and support plan and personal budget. So, it was unclear whether the £72 charged for the care needed to access the community was a top-up fee to be paid by a third party under an agreement, was an 'optional extra' to be paid for by the resident or formed part of the assessed needs and therefore was part of the personal budget. This was maladministration.[3]

Getting into the community: health care appointments. A failure even to consider a request for support with health care appointments (over and above NHS patient transport) – in relation to eating, drinking, going to the toilet over an 8-hour period – is maladministration.[4]

Nutrition: importance of fresh food. A visually impaired woman had been receiving personal assistant help with checking fridge contents, the reading of cooking instructions and occasionally being escorted to the local shopping centre. On a review, the local authority assessed that these were

1   *LGO, London Borough of Hillingdon*, 2016 (16 000 056), paras 9–10, 14.

2   *LGO, London Borough of Bromley*, 2016 (16 002 600), paras 7–11, 15.

3   *LGO, Luton Borough Council*, 2016 (16 000 474), paras 31, 37, 43.

4   *LGO, Barnsley Metropolitan Borough Council*, 2016 (15 015 000), paras 20–21.

not eligible needs, because she could instead make use of long-life foods, her freezer and ready meals. The ombudsman found maladministration, since the local authority had failed to recognise that fresh food is essential to meet nutritional needs, and that consumption of fresh food, once it has started to perish, carries a significant health risk. Overall, this meant the restrictive interpretation of this Care Act outcome did not take proper account of the woman's well-being.[1]

Being appropriately clothed: stained clothing. A visually impaired woman had been receiving personal assistant help with sorting her clothes, so that she did not end up wearing stained or inappropriate clothing. On a review, the local authority held that this was not an eligible need. This was on the ground that the Care Act outcome on clothing did not require clothes to match or be clean. The ombudsman found maladministration, because the local authority had failed to recognise the importance to the woman's personal dignity of wearing clean, presentable and appropriate clothes. Overall, this meant the restrictive interpretation of this Care Act outcome did not take proper account of the woman's well-being.[2]

Being appropriately clothed: undressing as well as dressing. A man had multiple sclerosis along with other health conditions. He had mobility difficulties, using both a wheelchair and a walking stick indoors. His wife, with whom he had been co-dependent in terms of care needs, had recently died. A decision was taken that he had an eligible need for help with dressing in the morning, but not with undressing in the evening. This was despite information from carers that he needed this latter help as well.

The ombudsman found maladministration, noting that it was logical to expect a person who needs assistance with dressing to need assistance with undressing. Being appropriately dressed for bed is equally as important as being dressed in day clothes. The local authority's views about his ability to undress were speculation. It had information from carers which showed him to require assistance with undressing at night. The lacuna in provision meant that his daughter had been helping him undress. She did not do so out of choice or willingness, but out of necessity, and had not been

---

1   *LGO, London Borough of Hammersmith & Fulham*, 2016 (15 011 661), paras 15, 18, 24.

2   *LGO, London Borough of Hammersmith & Fulham*, 2016 (15 011 661), paras 15, 18, 24.

offered or received a carer's assessment. The authority should not have made presumptions about his daughter.[1]

ELIGIBILITY OF ADULTS IN NEED: SIGNIFICANT IMPACT ON WELL-BEING. The third question is about whether there is a significant impact on the adult's well-being, requiring scrutiny of the definition of well-being in section 1 of the Care Act. The impact could be a likelihood only, but must be significant. Guidance states the local authority 'will have to consider whether the adult's needs and their consequent inability to achieve the relevant outcomes will have an important, consequential effect on their daily lives, their independence and their wellbeing'.[2]

The definitional elements of well-being are: personal dignity; physical and mental health and emotional well-being; protection from abuse and neglect; control by the individual over day-to-day life; participation in work, education, training or recreation; social and economic well-being; domestic, family and personal relationships; suitability of living accommodation; the adult's contribution to society (see: **Well-being**).

Professional consideration of emotional and psychological well-being. Under the Care Act, failure to take account of the definitional elements of well-being will undermine the lawfulness of a decision – for instance, in relation to emotional and psychological health and well-being. But, an evidenced and reasoned view by a professional as to the impact of a proposed care and support package on these matters would be evidence that they had been lawfully considered, even if the conclusion was at variance with that of the service user.[3]

Social activities. Social activities relate to social well-being and recreational activities under section 1 of the Act. However, a reduced care and support package – meaning that the person could not go on longer social outings, but could continue nonetheless with a wide range of other outings and

---

1   *LGO, Dorset County Council,* 2016 (15 014 893), paras 9–10, 44–47.

2   Statutory guidance, 2016, para 6.107.

3   *R(Davey) v Oxfordshire County Council* [2017] EWHC 354 (Admin), para 136.

activities – was not a breach of section 1 because it amounted to no more than limited curtailment of such activities.[1]

Domestic, family and personal relationships. Considering the definition of well-being, the local ombudsman found that the absence of a care and support plan – for a man being discharged from hospital – meant that the local authority could not show that it had considered the impact of proposed care arrangements on his domestic, family and personal relationships. This was maladministration.[2]

Taking account of social needs and emotional well-being in determining cost-effective option for meeting need. In offering a supported living option under the Care Act, and arguing it was a reasonable, cost-effective way of meeting a person's needs, the local authority could not show that its care and support plan took account of the man's social needs and emotional well-being in addition to his physical needs, even though an outcome, of developing peer group relationships and avoiding isolation, had been identified in the assessment. Nor could it show that it had considered his wishes. This was maladministration.[3]

ELIGIBILITY OF ADULTS IN NEED: MEETING ELIGIBLE NEEDS. If the answer to all three of the above questions is affirmative, then the adult will have eligible needs.

ELIGIBILITY OF ADULTS IN NEED: ROLE OF CARER. Broadly, the local authority must ensure that eligible needs are met under section 18 of the Care Act, unless a carer is able and willing to meet them. The determination of eligible need is therefore made 'carer-blind' – the carer is only brought into the equation after the determination.[4]

---

1   *R(Davey) v Oxfordshire County Council* [2017] EWHC 354 (Admin), para 153.

2   *LGO, London Borough of Bromley*, 2016 (15 016 292), para 44.

3   *LGO, London Borough of Barking and Dagenham*, 2016 (15 019 312), para 31.

4   Statutory guidance, 2016, para 6.113.

> **Failure to establish eligible need of the adult, followed by eligible needs of the carer**. A local authority assessed the needs of a man and his carer wife by listing briefly the activities that he required help with, then setting out the care needs that his wife did not meet, followed by the services provided to meet those gaps. This was maladministration, because the local authority had not assessed in line with the Care Act. The man's eligible needs should first of all have been established. Only then should the local authority have assessed the total needs of his wife as carer, in terms of which of the eligible needs of her husband she was able and willing to meet. And finally, it should have identified the eligible needs of the wife. The local authority had failed to do all this.[1]

ELIGIBILITY OF ADULTS IN NEED: LOCAL AUTHORITY MEETING NEEDS. For the local authority to have a duty to meet a person's eligible needs, the following additional rules apply: first, the person must be ordinarily resident in the local authority's area, or have no settled residence, but be physically present in the authority's area (see **Ordinary residence**); second, under the local authority's charging policy, there is no financial charge being made; or third, there is a financial charge being made, and one of the following applies:

- **The person's financial resources are below the limit**. The person's resources fall below the financial limit defined in regulations (currently, £23,250).

- **The person's financial resources are over the limit**. The person's resources are at or above the financial limit but the person asks the local authority to meet his or her needs anyway. (This duty applies, currently, to *non-residential* care and support only.)[2] For example, the ombudsman accepted as justified an administration fee being charged for a person's attendance at a day centre: the annual fee of £240 covering the cost of negotiating and managing the provider contract (£72), the cost of setting up the care package (£52) and its administration costs (£112).[3]

---

1   *LGO, London Borough of Bromley*, 2016 (15 020 384), paras 32–33.

2   Department of Health *Update on final orders under the Care Act*. London: DH, 2015. And see SI 2015/993. Care Act 2014 (Commencement No. 4) Order 2015, r.3.

3   *LGO, London Borough of Bromley*, 2016 (15 012 765), paras 13, 17.

In the case of a care home, the local authority would currently still have a power (discretion) to arrange care home provision in such circumstances.[1] In either case, the local authority can charge the person not only the full cost of the service but also extra for arranging the service.[2]

- **Lack of mental capacity**. The person lacks mental capacity to arrange care and support, and there is nobody authorised under the Mental Capacity Act to make the arrangements.

ELIGIBILITY OF ADULTS IN NEED: LOCAL AUTHORITY NOT NEC-ESSARILY MEETING ALL NEEDS DIRECTLY.

The determination of eligible need and what to do about it will not necessarily mean that the local authority must directly and absolutely ensure the achievement of all outcomes.

> **Not having to provide directly to achieve certain outcomes**. The courts have held that two of the outcomes – making use of the home safely and a habitable home environment – do not mean that the local authority would have to provide accommodation since they assume that the person already has accommodation. Likewise, the outcomes – of work, education, training or volunteering – do not mean that the local authority itself must provide any of these directly.[3]

Additional considerations are:

- **Other statutory services meeting needs**. Guidance suggests that if another statutory service can meet the eligible needs, those needs should still be recorded as eligible. So that if the alternative services fail, the local authority can consider what it should then do, either itself to meet the needs, assuming it has legal power to do so, or helping the person obtain the service they need under other legislation.[4]

---

1   Statutory guidance, 2016, para 8.56.

2   Care Act 2014, s.14(1)(a).

3   *R(GS) v London Borough of Camden* [2016] EWHC 1762, para 28.

4   Statutory guidance, 2016, paras 10.22–10.24.

- **Voluntary or community group meeting needs**. The local authority could look to use a voluntary or community group providing preventative services (sometimes free of charge) to meet an eligible need for care and support.[1]

But any such provision would need to be reliable. Otherwise the local authority might have to step in and pay for alternative provision to ensure the needs were met. Wishful thinking could lead to unlawfulness or maladministration.[2]

Wishful thinking about a voluntary organisation grant. A local authority declined to meet a visually impaired woman's needs under the Care Act on the grounds that a local voluntary organisation would give her a grant for technology to access the Internet. But the grant was discretionary, and the local authority did not consider how she would manage if the grant was not forthcoming. This was maladministration.[3]

Eligibility of carers

For a carer, three questions determine eligibility:

- **Necessary care**: whether the carer's needs arise as a consequence of providing necessary care

- **Health or outcomes**: whether the effect of the needs is that the carer's physical or mental health is at risk or the carer is unable to achieve at least one outcome, and

- **Well-being**: whether, as a consequence, there is or is likely to be a significant impact on the carer's well-being.[4]

The questions need to be asked in order. Eligibility depends on the answer 'yes' to all three questions. The responsible local authority is the authority in whose area the cared-for adult (but maybe not the carer) is ordinarily resident.

---

1   Statutory guidance, 2016, para 10.13.

2   *LGO, London Borough of Southwark*, 2001 (99/A/00988).

3   *LGO, London Borough of Hammersmith & Fulham*, 2016 (15 011 661), para 24

4   SI 2015/313. Care and Support (Eligibility Criteria) Regulations 2015.

ELIGIBILITY OF CARERS: NECESSARY CARE. The first is whether the carer's needs arise as a consequence of providing necessary care for an adult. Guidance states that if the adult could perform the task themselves, then the carer might be doing something that is not necessary.[1] The Act states that a local authority can meet a carer's needs by providing services for the adult, even though the local authority would not otherwise have a duty to meet the adult's needs for care and support.[2] Department of Health guidance confirms that this means that a carer might have eligible needs even though the adult being cared for might not.[3] So, this would seem to mean that necessary care cannot be equated simply to the cared-for adult having eligible needs.

ELIGIBILITY OF CARERS: IMPACT ON HEALTH OR OUTCOMES. The second question is whether the effect of the needs is such that 'any' of the specified circumstances applies to the carer. *Both circumstances are therefore not required, only one*. The first circumstance is that the carer's physical or mental health is, or is at risk of, deteriorating. The second, alternative, circumstance is that the carer is unable to achieve at least any one of the outcomes listed:

- carrying out any caring responsibilities the carer has for a child

- providing care to other persons for whom the carer provides care

- maintaining a habitable home environment in the carer's home (whether or not this is also the home of the adult needing care)

- managing and maintaining nutrition

- developing and maintaining family or other personal relationships

- engaging in work, training, education or volunteering

- making use of necessary facilities or services in the local community, including recreational facilities or services, and

- engaging in recreational activities.

---

1   Statutory guidance, 2016, para 6.116.

2   Care Act 2014, s.20(7).

3   Statutory guidance, 2016, para 6.116.

> **Failure to take account of health problems of carer.** If a local authority considers, but then in its final decision simply overlooks, the impact of the carer's own health and consequent difficulties (and, as a result, then reduces the level of care and support being provided for the cared for person), the ombudsman will find maladministration. In one case, it meant that the local authority viewed the wife as her husband's main carer – and capable of being so – on the basis of selective evidence only.[1]

ELIGIBILITY OF CARERS: LEGAL INABILITY TO ACHIEVE AN OUTCOME. A carer's inability to achieve an outcome is defined legally – as opposed to actually – if one of the following applies, namely that the carer is:

- unable to achieve it without assistance

- able to achieve it without assistance but doing so causes the carer significant pain, distress or anxiety, or

- able to achieve it without assistance but doing so endangers or is likely to endanger the health or safety of the carer, or of others.

ELIGIBILITY OF CARERS: GUIDANCE ON OUTCOMES. Statutory guidance expands upon the outcomes and what local authorities should consider:

- **Carrying out any caring responsibilities the carer has for a child**: Consider any parenting or other caring responsibilities the carer has for a child in addition to their caring role for the adult. For example, the carer might be a grandparent with caring responsibilities for their grandchildren while the grandchildren's parents are at work.

- **Providing care to other persons for whom the carer provides care**: Consider any additional caring responsibilities the carer may have for other adults. For example, a carer may also have caring responsibilities for a parent in addition to caring for the adult with care and support needs.

- **Maintaining a habitable home environment**: Consider whether the condition of the carer's home is safe and an appropriate environment to live in and whether it presents a significant risk to the carer's well-being.

---

1   *LGO, Royal Borough of Greenwich*, 2016 (15 016 122), paras 15–17.

A habitable home should be safe and have essential amenities such as water, electricity and gas.

- **Managing and maintaining nutrition**: Consider whether the carer has the time to do essential shopping and to prepare meals for themselves and their family.

- **Developing and maintaining family or other significant personal relationships**: Consider whether their caring role prevents the carer from maintaining key relationships with family and friends or from developing new relationships where the carer does not already have other personal relationships.

- **Engaging in work, training, education or volunteering**: Consider whether the carer can continue in their job, and contribute to society, apply themselves in education, volunteer to support civil society or have the opportunity to get a job, if they are not in employment.

- **Making use of necessary facilities or services in the local community**: Consider whether the carer has an opportunity to make use of the local community's services and facilities and, for example, consider whether the carer has time to use recreational facilities such as gyms or swimming pools.

- **Engaging in recreational activities**: Consider whether the carer has leisure time, which might for example be some free time to read or engage in a hobby.[1]

ELIGIBILITY OF CARERS: SIGNIFICANT IMPACT ON WELL-BEING. The third overall question is whether, as a consequence of one of the two circumstances (impact on health or outcomes) applying to the carer, there is – or there is likely to be – a significant impact on the carer's well-being.[2]

ELIGIBILITY OF CARERS: MEETING ELIGIBLE NEEDS. If the carer has eligible needs, the local authority must meet them. The specific rules about this are as follows, in section 20 of the Care Act. The adult being cared for

---

1   Statutory guidance, 2016, para 6.123.

2   SI 2015/313. Care and Support (Eligibility Criteria) Regulations 2015.

must be ordinarily resident in the local authority's area, or have no settled residence but be physically present in the authority's area. So, the responsible local authority for meeting a carer's needs is identified by where the cared-for adult is ordinarily resident or present, not by where the carer lives. One of the following must then apply for the duty to bite:

- **Meeting the carer's need through support to the carer**. The needs of the carer are to be met by provision of support to the carer, and there is no financial charge made for the support. Or, there is a charge, but the carer's resources are beneath the specified financial limit (currently £23,250). Alternatively, the carer's resources are at or above the financial limit, but the carer asks the local authority nonetheless to meet his or her needs.

- **Meeting the carer's need by providing care and support for the adult being cared for**. The needs of the carer are to be met by providing care and support to the adult, and the adult agrees to the care and support, and there is no financial charge made for the care and support. Or, if there is such charge, the adult agrees to the care, but his or her resources are below the specified financial limit. Alternatively, the adult's resources are at or above the financial limit, but the adult nonetheless asks the local authority to meet his or her needs.

ELIGIBILITY OF CARERS: NOT FEASIBLE TO PROVIDE FOR THE ADULT. Section 20 of the Act states that if a local authority has a duty to meet a carer's needs but it is not feasible to do this by providing care and support to the adult, the local authority must, as far as feasible, find another way of meeting the carer's needs.

Enquiries into abuse or neglect

A duty to make safeguarding enquiries is triggered under section 42 of the Care Act if a local authority has reasonable cause to suspect the following about an adult in its area (whether or not ordinarily resident there). The adult:

- has needs for care and support (whether or not the authority is meeting any of those needs)

- is experiencing, or is at risk of, abuse or neglect, and

- as a result of those needs is unable to protect himself or herself against the abuse or neglect or the risk of it.

If there is reasonable cause to suspect these three things, then the local authority must either make the enquiries itself or 'cause' them to be made – that is, ask somebody else to make them. This is so the local authority can then decide whether anything should be done and, if so, what and by whom.

ENQUIRIES INTO ABUSE OR NEGLECT: UNDERLYING PRINCIPLES. Guidance states that adult safeguarding should be underpinned by six principles: empowerment, prevention, proportionality, protection, partnership, accountability. And that it is about 'making safeguarding personal'. (It could simply have referred to 'making safeguarding lawful': adherence to the Care Act 2014, Human Rights Act 1998 and Mental Capacity Act 2005 would arguably make safeguarding personal as well as lawful.)

> **Not informing people about enquiries**. It might be maladministration not to inform a person about what the local authority is doing, what 'making enquiries' means, what the authority is likely to do and what options there are – in the absence of any particular reason not to give such an explanation.[1]

ENQUIRIES INTO ABUSE OR NEGLECT: REASONABLE CAUSE TO SUSPECT. This would seem to mean striking a balance somewhere between totally flimsy and conclusive evidence. Erring too far in either direction could mean either unjustified enquiries, or failure to make enquiries that are needed. Section 47 of the Children Act contains the same phrase in relation to a child suffering, or likely to suffer, significant harm. The courts have noted:

> - **Suspicion or belief**. Reasonable cause to 'suspect' is a lower threshold – more easily triggered – than reasonable cause to 'believe'.

---

1   LGO, *Durham County Council*, 2016 (15 014 024), para 34.

- **Objective grounds**. At least if a person's liberty is at risk, then there must be reasonably objective grounds for the reasonable suspicion, not just the subjective view of the local authority – but the courts would nonetheless be slow to interfere with the local authority's decision about this.[1]

- **Threshold**. The threshold is lower than the balance or probability. In other words, it does not have to be more likely than not for reasonable cause to suspect to arise.[2]

The following case illustrates a local authority failing to make enquiries when there was clearly cause to suspect experience or risk of abuse or neglect (under what would now be the Care Act).

Wrongly not making enquiries despite reasonable cause to suspect. A man was discharged from hospital to a care home. Concerns became known to the local authority about the role of a woman who had befriended him, his periodic confusion, her living in his home, her control of his finances, care home fees not being paid, the length of time she claimed to have known him and contradictory information provided by her. By this stage, the local authority should have initiated an investigation. Not to do so was maladministration.[3]

In the following cases the ombudsman considered 'reasonable cause to suspect' under the Care Act:

Reasonable cause to suspect not the same as accepting assertions at face value. The local authority was justified in making enquiries in relation to a man's not paying care home fees for his mother in a care home because of the consequent threat of eviction. However, it was at fault for accepting at face value the hearsay that he was about to remove his mother from the care home, and for making a best interests decision – and threatening legal action against the son – without first trying to understand the son's actions

---

1   *Gogay v Hertfordshire County Council* [2001] 1 F.C.R. 455 (Court of Appeal).

2   *R(S) v Swindon Borough Council* [2001] EWHC Admin 334, para 36.

3   LGO, *Essex County Council*, 2016 (14 012 127), paras 42–43.

(a protest against what he considered poor care: he was trying to arrange alternative care).[1]

Reasonable cause to suspect: wandering in the street and son's comments about his mother. A woman with dementia and schizophrenia lived with her son who was her main carer. The police told the local authority that the woman had been found wandering in the street. The emergency services reported that he had said he hoped she would die really. He then refused an assessment of either his mother's or his own needs. The local authority made enquiries under section 42, concluding there was no evidence of neglect. Further enquiries took place shortly after this, along similar lines including possible misuse of sedative tablets. The enquiries were again closed, although as a consequence she was offered, and began to attend, a day centre. The son complained, but the ombudsman found the section 42 enquiries justified.[2]

ENQUIRIES INTO ABUSE OR NEGLECT: ORDINARY RESIDENCE. The duty falls on the local authority where the person is present, not where they are (legally) ordinarily resident. See **Ordinary residence**.

ENQUIRIES INTO ABUSE OR NEGLECT: NEEDS FOR CARE AND SUPPORT. It is irrelevant whether the local authority is meeting the person's needs. For instance, the person might have low needs and not be eligible for care and support from the local authority.[3] Or he or she might be self-funding, might be looked after by their family, or simply not be having their needs met at all. The emphasis that eligibility is not required means, presumably, that even the first of the three eligibility conditions – that there be an impairment or illness – might not apply. Furthermore, *care and support* is not defined under the Act and, as such, is probably capable of broad interpretation.

---

1   *LGO, Durham County Council*, 2016 (15 009 788), paras 31–34.

2   *LGO, Birmingham City Council*, 2016 (16 007 420), paras 7–26.

3   Care Act 2014: explanatory notes, para 274.

ENQUIRIES INTO ABUSE OR NEGLECT: HEALTH CARE NEEDS. Care and support needs are legally not the same as health care needs. If a person were to have health care needs only, but no needs for care and support, then the section 42 duty to make enquiries would not apply.

> **Health care, but not social care, needs.** A man, with HIV positive status (possibly with AIDS), had needs for a home, subsistence and medication (and a refrigerator for it), but no other daily living needs. He was held by the courts under previous legislation not to be in need of care and attention (a term similar to care and support) for the purposes of adult social care.[1]

The Law Commission noted that many people with health care needs will also have social care needs.[2]

ENQUIRIES INTO ABUSE OR NEGLECT: CARERS. The reference to care and support means that section 42 clearly does not apply to carers. Otherwise there would be reference to 'support' in addition to 'care and support'. However, if a carer is subject to abuse or neglect, other duties under the Care Act apply, including the duty to promote well-being, to provide advice and information, to cooperate with other organisations and to assess.[3] All these apply to carers, and all contain reference to protection from abuse and neglect. In any case, the local authority can refer to other agencies – for example, the police – if necessary; section 42 enquiries are not required in order to do this.[4]

ENQUIRIES INTO ABUSE OR NEGLECT: INABILITY TO PROTECT. The inability of a person to protect themselves must be because of their needs for care and support. An example of this is given in guidance, which suggests that if a person is neglecting themselves but can control their own behaviour and decisions without external support, section 42 enquiries might not be

---

1   *R(M) v Slough Borough Council* [2008] UKHL 52, para 60.

2   Law Commission *Adult social care*. London: LC, 2013, para 9.36.

3   Care Act 2014, ss.1, 2, 6–7, 10.

4   Statutory guidance, 2016, para 14.48.

triggered.[1] Clearly, an inability to protect oneself would not just be about mental capacity, but could also relate, for example, to mental health, physical inability or some form of undue influence, coercion or duress. The issue of self-protection under section 42 has been considered by the courts, although the judge seemed to equate choice not to protect oneself with inability to do so. This, as a general proposition at least, does not sound quite right.

> **Inability to protect themselves**. When service users objected to the local authority making enquiries into possible fraud by a direct payment support provider – arguing they could perfectly well protect themselves – the judge held that section 42 enquiries were justified. The service users were vulnerable, and they were either unaware of the fraud or chose not to take any action – either way, this was 'clear evidence' that they could not protect themselves.[2]

ENQUIRIES INTO ABUSE OR NEGLECT: PRESENT TENSE. It is clear from the wording of section 42 that the duty to make enquiries arises only in relation to current experience of risk of abuse or neglect. If it is in the past, in respect of the particular person, then the duty does not arise. The intent of the legislation is that past abuse or neglect should be considered by safeguarding adults boards by way of safeguarding adults reviews.[3] See **Safeguarding adults reviews**.

> **Safeguarding alert: past risk**. A safeguarding alert was raised on the day a woman was leaving her present care home to go to another. The ombudsman pointed out that the resident was no longer at any potential risk from the previous home, meaning that section 42 enquiries would not be triggered. Unless, of course, any of the suspected risks might apply to other residents of the previous home.[4]

---

1   Statutory guidance, 2016, para 14.17.

2   *R(Collins) v Nottinghamshire County Council, Direct Payments Service* [2016] EWHC 996 (Admin), paras 19, 28.

3   Secretary of State for Health *Care Bill explained including a response to consultation and pre-legislative scrutiny on the Draft Care and Support Bill*. London: TSO, 2013, p.67.

4   *LGO, Durham County Council*, 2016 (15 009 788), paras 47–48

ENQUIRIES INTO ABUSE OR NEGLECT: CONSENT. There is no requirement that the adult consent to the enquiries, although consent should be obtained where practicable.[1] However, with or without consent, the duty might remain. Equally, the local authority has no legal power to force the adult to engage in the enquiries or indeed to allow the local authority to enter the adult's home. Any coercive entry to the adult's home would, if appropriate, have to take place under other legislation and, therefore, not directly for Care Act purposes. In case of lack of capacity, enquiries could be undertaken if they are believed to be in the adult's best interests.

ENQUIRIES INTO ABUSE OR NEGLECT: CARRYING THEM OUT. Section 42 states that either the local authority must itself make the enquiries or it must 'cause' them to be made by somebody else. This could be, for example, the police, a hospital or a care home. The local authority cannot legally force anybody else to make the enquiries. However, in case of a defined statutory partner under sections 6 and 7 of the Act – about cooperation – the local authority could bring a degree of legal pressure to bear. See **Cooperation**.

> **Using the cooperation duty in safeguarding**. A vulnerable man, maybe with autism and learning disabilities, but so far undiagnosed, was the focus of both assessment and safeguarding (after he was assaulted) duties on the part of the local authority. One of the difficulties in reaching a conclusion about his needs and what to do was a continuing absence of assessment by the Autism Spectrum Conditions (ASC) Team, an NHS-based team. In relation to both the assessment and the safeguarding investigation, the ombudsman referred to the duties of cooperation in sections 6 and 7 of the Care Act. It was maladministration that the local authority had not made greater efforts to get the NHS ASC Team involved: after two years the assessment was still outstanding.[2]

ENQUIRIES INTO ABUSE OR NEGLECT: NATURE AND DEPTH. Guidance states that enquiries could range from an informal conversation to more

---

1   Statutory guidance, 2016, para 14.95.

2   *LGO, Kent County Council*, 2016 (15 018 466), para 28.

formal, involving a multi-agency approach.[1] It is for the local authority to decide therefore how the enquiries should be carried out and to what depth.

Asking NHS to enquire. The local authority conducted adequate enquiries by requesting the NHS to look into the care of a care home resident, and then deciding that no further, formal safeguarding action was required once the care home had agreed to certain recommendation about its practices.[2]

Unannounced visit. The local authority made an unannounced visit with a senior social worker and contracts compliance officer, inspected records of the woman suspected to be at risk and of several other residents potentially so and talked to the NHS body which had placed the woman in the care home, and concluded that there was no evidence of neglect or abuse. The ombudsman found no fault.[3]

Asking range of professionals. A local authority considered information provided by a care home resident's sister, the care home, the GP, the NHS Safeguarding Nurse and the manager of the integrated care team. The local authority reported care standards concerns to the Care Quality Commission. It could have scrutinised the deputy manager in relation to medication practices, and its minute-taking could have been better. But, overall, there was no maladministration.[4]

Limitations to enquiries. A woman wanted the local authority to investigate her mother's bank accounts; she suspected (correctly, as it turned out) that her mother was being financially abused by her brother-in-law. The local authority established that the mother had capacity to decide who should help her with her finances and declined to act on the daughter's suggestion; the ombudsman found that it would have been beyond the local authority's role and legal powers. It was not maladministration.[5]

---

1   Statutory Guidance, 2016, para 14.77.

2   *LGO, Durham County Council*, 2016 (15 014 024), paras 30–31.

3   *LGO, Thurrock Council*, 2016 (16 001 733), para 17.

4   *LGO, North Somerset Council*, 2016 (16 000 240), paras 23–24.

5   *LGO, North Lincolnshire Council*, 2016 (15 015 381), para 51.

ENQUIRIES INTO ABUSE OR NEGLECT: STANDARD OF. The purpose of the enquiries is to enable the local authority to decide whether anything should be done, either under the Care Act or otherwise – and, if so, what and by whom. For the local authority to take this decision, the enquiries clearly need to be of a certain standard. Sometimes the local authority might have to challenge the organisation which it has asked to make the enquiries.[1]

Grossly flawed enquiries by a local authority can lead to draconian, wrong and unlawful decisions being taken.

> **Failure of enquiries and draconian decision**. A 19-year-old woman with learning disabilities came back from a school trip with bruising on her chest. The local authority failed to conduct a competent investigation by doing the obvious: talking to other people on the trip who had witnessed her injuring herself. Instead the local authority jumped to the conclusion that the mother was responsible. It unlawfully removed the woman from her family for a year, depriving her of her liberty and breaching many of the rules under the Mental Capacity Act 2005.[2]

The local ombudsman has drawn attention to the adequacy of enquiries.

> **Allowing delay and relying on unsatisfactory enquiries about hospital care**. A local authority requested that a hospital investigate how an elderly patient was being cared for. The local authority waited five months before chasing up the hospital. (The woman had during this time died.) The hospital provided nothing in writing, claimed there was nothing untoward and that it had spoken to the woman's daughter (which it hadn't). The local authority decided to do nothing more; this was maladministration.[3]
>
> **Relying on unsatisfactory care home enquiries without checking**. A local authority asked a care home to provide information about the care of a resident who had suffered an accident (and subsequently died). The care home manager reported back that the accident could not have been

---

1   Statutory guidance, 2016, para 14.100.

2   *Somerset County Council v MK* [2014] WL 8106551.

3   Local Government Ombudsman *Review of adult social care complaints 2014/15*. London: LGO, 2015, p.12.

foreseen or prevented. The local authority accepted the findings without checking the care records, which showed 11 previous incidents similar to the final accident. This was maladministration.[1]

Not making further enquiries after police enquiries were terminated. The ombudsman found fault when a local authority failed to make its own enquiries – into potentially serious abuse of a man with learning disabilities in a care home – once the police investigation had ended because of a lack of forensic evidence.[2]

Hearsay evidence and lack of evidence. A local authority made enquiries into alleged verbal abuse, emotional abuse and control and neglect, perpetrated by a daughter against her mother. The safeguarding report substantiated these allegations but on the basis of hearsay, assumptions, lack of factual evidence and inflammatory language.[3]

Adequate knowledge of investigator. The safeguarding investigator was experienced in social work but did not pick up important discrepancies in recording in the nursing home or that the resident had been inappropriately moved after his fall. The ombudsman found that someone with a knowledge of care standards should have been part of the investigation, or that investigating staff should have been provided with tools to ensure they considered relevant information. This did not happen and was maladministration.[4]

Asking others to carry out enquiries: appropriateness. A local authority asked a care provider to investigate safeguarding concerns against staff raised by parents about their autistic son living in supported residential accommodation. The ombudsman found fault with the local authority because there was no evidence that the local authority had considered whether the care home staff were sufficiently independent to consider the issues raised.[5]

---

1   Local Government Ombudsman *Adult social care matters: Safeguarding vulnerable adults*. London: LGO, 2014, p.5.

2   *LGO, Essex County Council*, 2013 (11 001 206), paras 33, 45.

3   *LGO, Lancashire County Council*, 2016 (15 017 811), para 48.

4   *LGO, Lancashire County Council*, 2016 (14 001 973), para 32.

5   *LGO, North Yorkshire County Council*, 2016 (14 003 742), para 34.

ENQUIRIES INTO ABUSE OR NEGLECT: FAIRNESS. Equally, enquiries should be fair and reasonably efficient.

Deplorable treatment of a care home owner. Investigating alleged failings in care at a family-run care home, a local authority subjected the elderly care home owner (not the care home manager) to a meeting of eight hours, gave her no proper opportunity to prepare for the meeting, refused to consider her solicitor's letter, had ten people at the meeting on their side opposed to the solitary care home owner, abused the informality of a lunch break, and then drew conclusions about her credibility and fitness to run the home. The court described her treatment as deplorable.[1]

Lack of fair hearing. Abuse allegations were investigated in relation to a daughter and her mother. It was understandable that the daughter was not invited to the safeguarding meetings, since she was the alleged abusive person. However, the allegations were not put to her, depriving her of any opportunity to respond, either then or when the final report – substantiating the allegations – was produced. This was maladministration.[2]

Safeguarding investigation: multiple failings. The ombudsman found maladministration having considered the following points about the investigation carried out: management of the safeguarding investigation was inadequate; the investigation was not completed quickly enough (six months); the investigation report was poorly written; an invitation to the case conference did not advise what was the purpose of the meeting or who was attending; the investigation report was not issued in good time before the meeting; recording of discussion at meetings was poor or absent.[3]

Not explaining finding of lack of neglect. It was maladministration when an investigation concluded, without explaining why, that there was no neglect in a care home, despite inconsistencies in the care home's records, and why it had failed to address all the concerns that had been raised.[4]

---

1   *Davis v West Sussex County Council* [2012] EWHC 2152 (QB), paras 45–47.

2   *LGO, Lancashire County Council*, 2016 (15 017 811), paras 42, 48.

3   *LGO, London Borough of Bromley*, 2016 (15 013 228), para 28.

4   *LGO, Nottinghamshire County Council*, 2016 (15 010 488), paras 17–18.

ENQUIRIES INTO ABUSE OR NEGLECT: DECIDING WHAT TO DO. The legislation states that once enquiries have been made, the local authority must decide whether anything should be done, and, if so, what and by whom. The language is slightly misleading, because the local authority cannot directly force anybody else to do anything. It can, at best, seek cooperation from statutory partners under sections 6 and 7 of the Care Act. The courts have in the past considered what enquiries should be undertaken by a local authority – and what actions then considered or taken by the authority. In one case, the court set out the enquiries the local authority should make in case of a proposed assisted suicide and a trip to Switzerland:

- **intention**: investigate the position of the vulnerable adult to consider her true position and intention

- **legal capacity**: consider whether she was legally competent to make and carry out her decision and intention

- **influence**: consider whether (or what) influence may have been operating on her position and intention and ensure that she had all the relevant information and knew all available options

- **court application**: consider whether to invoke the courts to decide about the issue of her competence

- **assistance if mentally incapacitated**: if she was not competent, to provide assistance in her best interests

- **assistance if mentally capacitated**: if she was competent, to allow her in any lawful way to give effect to her decision, although this should not preclude advice or assistance being given about what are perceived to be her best interests

- **informing the police**: inform the police if there were reasonable grounds for suspecting that a criminal offence would be involved

- **court injunction**: in very exceptional circumstances only, seek an injunction from the courts (using s.222 of the Local Government Act 1972).[1]

---

1   *Re Z* [2004] EWHC 2817 (Fam).

The local ombudsman has examined the adequacy of enquiries and decisions then taken.

> **Salad and chips: lack of expeditious enquiries and decisions through inertia**. A woman used to visit her sister in a care home. In September 2010, two safeguarding concerns were raised, about the visiting sister taking money out of the sister's account, and changing her sister's menu choice from salad to chips. Informal investigations in March 2011 and December 2011 made no findings of abuse. However, by now the woman had been told not to visit her sister and felt unable to, being made to feel like a 'criminal'. By the time the complaint reached the ombudsmen (local and health), the woman had in effect been unable, or felt unable, to visit for three years. The two ombudsmen concluded that this was maladministration, not least because the allegations had never been investigated, substantiated and followed up.[1]
>
> **Unsatisfactory response and decision about dehydration of care home resident**. A woman stayed a few days in a care home, became dehydrated, suffered kidney damage and died a few days later. The care home took months to report back and denied any poor care practices. The local authority decided to take no action despite incomplete paperwork and fluid charts which contradicted the care home's report, other seriously conflicting information and the concerns of the woman's GP. Confusingly, it made no finding of neglect, yet reported partial neglect. It did not inform its own contracts department, nor the Care Quality Commission. All this – and more – was maladministration.[2]
>
> **Justifiable conclusion of safeguarding investigation but still failure to follow up**. Under section 42 of the Care Act, the local authority made enquiries into concerns about a home care agency. The local authority concluded by stating that there was little tangible evidence; it was largely the family's word against that of the carers; there was no evidence the carers were responsible for damage, given that it was a family home

---

1   LGO and HSO: *Essex County Council, Suffolk County Council, North Essex Partnership NHS Foundation Trust and Norfolk and Suffolk NHS Foundation Trust*, 2014 (12 004 807 and 12 013 660), paras 79–80.

2   *LGO, Oxfordshire County Council and Caring Homes Healthcare Group Ltd*, 2016 (15 007 968 and 15 006 620).

with other people around; the issue of falsified care records was for the contracts team, rather than safeguarding. The ombudsman held that this decision was justifiable. The local authority asked the care agency to consider the family's concerns as a complaint. And said that it, the local authority would ask the care agency for the complaint outcome and check that any appropriate action was taken. The authority failed to do this and this was maladministration.[1]

ENQUIRIES INTO ABUSE OR NEGLECT: ELIGIBILITY FOR ONGOING HELP. Following the enquiries, the local authority would only have an ongoing duty to provide help for the person if they were assessed to have eligible needs. See **Eligibility**.

ENQUIRIES INTO ABUSE OR NEGLECT: ASSESSMENT. Making enquiries and assessment of need are separate and distinct functions under the Care Act, but might in practice be intertwined and sometimes run in parallel.[2] For instance, an assessment of an adult or carer under sections 9 and 10 of the Care Act might reveal suspected abuse or neglect, in which case the duty to make enquiries would be triggered as well. Conversely, enquiries being made under section 42 in relation to somebody previously unknown might trigger the duty to assess or, in the case of somebody known, to review and to reassess in the light of changed circumstances. Either way, there is no requirement that an assessment has been carried out prior to conducting section 42 enquiries.

ENQUIRIES INTO ABUSE OR NEGLECT: 'NON-STATUTORY'. Many local authorities appear to have adopted the notion of conducting what they call 'non-statutory' enquiries,[3] meaning enquiries that for one reason or another do not meet the legal conditions set out in section 42.

---

1 *LGO, London Borough of Havering*, 2016 (16 002 895), para 25.

2 Statutory guidance, 2016, para 6.57.

3 See discussion of this: Social Care Institute for Excellence *Adult safeguarding practice questions*. London: SCIE, 2015, p.17. And Spencer-Lane, T. *Care Act manual*. 2nd edition. London: Sweet and Maxwell, 2015, p.310.

- **Duty to enquire**. First, there are other parts of the Care Act that distinguish explicitly between a duty and a power: for example, a duty to meet eligible need, and a power to meet non-eligible need (sections 18 and 19). There is no such duty/power option in section 42. Nor is it referred to in Chapter 14 of the statutory guidance. So, it is likely that any such additional enquiries would not be made under section 42.

- **Other functions under the Care Act and clarity**. Second, 'non-statutory enquiries' would be surely better described, at least in the first instance, as a function under other parts of the Care Act, a number of which can relate to protection from abuse or neglect – for example, conducting a carer's assessment under section 10 in response to concerns about neglect or abuse of a carer (which does not come under section 42). This would then make clearer the legal underpinning.

  A similar point has been made under section 47 of the Children Act 1989, in relation to a reasonable cause to suspect a child is suffering significant harm. The courts have pointed out that if the section 47 threshold is not crossed, then enquiries could be made under other sections of the Children Act 1989 (or, in some circumstances, under a common law duty of care to take care of looked after children).[1]

- **Meaning of 'non-statutory'**. Third, 'non-statutory' refers, literally, to something outside of legislation (and therefore to a common law function), which means that any such enquiries would be outside of the Care Act altogether. Yet local authorities and other organisations have long called for adult safeguarding to be put on a statutory footing. The Care Act has now done this and delineated, quite widely, the safeguarding role of local authorities. It would therefore seem odd to adopt, unnecessarily, the notion of 'non-statutory'. If common law is to be used, surely it should be a last resort, and only after close examination of statutory options already within the Care Act.

Equality Act 2010

The Equality Act 2010 seeks to protect from discrimination people with a 'protected characteristic'. These characteristics are age, disability, gender

---

1   *Gogay v Hertfordshire County Council* [2001] 1 F.C.R. 455.

reassignment, marriage and civil partnership, pregnancy and maternity, race, religion or belief, sex and sexual orientation. Provisions in the Act include:

- **Social and health care provision, etc**. Providers of goods and services (including social services and the NHS), of education and of housing must not discriminate against people because of their protected characteristic. And they must make reasonable adjustments to aspects of provision, such as policies, criteria, auxiliary aids and services.

- **Public sector equality duty**. In addition, public bodies have a 'public sector equality duty' to consider the impact of their policies on those groups with protected characteristics.

  For example, under previous legislation, a local authority consultation exercise was held to be unlawful. It proposed to restrict adult social care eligibility to higher levels of need, but failed to demonstrate that consideration had been given to the impact of the policy on disabled people – under what was then the Disability Discrimination Act 1995 and is now the Equality Act.[1] Similarly, general consideration of the likely impact of stricter eligibility criteria – without assessing the practical impact on people – was also unlawful.[2] On the other hand, in an individual case about disputed provision – and given that Care Act provision is anyway all about the welfare of disabled people – the courts stated that explicit reference to the public sector equality duty might be 'entirely superfluous'.[3]

- **Landlord permission for adaptations to be carried out**. Home adaptations (or other works to the dwelling) require landlord permission (in any tenure). This permission cannot be withheld unreasonably. And if permission is given, but with conditions, those conditions would need to be reasonable.[4]

- **Reasonable adjustments by the landlord – and landlord adaptations**. For disabled tenants, landlords must themselves make reasonable adjustments by

---

1   *R(Chavda) v London Borough of Harrow* [2007] EWHC 3064 (Admin). And *R(W) v Birmingham City Council* [2011] EWHC 1147 (Admin), para 183.

2   *R(W) v Birmingham City Council* [2011] EWHC 1147 (Admin), para 176. And see *R(JM and NT) v Isle of Wight Council* [2011] EWHC 2911 (Admin).

3   *R(McDonald) v Royal Borough of Kensington and Chelsea* [2011] UKSC 33, para 24.

4   For non-protected, non-statutory and non-secure tenancies, see Equality Act 2010, s.190. For protected and statutory tenancies, see Housing Act 1980 (ss.81–85), and for secure tenancies, see Housing Act 1985 (ss.97–99).

way of provision, criterion or practice (in relation to a term of the tenancy) or by way of providing auxiliary aids or services to prevent comparative disadvantage to the tenant. However, this duty to make reasonable adjustments does not extend to altering or removing a physical feature. Physical features are defined as not including furniture, furnishings, materials, equipment or other items of property in or on the premises, meaning that all of these could potentially relate to the duty to make reasonable adjustments. Noticeably, also, altering or removing physical features does not include any of the following, which therefore could in principle be a reasonable adjustment:

» the replacement or provision of a sign or notice

» the replacement of a tap or door handle

» the replacement, provision or adaptation of a door bell or door entry system

» changes to the colour of a wall, door or any other surface.[1]

Equipment, see Community equipment

---

1   Equality Act 2010, s.20 and schedule 4.

F

Fettering of discretion, see Blanket policies

Fifteen minutes, see Home care visits

Funded nursing care

Funded nursing care (FNC) is an amount paid in respect of residents of nursing homes, who do not qualify for NHS continuing health care but who require registered nursing care.[1] The amount currently stands at £156.25 per week. It represents the notional cost of the registered nursing care required by the resident. It must be considered, only after a decision has first been taken about whether the resident qualifies for NHS continuing health care (which is fully funded by the NHS).[2] The courts have held that the amount represents the cost of the actual registered nursing care provided to the resident each week, not necessarily the amount of time that the registered nurse is, in total, at work in the care home each week.[3]

---

1 Department of Health *National framework for NHS continuing healthcare and NHS-funded nursing care*. London: DH, 2012, Annex D.

2 NHS Commissioning Board and CCGs (Responsibilities and Standing Rules) Regulations 2012, r.21(3).

3 *Forge Care Homes Ltd v Cardiff & Vale University Health Board* [2016] EWCA Civ 26, paras 31, 75.

G

Guidance

Government guidance is, by definition, not legislation. Statutory guidance is issued directly under a provision in legislation. A public body requires sound reasons not to follow the word 'must' in guidance.[1] For example, a social services charging policy inconsistent with the guidance might be struck down as unlawful.[2] The word 'should' is less strong, and the word 'may' indicates discretion. Under section 78 of the Care Act, the Department of Health has published just such statutory guidance – over 500 pages of it.[3] Government guidance which is non-statutory – not issued directly under a provision in legislation – should nonetheless still be taken account of.[4]

A few considerations about guidance are as follows:

- **Uncertainties in guidance**. Guidance has been characterised in the past as 'four times cursed': not going through Parliament, unpublished and inaccessible to those affected, a jumble of provisions – legal, administrative or directive – and not expressed in precise legal language. This is compared with 'twice blessed' legislation, which has passed through both Houses of Parliament.[5] The Care Act guidance may be published on the Internet but its 500-page medley of legal interpretation, policy, aspiration, wishful thinking and repetitiveness fits this 1949 characterisation of guidance. Furthermore, even on the publication point, and since it was initially issued in October 2014, the Department of

---

1   *R(Rixon) v Islington London Borough Council* [1997] E.L.R. 66, pp.2–3.

2   *R(KM) v Northamptonshire County Council* [2015] EWHC 482 (Admin).

3   Statutory guidance, 2016.

4   *R(Rixon) v Islington London Borough Council* [1997] E.L.R. 66, pp.6, 11.

5   *Patchett v Leathem* (1949) TLR 4 February 1949, High Court, Kings Bench Division.

Health has been amending it piecemeal, but has not issued an easily accessible consolidated version online.

- **Departing from guidance**. The courts have already stated in one Care Act case – about direct payments and safeguarding – that the guidance was there to be departed from with good reason and that the local authority was justified in doing so.[1]

- **Loose language in guidance?** Guidance can be misleading. Various examples are present in the Care Act guidance. One such is a statement that a person is best placed to judge their own well-being – which does not in fact reflect accurately the wording, or its implications, in section 1 of the Care Act.[2]

---

1   *R(Collins) v Nottinghamshire County Council, Direct Payments Service* [2016] EWHC 996 (Admin), para 32.

2   Statutory guidance, 2016, paras 6.30, 6.35.

H

Health and Social Care Act (Regulated Activities) Regulations 2014, see *Care Quality Commission (CQC)*

Health care, see *National Health Service (NHS)*

Health service ombudsman (HSO)

Under the Health Service Commissioners Act 1993, the health service ombudsman (HSO) investigates complaints against the NHS. Normally the complainant must have gone through the NHS body's own complaints procedure first. The ombudsman's remit extends to complaints about NHS-funded health care services provided in a private hospital and to complaints about any NHS-funded health care services for privately funded patients in an NHS hospital.

HSO: MALADMINISTRATION, FAILURE IN SERVICE. The ombudsman looks to see whether hardship or injustice has resulted from maladministration, failure in a service that has been provided or failure to provide a service which it was a function of the NHS body concerned to provide. The ombudsman can question clinical judgements. With increased joint working and integration within health and social care, the health service ombudsman can investigate jointly with the local ombudsman.[1]

Home adaptations

Housing adaptations, major or minor, can be a cost-effective way of enabling people with a disability or illness to remain in their own homes. Examples range from a handrail or grab rail at one extreme to stairlifts, ceiling track hoists or downstairs bathrooms at another.

Legally, there are different possible routes for obtaining adaptations. The main ones are:

- the Care Act 2014

- the Housing Grants, Construction and Regeneration Act 1996

- the Regulatory Reform (Housing Assistance) (England and Wales) Order 2002

- the NHS Act 2006

- the Equality Act 2010.

(For children, the above list is the same, except section 17 of the Children Act 1989 and section 2 of the Chronically Sick Disabled Persons Act 1970 should be substituted for the Care Act.) For major adaptations, legislation other than the Care Act 2014 will often be the first port of call (see **Housing Grants, Construction and Regeneration Act 1996** and **Regulatory Reform (Housing Assistance) (England and Wales) Order 2002**).

HOME ADAPTATIONS: CARE ACT 2014. The Act itself does not mention adaptations by name. But section 8 of the Act – giving non-exhaustive examples of how care and support needs can be met – appears wide enough to include adaptations. Statutory guidance emphasises the importance of adaptations, both as a preventative measure under section 2 of the Act and as

---

1   Health Service Commissioners Act 1993, ss.2A, 2B, 3, 18ZA.

a means of meeting need under section 18 of the Act.[1] In addition, regulations stipulate that any minor adaptation arranged by a local authority under the Care Act must be free of charge if its cost is £1000 or less.[2]

HOME ADAPTATIONS: MAJOR ADAPTATIONS. The rule about minor adaptations does not prevent a local authority from assisting with more major adaptations, either preventatively or as a way of discharging its duty to meet eligible need. But this does mean a local authority, under section 14 of the Act, could choose to apply a financial test of resources to an adaptation costing more than £1000.

Government guidance has in the past stated that social care legislation, in its own right, creates a strong duty to meet people's needs for adaptations, and that if a person's need for a major adaptation is not being met either at all or fully under the Housing Grants, Construction and Regeneration Act, 1996, local social services authorities may have a strong duty to assist.[3] This could be, for example, if:

- the cost of the adaptation exceeds the £30,000 limit, above which housing authorities do not have a duty to go

- the adaptation required doesn't come under the 1996 Act at all, because it does not fall within the list of works in that Act

- in a situation of shared care, an adaptation is required in a second dwelling – a disabled facilities grant (DFG) is not normally available in a second dwelling

- the person is genuinely unable to fund their assessed financial contribution to the adaptation, as calculated by the financial test of resources applied under the 1996 Act.

---

1   Statutory guidance, 2016, para 15.52.

2   SI 2014/2672. Care and Support (Charging and Assessment of Resources) Regulations 2014, r.3. And SI 2014/2673. Care and Support (Preventing Needs for Care and Support) Regulations 2014.

3   Department of Communities and Local Government *Housing adaptations for disabled people: A good practice guide*. London: DCLG, 2006, paras 2.7–2.8. Superseded in February 2015 by: Home Adaptations Consortium. *Home adaptations for disabled people: a detailed guide to related legislation, guidance and good practice*. Nottingham: Care and Repair, 2013 (not, though, government guidance).

This guidance referred to previous legislation, the Chronically Sick and Disabled Persons Act 1970, and its gist is supported by case law.[1] The principle would seem to be equally applicable to the position under the Care Act, which has superseded the 1970 Act for adults.[2] Any duty to assist in such circumstances, under the Care Act, would of course depend on assessment, eligible need, the adaptation being the most cost-effective way of meeting that need, and on possible means testing and charging.

HOME ADAPTATIONS: NHS ACT 2006. Government guidance makes clear that in some circumstances the NHS – in the form of clinical commissioning groups – might have responsibility for adaptations to a person's home. This could be when the person has been assessed as having NHS continuing health care status and the need is either outside of, or in excess of, a grant obtainable under the Housing Grants, Construction and Regeneration Act 1996.[3]

Home care visits

Significant concerns have been raised about home care visits commissioned by local authorities from independent care agencies as being too short, truncated, late or missed.[4] Guidance states that commissioned care must be appropriate and adequately resourced to be consistent with meeting need and the well-being principle. It emphasises that 15-minute visits are not appropriate for help with personal care tasks but may be appropriate for

---

1   *Re Teresa Judge* [2001] NIQB 14, High Court (Northern Ireland). And *Withnell v Down Lisburn Health and Social Services Trust* (2004) High Court (Northern Ireland). And English cases in which this approach seemed to be assumed: *R v Kirklees Metropolitan Borough Council, ex p Daykin* [1996] 3 CL 565, High Court. And *R v Kirklees Metropolitan Borough Council, ex p Good* [1996] 11 CL 288, High Court. And *R(Fay) v Essex County Council* [2004] EWHC Admin 879. And *R(Spink) v Wandsworth LBC* [2005] EWCA Civ 302, Court of Appeal.

2   Statutory guidance, 2016, paras 15.51–15.52.

3   Department of Health *National framework for NHS continuing healthcare and NHS-funded nursing care*. London: DH, 2012, pp.103–104.

4   See e.g. Care Quality Commission *Not just a number: Home care inspection programme, national overview*. London: CQC, 2013, pp.27–28. And Local Government Ombudsman *Review of local government complaints 2015–16*. London: LGO, 2016, p.9.

checking someone has returned safely home from a day centre or that they have taken medication – or if the short visit is through personal choice.[1]

Hospital discharge

The Care Act contains rules about the discharge of patients from acute hospital beds.[2] In summary, the rules provide for hospitals to serve first an assessment notice, followed by a discharge notice, on the local authority. If the local authority has failed to discharge the patient by the discharge date, the hospital can – but does not have to – seek reimbursement from the local authority. The basic rules are as follows:

- **Assessment notice**. The assessment notice must be served on the local authority if the hospital believes that it would not be safe to discharge the patient without care and support being provided by the local authority. Before serving the notice, the hospital must consult with the patient and, if feasible, any carer that the patient has.

- **NHS continuing health care**. Amongst other things, the assessment notice must specify whether the NHS has considered whether to provide the patient with NHS continuing health care and the result of that consideration.

- **Consultation with local authority**. The hospital must then consult the local authority, before deciding what it (the hospital) will do for the patient to achieve a safe discharge.

- **Discharge notice**. The hospital must also give a discharge notice to the local authority, specifying a discharge date. This date cannot be less than a day after the assessment notice is given, and there must be a gap of at least two days between the discharge date and the assessment notice having been given. But if an assessment notice is given after 2pm on a particular day, it is taken to have been given on the following day.

- **Health care provision**. The discharge notice must specify what, if any, health services are going to be provided under the NHS Act 2006.

---

1   Statutory guidance, 2016, para 4.101.

2   Care Act 2014, schedule 3. And SI 2014/2823. Care and Support (Discharge of Hospital Patients) Regulations 2014.

- **Local authority assessment**. Having received the assessment notice, the local authority must carry out an assessment of the adult (and sometimes carer) under the Care Act. It must inform the hospital:

  » whether the patient has needs for care and support

  » (where applicable) whether a carer has needs for support

  » whether any of the needs meet the eligibility criteria, and

  » how the authority plans to meet such of those needs as meet the eligibility criteria.

- **Reimbursement to penalise the local authority**. If the local authority fails either to do the assessment or provide care and support which it proposes to provide – and this is the sole reason why the patient has not been discharged by the date of discharge – the hospital can seek reimbursement for the cost of the patient's subsequent days at the hospital.

- **Rules apply to acute care only**. These rules apply to acute care only. Acute care means intensive medical treatment provided by or under the supervision of a consultant. It lasts only for a limited period, after which the person receiving the treatment no longer benefits from it. Private patients are not covered by the rules. Acute care cannot be:

  » care of an expectant or nursing mother

  » mental health care

  » palliative care

  » a structured programme of care provided for a limited period to help a person maintain or regain the ability to live at home

  » care provided for recuperation or rehabilitation.

  In turn, mental health care means psychiatric services or other services provided for preventing, diagnosing or treating illness, the arrangements for which are the primary responsibility of a consultant psychiatrist.[1]

---

1   Care Act 2014, schedule 3. And SI 2014/2823. Care and Support (Discharge of Hospital Patients) Regulations 2014.

HOSPITAL DISCHARGE: SERVICE FAILURE. Unsafe hospital discharges are regularly referred to the health service ombudsman for investigation, who might identify service failure. In 2016, the ombudsman highlighted the 'harrowing impact of poorly managed hospital discharges on individuals and their families', in the case of highly vulnerable, elderly people. The most frequent, and regularly complained about, problems were:

- patients being discharged before they were clinically ready to leave hospital

- patients not being assessed or consulted properly before their discharge

- relatives and carers not being told that their loved one had been discharged

- patients being discharged with no home care plan in place or being kept in hospital due to poor coordination across services.[1]

The ombudsman noted that matters had not improved since 2011 when she had previously highlighted the 'shambolic and ill-prepared' nature of hospital discharge arrangements.[2] A House of Commons Committee echoed this later in 2016, finding discharge failures to be a wide and persistent problem.[3]

Housing Grants, Construction and Regeneration Act 1996 (HGCRA)

A significant statutory route for major adaptations to a person's home is the Housing Grants, Construction and Regeneration Act 1996 (HGCRA). If certain conditions are met, this Act creates, in its own right, a strong duty on the local housing authority to approve an application for a disabled facilities grant (DFG). Government guidance emphasised in the past that the obligation 'is primary, absolute and remains irrespective of whether other

---

1 Health Service Ombudsman *A report of investigations into unsafe discharge from hospital*. London: HSO, 2016, pp.2, 5–6.

2 Health Service Ombudsman *Care and compassion? Report of the Health Service Ombudsman on ten investigations into NHS care of older people*. London: HSO, 2011.

3 House of Commons Public Administration and Constitutional Affairs Committee *Follow-up to PHSO report on unsafe discharge from hospital*. Fifth Report of Session 2016–17. London: TSO, 2016, p.3.

assistance is provided by a social services authority or other body' (such as a registered social landlord).[1]

HGCRA: KEY POINTS. A DFG application must be approved if the following conditions are met:

- the adaptation is for a disabled occupant

- the works fall within the list of purposes set out in the legislation

- the works are necessary and appropriate

- the works are reasonable and practicable.

HGCRA: DISABLED OCCUPANT. A disabled occupant is defined as a person who is disabled, or taken to be disabled, because:

- his or her sight, hearing or speech is substantially impaired

- he or she has a mental disorder or impairment of any kind

- he or she is physically substantially disabled by illness, injury, impairment present since birth, or otherwise, or

- he or she is on a sight-impaired or disability register kept by the local authority under section 77 of the Care Act.[2]

HGCRA: STATUTORY PURPOSES OF A DFG. The works must be for one of the following purposes:

- **Access to dwelling**: facilitating access by the disabled occupant to and from (i) the dwelling, qualifying houseboat or caravan, or (ii) the building in which the dwelling or, as the case may be, flat is situated

- **Safety**: making (i) the dwelling, qualifying houseboat or caravan, or (ii) the building, safe for the disabled occupant and other persons residing with him

---

1   Department for Communities and Local Government *Delivering housing adaptations for disabled people: A good practice guide*, June 2006 edition. London: DCLG, 2006, para 2.13.

2   HGCRA 1996, s.100.

- **Family room**: facilitating access by the disabled occupant to a room used or usable as the principal family room

- **Sleeping room**: facilitating access by the disabled occupant to, or providing for the disabled occupant, a room used or usable for sleeping

- **Lavatory**: facilitating access by the disabled occupant to, or providing for the disabled occupant, a room in which there is a lavatory, or facilitating the use by the disabled occupant of such a facility

- **Bath or shower**: facilitating access by the disabled occupant to, or providing for the disabled occupant, a room in which there is a bath or shower (or both), or facilitating the use by the disabled occupant of such a facility

- **Wash-hand basin**: facilitating access by the disabled occupant to, or providing for the disabled occupant, a room in which there is a wash-hand basin, or facilitating the use by the disabled occupant of such a facility

- **Food**: facilitating the preparation and cooking of food by the disabled occupant

- **Heating**: improving any heating system in the dwelling, qualifying houseboat or caravan to meet the needs of the disabled occupant or, if there is no existing heating system there or any such system is unsuitable for use by the disabled occupant, providing a heating system suitable to meet his needs

- **Power**: facilitating the use by the disabled occupant of a source of power, light or heat by altering the position of one or more means of access to or control of that source or by providing additional means of control

- **Caring role**: facilitating access and movement by the disabled occupant around the dwelling, qualifying houseboat or caravan in order to enable him to care for a person who is normally resident there and is in need of such care

- **Garden**: facilitating access to and from a garden by a disabled occupant, or making access to a garden safe for a disabled occupant.[1]

---

1   HGCRA 1996, s.23(1), except for gardens. And see SI 2008/1189. Disabled Facilities Grants (Maximum Amounts and Additional Purposes) (England) Order 2008, r.3.

HGCRA: NECESSARY AND APPROPRIATE. The works must be judged by the local housing authority to be necessary and appropriate. The courts have held that this is a 'technical question' and that resources should not be taken into account.[1] In deciding this, the housing authority must consult the social services authority, assuming they are not one and the same authority.[2] In the case of a unitary authority, past guidance pointed out that the housing department should of course consult the social services department. It stated that the purpose of a home adaptation is to 'restore or enable independent living, privacy, confidence and dignity for individuals and their families'.[3]

HGCRA: NOT CONFUSING RULES WITH CARE ACT ELIGIBILITY. When social services is consulted about whether a DFG is necessary and appropriate, it must consider the request under the HGCRA and not the Care Act – legally, because the two Acts are separate pieces of legislation, and practically, because eligibility under the Care Act is not necessarily co-extensive with eligibility under the HGCRA.[4] Muddling up the separate legal eligibility rules would be potentially unlawful and has been held to be maladministration.[5] For instance, a decision seemingly under the Care Act, that a woman did not need access to her bath, but could strip wash instead, did not meant that she was not eligible under the HGCRA 1996, which refers explicitly to a disabled occupant having access to a bath or shower.[6] The ombudsman

---

1   *R v Birmingham City Council, ex p Taj Mohammed* [1998] 1 CCLR 441, High Court.

2   HGCRA 1996, s.24.

3   Department for Communities and Local Government *Delivering housing adaptations for disabled people: A good practice guide*, June 2006 edition. London: DCLG, 2006, para 1.6. Superseded in February 2015 by: Home Adaptations Consortium. *Home adaptations for disabled people: a detailed guide to related legislation, guidance and good practice*. Nottingham: Care and Repair, 2013 (not, though, government guidance).

4   Department for Communities and Local Government *Delivering housing adaptations for disabled people: A good practice guide*, June 2006 edition. London: DCLG, 2006, para 4.7. Superseded in February 2015 by: Home Adaptations Consortium. *Home adaptations for disabled people: a detailed guide to related legislation, guidance and good practice*. Nottingham: Care and Repair, 2013 (not, though, government guidance).

5   *LGO, Neath Port Talbot County Borough Council 1999* (99/0149/N/142).

6   *LGO, Birmingham City Council*, 2016 (15 015 721), paras 8–9.

previously has referred to the importance of dignity in relation to bathing and washing.[1]

HGCRA: REASONABLE AND PRACTICABLE. The works must also be reasonable and practicable. Legally this question can relate to the age and condition of the dwelling only.[2] The local authority's financial resources, however, could be relevant if, for example, the building were old and dilapidated, requiring excessive expenditure to make the adaptation possible.[3]

HGCRA: APPROVAL OF THE GRANT. If the grant application is approved, means testing will establish whether the applicant must contribute.[4] (There is no means testing in the case of children.) Approval must take place within six months of the application being submitted, and payment of the grant must be no longer than 12 months from the date of submission of the application.[5] The maximum payable before any contribution is calculated is £30,000 (£35,000 in Wales). In some circumstances (owner occupation), the local authority can demand repayment of up to £10,000 of any part of the grant exceeding £5000 if the person leaves the dwelling within ten years.[6]

HGCRA: TENURE. Owner occupiers and tenants in private housing can apply for DFGs, as can council and housing association tenants. If local authorities and housing associations carry out adaptations themselves and meet the needs of the disabled occupant – equivalent to what a DFG would

---

1   *LGO, Bolsover District Council*, 2003 (02/C/08679, 02/C/08681 & 02/C/10389), para 19.

2   HGCRA 1996, s.24.

3   See e.g. comments in *R v Birmingham City Council, ex p Taj Mohammed* [1998] 1 CCLR 441, High Court.

4   HGCRA 1996, s.30. And SI 1996/2367. Housing Renewal Grants Regulations 1996.

5   HGCRA 1996, ss.34, 36.

6   *The Housing Grants, Construction and Regeneration Act 1996: Disabled Facilities Grant (conditions relating to approval or payment of grant) general consent 2008*, Secretary of State for Communities and Local Government, 2008.

have achieved – a DFG might not be necessary. There would be no point. But otherwise, the tenant has a statutory right to apply for a DFG.[1]

Human rights

The European Convention on Human Rights has been imported into United Kingdom law by the Human Rights Act 1998. Human rights law applies to public bodies and other bodies carrying out functions of a public nature. Local authorities and NHS bodies are public bodies.

HUMAN RIGHTS: AND THE CARE ACT 2014. The courts held in the past that independent care providers were neither public bodies nor, in the main, bodies carrying out functions of a public nature.[2] (However, for example, a private hospital, treating a detained patient under the Mental Health Act, is carrying functions of a public nature.)[3]

Section 73 of the Care Act modifies this by stating that a registered care provider exercises functions of a public nature (and is therefore subject to human rights law) but only if a local authority has arranged, or paid for (directly or indirectly), the care and support under sections 2, 18, 19, 20, 38 and 48 of the Care Act. 'Indirectly' means that use of a direct payment would be included in this rule, which means that if an individual themselves arranges care on a self-funding basis, from a care agency or care home, the Human Rights Act would not apply.

HUMAN RIGHTS: RIGHT TO LIFE. Article 2 of the European Convention states that everyone's right to life shall be protected by law. Article 2 arises sometimes in health and social care, requiring procedurally an independent

---

1 Department for Communities and Local Government *Delivering housing adaptations for disabled people: A good practice guide*, June 2006 edition. London: DCLG, 2006, paras 2.20, 3.26. Superseded in February 2015 by: Home Adaptations Consortium. *Home adaptations for disabled people: a detailed guide to related legislation, guidance and good practice*. Nottingham: Care and Repair, 2013 (not, though, government guidance).

2 *YL v Birmingham City Council* [2007] UKHL 27, House of Lords.

3 *R v Partnerships in Care Ltd, ex p A* [2002] EWHC Admin 529.

investigation into some deaths in which there might have been a breach of human rights, with the State implicated.[1]

HUMAN RIGHTS: INHUMAN AND DEGRADING TREATMENT. Article 3 of the Convention states that no one shall be subjected to torture or to inhuman or degrading treatment or punishment. The courts have held that ill treatment must reach a minimum level of severity and involve actual bodily injury or intense physical or mental suffering. Degrading treatment would occur if it 'humiliates or debases an individual showing a lack of respect for, or diminishing, his or her human dignity or arouses feelings of fear, anguish or inferiority capable of breaking an individual's moral and physical resistance'.[2]

HUMAN RIGHTS: DEPRIVATION OF LIBERTY. Article 5 of the Convention states that 'everyone has the right to liberty and security of person. No one shall be deprived of his liberty save in the following cases and in accordance with a procedure prescribed by law.' One of the categories for who can be deprived of their liberty is 'persons of unsound mind'. Therefore, when people are deprived of their liberty under the Mental Capacity Act 2005, the rules of the 2005 Act must be followed. If they are not, a breach of article 5 will occur – for example, a local authority depriving of his liberty a man who in fact had, during most of the period of detention, mental capacity – meaning that the grounds for holding him did not exist.[3]

HUMAN RIGHTS: RIGHT TO RESPECT FOR PRIVATE LIFE, FAMILY LIFE AND HOME. Article 8 of the Convention states:

- **Right**. Everyone has the right to respect for his private and family life, his home and his correspondence.

- **Interference with the right**. There shall be no interference by a public authority with the exercise of this right except such as is in accordance with the law and is necessary in a democratic society in the interests of national

---

1   *R(Middleton) v West Somerset Coroner* [2004] UKHL 10.

2   *Pretty v United Kingdom* [2002] 2 FCR 97 (European Court of Human Rights).

3   *Essex County Council v RG* [2015] EWCOP 1.

security, public safety or the economic well-being of the country, for the prevention of disorder or crime, for the protection of health or morals, or for the protection of the rights and freedoms of others.

This means that interference with private life, family life and home is possible but must be justified. Private life has been held to include physical and psychological integrity, and therefore a notion of dignity.[1]

Examples of breaches of article 8 by local authorities have included the operation of a blanket manual handling policy,[2] leaving an immobile stroke victim in squalid conditions in her living room for two years,[3] and wholly inadequate assessment of a woman with dementia aged 90 about where she should live.[4]

On the other hand, interference with article 8 rights can sometimes be justified if the interference is according to relevant law, necessary and proportionate. For instance, offering a woman the more cost-effective option of incontinence pads – rather than the night-time carer she wished for – was held to be justified for the economic well-being of the country.[5]

Proper application of the Care Act is, in principle, likely to make a breach of article 8 uncommon[6] since the Care Act is likely to be viewed generally by the courts as broad, humane and all about taking account of private and family life.[7]

---

1   *Botta v Italy* (1998) 26 EHRR 241.

2   *R(A and B) v East Sussex County Council* [2003] EWHC 167 (Admin).

3   *R(Bernard) v Enfield London Borough Council* [2002] EWHC 2282 (Admin).

4   *R(Goldsmith) v Wandsworth London Borough Council* [2004] EWCA Civ 1170.

5   *McDonald v United Kingdom* (2015) 60 E.H.R.R. 1.

6   *R(Cowl) v Plymouth City Council* [2001] EWHC Admin 734, para 36. And see Court of Appeal: [2001] EWCA Civ 1935.

7   *R(Khana) v London Borough of Southwark* (2001), unreported. And see Court of Appeal: [2001] EWCA Civ 999.

I

Immigration

There are legal rules and restrictions about accessing health and social care by various categories of people subject to immigration control – often referred to loosely as having 'no recourse to public funds' (NRPF). The following paragraphs provide only a brief overview of what is a complex area of law. The organisation, No Recourse to Public Funds, publishes detailed guides.[1]

IMMIGRATION: CARE ACT AND ACCOMMODATION. Since the implementation of the Care Act, the courts have raised a problem in this area of law. Even if a person, subject to the immigration rules, is eligible under the Care Act for help with care and support needs, ordinary accommodation – a bare roof over one's head – can only be provided if the need for it is care and support related. Put another way, the care and support services the person needs would have effectively to be useless without the accommodation. In some circumstances, this labyrinthine complexity could result in the Localism Act 2011 having to be considered to underpin provision of the accommodation in order to avoid a breach of human rights.[2]

IMMIGRATION: IMMIGRATION AND ASYLUM ACT 1999 (IA 1999). Section 21 of the Care Act 2014 states that a local authority is not permitted to meet the care and support needs of a person subject to immigration control – to whom section 115 of the Immigration and Asylum Act 1999 (IA 1999)

---

1   For example, NRPF Network *Practice guidance for local authorities (England): Assessing and supporting adults who have no recourse to public funds (NRPF)*. London: NRPF, April 2016.

2   *R(GS) v London Borough of Camden* [2016] EWHC 1762, paras 75–78.

applies (see below). This prohibition applies only if the person's needs for that care and support have arisen solely (a) because the adult is destitute, or (b) because of the physical effects, or anticipated physical effects, of being destitute.[1]

If the prohibition does not apply, asylum seekers are entitled to help with care and support needs under the Care Act 2014 but subject to the same eligibility criteria as anybody else. (In case of urgency, under section 19 of the Act, the local authority can help ahead of any assessment or eligibility decision.) The power under section 19 of the Care Act, to meet needs in case of urgency in advance of any assessment and eligibility decision, could be used in some cases (e.g. before it is known whether the need is just destitution based or not). This prohibition, under section 21 of the Care Act, does not apply to after-care services under section 117 of the Mental Health Act 1983.

IMMIGRATION: IA 1999 – SUBJECT TO IMMIGRATION CONTROL. Section 115 applies to a person who is not a European Economic Area (EEA) national and who:

- requires leave to enter or remain in the United Kingdom but does not have it

- has leave to enter or remain in the United Kingdom which is subject to a condition that he does not have recourse to public funds, or

- has leave to enter or remain in the United Kingdom given as a result of a maintenance undertaking.

Under section 115, a person is denied access to a range of public funds (various social security benefits and, under section 117 of the Act, assistance with housing). However, the definition of public funds does not include, for example, social care assistance or health care, which is why the Care Act 2014 contains its own prohibition related to need and destitution.

IMMIGRATION: IA 1999 – DESTITUTION TEST. Destitution means that a person does not have adequate accommodation or means of obtaining it

---

1   Immigration and Asylum Act 1999, s.95.

(whether or not other essential living needs are met), or the person does have adequate accommodation or the means of obtaining it, but cannot meet other essential living needs.[1] If a person's needs preceded the destitution, this could well suggest that their current needs have not arisen solely from that destitution. Furthermore, mental health needs are embraced by the term 'physical effects'.[2]

IMMIGRATION: IA 1999 – ASYLUM SEEKERS. Asylum seekers whose needs are related solely to destitution are not therefore a local authority responsibility – excluded by section 21 of the Care Act. However, they are still entitled to support from the Home Office under section 95 of the 1999 Act. Local authorities are not allowed to support an asylum-seeking family with children, who come under section 95 of the Immigration and Asylum Act 1999 and so are supported by the Home Office.[3] When certain provisions of the Immigration Act 2016 come into force, failed asylum-seeking families who face genuine obstacles to departure will continue to be supported by the Home Office under section 95A of the 1999 Act.

IMMIGRATION: IA 1999 – OTHER PEOPLE SUBJECT TO IMMIGRATION CONTROL. Somebody other than an asylum seeker – for example, an illegal entrant or over-stayer falling into the above definition (of being subject to immigration control) – would be excluded from having their care and support needs met under the Care Act 2014, unless their needs have arisen other than because of destitution. If their needs are solely destitution related, then they would be entitled to support from neither the local authority nor the Home Office. This would seem to leave open local authority support under the Care Act for people subject to immigration control, whose care and support needs are not related solely to destitution. However, the National, Immigration and Asylum Act 2002 (NIA 2002; see below) imposes further prohibitions.

---

1   Immigration and Asylum Act 1999, s.95.

2   *R(PB) v Haringey London Borough Council* [2006] EWHC Admin 2255, para 49.

3   Immigration and Asylum Act 1999, s.122.

IMMIGRATION: NATIONALITY, IMMIGRATION AND ASYLUM ACT 2002 (NIA 2002) – PROHIBITIONS. Under the NIA 2002, local authorities are prohibited from providing 'support or assistance' for certain categories of people.[1] The prohibitions include adult social care under Part 1 of the Care Act 2014 and also help for adults under sections 17, 23C, 24A and 24B of the Children Act 1989 – that is, provisions covering children in need (under section 17) of the Act, and former looked after children.

However, these prohibitions are disapplied if a failure to provide support or assistance would result in a breach of human rights or of a European Union (EU) treaty. They anyway apply neither to children, nor to the provision of after-care under section 117 of the Mental Health Act 1983. If the prohibitions do not apply, the Care Act 2014 applies as normal, but subject to the same eligibility criteria as for anybody else. In case of urgency, under section 19 of the Act, the local authority can help ahead of any assessment or eligibility decision, on the basis of avoiding a potential breach of human rights.

IMMIGRATION: NIA 2002 – PROHIBITION ON PROVIDING SUPPORT OR ASSISTANCE. The rules prohibit 'support or assistance' under the Care Act, thereby ruling out care and support for adults in need, and support for carers. Department of Health advice states, however, that (in its view) assessment, information and advice are not prohibited.[2] And, presumably, therefore, independent advocacy, in relation to assessment, is not prohibited either.

IMMIGRATION: NIA 2002 – PEOPLE SUBJECT TO THE PROHIBITIONS. The prohibitions apply to the following groups of people:

- refugee status abroad

- EEA status

- failed asylum seeker who has failed to cooperate with removal directions

---

1   Nationality, Immigration and Asylum Act 2002, schedule 3.

2   NRPF Network *Schedule 3 of the Nationality Immigration and Asylum Act 2002 and the Care Act 2014*. London: NRPF, July 2015.

- anybody else in breach of immigration law

- failed asylum seekers with dependent children, certified by the Home Office as having failed to take steps to leave the UK voluntarily.[1]

When certain provisions of the Immigration Act 2016 come into force, two more prohibited categories will be added – namely, a person in England without leave to enter or remain, and a primary carer without leave to enter or remain. The third category applies only to asylum seekers who applied for asylum at port of entry. Whereas an 'in-country' applicant falls into the fourth category, immediately their application has failed.[2]

IMMIGRATION: NIA 2002 – HUMAN RIGHTS AND RETURN TO COUNTRY OF ORIGIN. The prohibitions do not apply if a breach of human rights would result. One key question as to whether human rights would be breached is whether the person can travel back to their country of origin. Local authorities can offer assistance with travel arrangements.[3] Reasons for not being able to travel could include ill health, medical condition or getting the appropriate paperwork.[4] If a person could travel back but chooses not to, what would otherwise be a breach of human rights is not in fact so.[5]

IMMIGRATION: NIA 2002 – HUMAN RIGHTS THRESHOLD. The courts have held that 'if there were persuasive evidence that [the person] was obliged to sleep in the street, save perhaps for a short and foreseeably finite period, or was seriously hungry, or unable to satisfy the most basic requirements

---

1   Nationality, Immigration and Asylum Act 2002, schedule 3.

2   *R(AW) v Croydon London Borough Council* [2005] EWHC 2950, High Court; [2007] EWCA Civ 266, Court of Appeal.

3   Under the Withholding and Withdrawal of Support (Travel Assistance and Temporary Accommodation) Regulations 2002 for EEA nationals. Otherwise, Local Government Act 2000.

4   See e.g. *R(Almeida) v Royal Borough of Kensington and Chelsea* [2012] EWHC 1082 (Admin): medical condition (HIV/AIDS). And *R(PB) v Haringey London Borough Council* [2006] EWHC Admin 2255: woman could not participate in child care proceedings if she left the country.

5   *R(Grant) v Lambeth London Borough Council* [2004] EWCA Civ 1711. And *R(K) v Lambeth London Borough Council* [2003] EWCA Civ 1150, para 35.

of hygiene, the [human rights] threshold would, in the ordinary way, be crossed'.[1]

Questions of deportation and human rights are considered by the Home Office. Legally, the threshold for arguing human rights as an obstacle to deportation is sometimes high. For instance, a person might be seriously ill – with HIV/AIDS or renal failure – and would live for many years with treatment in the United Kingdom but die quickly if they returned to their country of origin. Yet deportation in such cases might not breach articles 3 and 8 of the European Convention,[2] although in a local authority case, a different sort of decision was reached.[3] In one case, a mother's inability to participate in child care proceedings – were she to return to country of origin – would have been a breach of article 8.[4]

IMMIGRATION: NIA 2002 – LOCAL AUTHORITIES SHOULD NOT BE SECOND GUESSING THE HOME OFFICE. If an application to the Home Office is still ongoing for leave to remain on grounds of human rights, the local authority must (subject to the person's eligibility under the Care Act) offer care and support.[5] It should not be second-guessing a Home Office decision on an immigration application, other than in rare, hopeless or abusive cases.[6]

IMMIGRATION: NIA 2002 – EU TREATY ISSUES. The prohibition on assisting EEA nationals is disapplied if the failure to assist would result in a breach of an EU treaty. The rules about this are complex. EU countries are Austria, Belgium, Bulgaria, Croatia, Cyprus, Czech Republic, Denmark, Estonia, Finland, France, Germany, Greece, Hungary, Ireland, Italy, Latvia,

---

1   *R v Secretary of State, ex p Limbuela* [2005] UKHL 66, House of Lords.

2   *N v Secretary of State for the Home Department* [2005] UKHL 31, House of Lords. And *GS (India), EO (Ghana), GM (India), PL (Jamaica), BA (Ghana) & KK (DRC) v The Secretary of State for the Home Department* [2015] EWCA Civ 40.

3   *R(Almeida) v Royal Borough of Kensington and Chelsea* [2012] EWHC 1082 (Admin).

4   *R(PB) v Haringey London Borough Council* [2006] EWHC Admin 2255.

5   *Birmingham City Council v Clue* [2010] EWCA Civ 460.

6   *R(AW) v Croydon London Borough Council* [2007] EWCA Civ 266, Court of Appeal.

Lithuania, Luxembourg, Malta, the Netherlands, Poland, Portugal, Romania, Slovenia, Spain, Sweden and the United Kingdom. And, also, in the EEA are Iceland, Norway and Lichtenstein.

People from these countries have a right to enter the United Kingdom and to exercise EU treaty rights. These rights apply to a 'qualified person' with a right to reside. Broadly, this means somebody who is job seeking, working, self-employed, self-sufficient or a student. Job-seeking status lasts longer than six months only if the person is still seeking work and has a genuine chance of getting it. If a person is temporarily unable to work because of illness or accident, the person is still exercising treaty rights. EEA nationals can also acquire permanent residence after being in the United Kingdom for five years as a qualified person.[1]

IMMIGRATION: NIA 2002 – MENTAL HEALTH ACT AFTER-CARE. The prohibitions in the 2002 Act do not apply to after-care provided by a local authority under section 117 of the Mental Health Act 1983. This means that local authorities should provide services as normal under section 117, even if the person falls within one of the excluded categories in the NIA. However, the courts have held that the provision of ordinary accommodation, a bare roof over one's head (as opposed to accommodation with care), will either be rare under section 117 or is simply not within its scope at all.[2] Looking to the Care Act to provide the accommodation and to avoid a breach of human rights is not straightforward (see the introduction to this section on **Immigration**).

IMMIGRATION: NIA 2002 – CHILDREN ACT. The prohibitions do not apply to children but do apply to adults under sections 17, 23C, 24A and 24B of the Children Act 1989, in which case an adult could be helped under these sections only if not to do so would result in a breach of human rights or an EU treaty. When a child reaches the age of 18, and is unlawfully in the

---

1   For details, see SI 2006/1003. Immigration (European Economic Area) Regulations 2006.

2   *R(Mwanza) v London Borough of Greenwich* [2010] EWHC 1462 (Admin), paras 65–67. And *R(Afework) v London Borough of Camden* [2013] EWHC 1637 (Admin), para 16.

country, a human rights assessment must be carried out to determine whether, despite the prohibitions under the Care Act, assistance should be provided.

IMMIGRATION: NOTE. When certain provisions of the Immigration Act 2016 come into force, the position for children reaching 18 without immigration status – and with a non-asylum application pending – will be support by the local authority either under the Children Act (if it is a first application or appeal) or otherwise under the NIA 2002 (paragraph 10B of schedule 3). In the case of families with children, following a failed asylum claim there will be a 90-day 'grace' period. In the case of further non-asylum application or appeal, support will be by the local authority under the NIA 2002 (paragraph 10A of schedule 3). Alternatively, and pending departure, if support is necessary it will also be provided by the local authority under paragraph 10A.

Immigration: NHS, see Overseas visitors (NHS)

Independent advocacy, see Advocacy

Independent Living Fund (ILF)

The ILF, which gave grants to disabled people to assist with independent living, was closed in June 2015. Funding for former users of the ILF was distributed to local authorities to become part of general social care funding under the Care Act.

Information and advice, see Advice and information

Integration

Section 3 of the Care Act imposes a duty on local authorities in respect of integration with the NHS. It is a general duty and is in any case subject to a number of provisos. The local authority must exercise its functions 'with a view to ensuring the integration of care and support provision with health provision and health-related provision'.

This duty applies only if the local authority considers that integration would promote the well-being of adults in need and carers, contribute to prevention or delay of needs in the area, or improve quality of local services for adults and carers. The duty to integrate applies not only in relation to health provision but also to 'health-related provision'. This includes provision of services which may have an effect on people's health and includes the provision of housing.

INTEGRATION: POTENTIAL LEGAL AND PRACTICAL PITFALLS. Integration does not diminish the respective legal duties of the two parties integrating. The urging of central government for health and social care services to integrate (in order, as government sees it, to save money) has taken little account of legal obstacles, the main one being that the Care Act 2014 and the NHS Act 2006 are like chalk and cheese in legal terms – never mind the quite distinct policies, priorities, pressures and constitutional basis of NHS bodies and local authorities. Some of the legal pitfalls have been illustrated in several mental health cases:

- **Health but no social care assessment**: a mental health team carrying out only a health assessment (Care Programme Approach) but no social care assessment.[1]

- **Not meeting social care needs**: an NHS Trust taking on social care responsibilities for adults with Asperger's syndrome but failing to discharge those functions properly.[2]

---

1   *R(B) v Camden London Borough Council and Camden and Islington Mental Health and Social Care Trust* [2005] EWHC Admin 1366.

2   *LGO, Somerset County Council*, 2015 (13 019 566).

- **Inability to meet physical and mental health needs in one person**: despite integration, an NHS Trust and local authority failed to agree for a year about how to meet the health and social care needs of a person with both health (depression) and physical (double leg amputation) needs, the complication being that she had both physical and mental health needs, an occurrence – not so unusual – which the Trust seemed unable to grasp.[1]

- **Falling between the physical and mental health stools**: an NHS Trust carrying out mental health social care functions on behalf of the local authority. It discharged the person from a mental health service on grounds of the person no longer needing it. The local authority then began to assess his other needs for help with personal care, domestic help and managing risks – which were eligible needs. The local authority referred him back to the NHS Trust for the latter to meet the needs by direct payments, but the NHS Trust had already discharged him and didn't respond. This meant that the man went without support. The ombudsman found maladministration.[2]

- **Failure to produce care and support plan and terminating services arbitrarily**: an NHS Trust, acting on behalf of the local authority and failing to produce a care plan as required under previous legislation and under the Care Act, for a person with mental health needs. And offering 12 weeks' only of direct payments, after which they would be stopped, with no explanation as to why.[3]

Intermediate care, see Reablement

---

1   *A joint Parliamentary and Health Service Ombudsman and Local Government Ombudsman investigation into complaints JW-199678 and 14 006 021 about Sheffield Health and Social Care NHS Foundation Trust and Sheffield City Council*, 2015.

2   *LGO, Portsmouth City Council*, 2016 (15 010 217), paras 63–67.

3   *LGO, Kent County Council*, 2016 (15 010 503), paras 57–58.

J

Joint working, see *Integration*

Judicial review

Judicial review is a type of legal case in which the courts scrutinise the decision-making process underlying a decision made by a public body.

JUDICIAL REVIEW: PERMISSION. Permission is required from a judge to bring a judicial review case. If the challenge succeeds, the decision is overturned and, typically, the public body must reconsider the decision, this time adhering to the rules. (Second time around, therefore, the final decision may or may not be different.) If a human rights claim is included in the case, financial compensation might sometimes be payable.

JUDICIAL REVIEW: AVOIDING UNDUE INTERFERENCE. The courts are wary of interfering unduly and will not do so unless the decision has breached legislation or strayed too far from certain legal principles (see below). They might avoid 'over-zealous textual analysis' of a decision and give practitioners some leeway.[1] For instance, two differing assessment decisions, relating to the same person, could both be lawful if the correct process was followed in both.[2] Sometimes the local authority (or NHS) complaints process might be deemed to be anyway a more appropriate, alternative remedy.[3]

---

1   *R(Ireneschild) v Lambeth LBC* [2007] EWCA Civ 234, paras 57, 71.

2   *R(GS) v London Borough of Camden* [2016] EWHC 1762, paras 32–33, 47.

3   *R(Cowl) v Plymouth CC* [2001] EWCA Civ 1935, para 27. And *R(Ireneschild) v Lambeth LBC* [2007] EWCA Civ 234, para 72.

JUDICIAL REVIEW: MORE ANXIOUS SCRUTINY. All this said, human rights issues might sometimes lead to closer, or more 'anxious', scrutiny, checking not just that relevant factors have been considered but also what weight has been given them in terms of proportion and balance.[1]

JUDICIAL REVIEW: PRINCIPLES APPLIED. Unlawful decision-making might come in the form of, for example:

- **breaching legislation**: breaching clear rules set out in legislation (e.g. not appointing an advocate when the Care Act rules demanded the appointment)[2]

- **ignoring relevant factors**: e.g. not taking account of a major health condition, osteoporosis, when deciding whether to hoist a person[3] – or proposing a care plan that ignored expert advice and would put the life of a man with severe epilepsy at risk[4]

- **taking account of irrelevant factors**: e.g. declining to assess a person on the grounds that it would have been poor use of resources – which then, as now under the Care Act, was irrelevant to the duty[5]

- **acting irrationally**: a decision representing an absurdity, or a taking leave of senses – e.g. treating the night-time element of disability living allowance as disposable income, in order to calculate a financial charge to be made for day care[6]

- **fettering of discretion**: applying a policy so rigidly as to preclude the making of exceptions (see **Blanket policies**).

---

1   *R(Daly) v Secretary of State for the Home Department* [2001] UKHL 26, para 26. And *R(A and B) v East Sussex County Council* [2003] EWHC 167 (Admin), para 166.

2   *R(SG) v Haringey LBC* [2015] EWHC 2579 (Admin).

3   *R(Clegg) v Salford City Council* [2007] EWHC 3276 (Admin).

4   *R(Clarke) v London Borough of Sutton* [2015] EWHC 1081 (Admin).

5   *R v Bristol City Council, ex p Penfold* [1998] 1 CCLR 315, High Court.

6   *R(Carton) v Coventry City Council* (2001) 4 CCLR 41.

Local government ombudsman (LGO)

Under the Local Government Act 1974, the local government ombudsman (LGO) independently investigates complaints against local authorities. Normally, under section 26 of the Act, the complainant must first have gone through the local authority's own complaints process. A few key points are as follows:

- **Maladministration and failure in service**. The ombudsman investigates maladministration, failure in a service which it was a local authority's function to provide, or failure to provide such a service. Maladministration is a wide concept, not defined in the Act, but it does not include questioning the merits of professional judgement.[1] Findings of maladministration may include reference to unlawfulness. But a finding of maladministration is not a legal ruling as such. And maladministration is a different concept from unlawfulness. There could be maladministration without unlawfulness and vice versa.[2]

- **Legal case an alternative remedy**. The ombudsman is prohibited from investigating a case for which a legal remedy could be pursued. However, this rule can be waived if the ombudsman is satisfied that in the circumstances it is not reasonable to expect the person to pursue a legal case.[3]

---

1   Local Government Act 1974, ss.26, 34(3).

2   *R(Goldsmith IBS Ltd) v Parliamentary & Health Service Ombudsman* [2016] EWHC 1905 (Admin), para 12.

3   Local Government Act 1974, s.26.

- **Local authority responsible for actions of a provider**. In the case of providers acting on behalf of the local authority, the ombudsman will hold the authority responsible for the actions of the provider.[1]

- **Independent social care providers**. The ombudsman's remit extends to complaints about independent adult social care providers, engaging in regulated activity under the Health and Social Care Act 2008 and to investigating alleged injustice.[2]

- **Investigation against local authority and independent social care provider**. The ombudsman might combine the separate powers – to investigate the local authority or to investigate a care provider – into one investigation against both if the local authority has commissioned the service from the provider.[3]

- **Joint investigation with the health service ombudsman**. With increased joint working and integration involving health and social care, the local government ombudsman can investigate local authorities and NHS bodies jointly with the health service ombudsman.[4]

- **Recommendations**. The local government ombudsman makes recommendations by way of remedy. These might relate, for example, to providing a service, changing a policy or paying financial compensation.

The recommendations are not legally binding (although findings of fact are).[5] If local authorities do not comply, the ombudsman can force the authority to make a statement in local newspapers about the case.[6] As a matter of practice, most ombudsman recommendations are complied with. However, on occasion, they are not. The ombudsman may then publish a further report, calling for compliance.[7] Occasionally, a local authority might remain obdurate. However, a rejection of findings (legally binding) – not just

---

1   Local Government Act 1974, s.25.

2   Local Government Act 1974, ss.34A–34T.

3   For example, *LGO, Oxfordshire County Council and Caring Homes Healthcare Group Ltd*, 2015 (15 007 968 and 15 006 620).

4   Local Government Act 1974, ss.26, 31, 34, 34A–34L, 33ZA.

5   *R(Gallagher) v Basildon District Council* [2010] EWHC 2824 (Admin).

6   Local Government Act 1974, s.31.

7   *LGO, Tameside Metropolitan Borough Council*, 2015 (12 019 862). (Further report.)

of recommendations (which are not legally binding) – might mean it is acting unlawfully.[1]

Localism Act 2011

Subject to some restrictions, the Localism Act 2011 gives local authorities discretion to do things that they might not, or cannot, do under other legislation. Because it is a discretion, rather than a duty, its use in relation to social care is likely to be limited in a climate of tight resources. However, the courts have ruled that to avoid a breach of human rights, a local authority might sometimes be obliged to use the discretion.[2]

---

1 Local Government Ombudsman *Maladministration causing injustice by Tameside Metropolitan Borough Council Statement of Non-Compliance with Ombudsman's Recommendations*, 2015, p.2.

2 *R(GS) v London Borough of Camden* [2016] EWHC 1762, paras 75–78.

M

Market oversight, see Business failure

Market shaping

Section 5 of the Care Act states that a local authority must promote the efficient and effective operation of a market in services for meeting care and support needs (and the needs of carers for support). This is so that people have a choice of providers, high quality services to choose from and sufficient information. In performing this duty, the local authority must have regard to various matters, including:

- **information**: making available information about providers

- **demand**: awareness of current and future demand

- **work, etc.**: the importance of enabling adults with needs for care and support, and carers with needs for support, to participate in work, education and training if they wish to

- **sustainability**: the importance of ensuring sustainability of the market

- **improvement**: the importance of fostering continuous improvement in the quality of services, in their efficiency and effectiveness and of encouraging innovation

- **workforce**: the importance of fostering a workforce delivering high quality services, and with relevant skills and appropriate working conditions.

MARKET SHAPING: NATURE OF DUTY. The duty is a general, target duty and likely to be difficult to enforce. Given the financial pressures on the social care market, there is a strong possibility that the section 5 duties will remain largely aspirational. Nonetheless, section 5 might feed into more specific duties that are more readily enforceable.

> **Doing nothing about the local market to remedy areas of unmet need**. A local authority had identified the need for recreational facilities for a severely disabled man (and others like him). Those facilities did not exist locally. But three years later, the local authority had still not remedied the deficiencies in the local market. This meant it was in breach of its individual and enforceable duty to meet the man's eligible needs, as set out in his care plan.[1]

Mental capacity

It is beyond the scope of this book to consider the Mental Capacity Act 2005 (MCA) in any detail, although it is of course highly relevant to social and health care decisions under the Care Act 2014 and NHS Act 2006.

MENTAL CAPACITY: KEY PRINCIPLES. When decisions are made and actions taken under the MCA, it is all important legally that the five principles in section 1 of the Act are applied, in order:

- **Assumption of capacity**. A person must be assumed to have capacity unless it is established that he lacks capacity.

- **Practicable steps**. A person is not to be treated as unable to make a decision unless all practicable steps to help him to do so have been taken without success.

- **Unwise decisions**. A person is not to be treated as unable to make a decision merely because he makes an unwise decision.

---

1   *R v Islington London Borough Council, ex p Rixon* [1997] 1 ELR 477.

- **Best interests**. An act done, or decision made, under this Act for or on behalf of a person who lacks capacity must be done, or made, in his best interests.

- **Less restriction**. Before the act is done, or the decision is made, regard must be had to whether the purpose for which it is needed can be as effectively achieved in a way that is less restrictive of the person's rights and freedom of action.

For example, to deprive somebody of their liberty without having first established a lack of mental capacity risks a serious breach of both the MCA and the Human Rights Act,[1] as does establishing a lack of relevant mental capacity but then not reaching a best interests decision according to the rules (under section 4 of the MCA) and not considering less restriction under the fifth principle in section 1.[2]

MENTAL CAPACITY: DECISION UNDER THE MCA BUT PROVISION UNDER THE CARE ACT. Local authorities make best interests decisions under the MCA, but consequent care and support arrangements are made under the Care Act 2014. This is what enables, for example, a financial charge to be made when it is decided – under the MCA – to deprive a person of their liberty.[3]

MENTAL CAPACITY: BEST INTERESTS DECISION RESTRICTED TO AVAILABLE OPTIONS UNDER OTHER LEGISLATION. A best interests decision under the MCA is generally about choosing the best of the options available in the particular context. In the case of social care or health care provision, the context is the Care Act 2014 or NHS Act 2006. Therefore, a best interests decision – even if made by the Court of Protection – cannot compel a local authority to adopt an option it is not willing to offer, meaning that any challenge to the options on offer would normally have to be made under the Care Act 2014 and sometimes the Human Rights Act 1998.[4]

---

1   *Essex County Council v RG* [2015] EWCOP 1.

2   *London Borough of Hillingdon v Neary* [2011] EWHC 1377 (COP).

3   *DM v Doncaster Metropolitan Borough Council* [2011] EWHC 3652 (Admin).

4   *In the matter of MN* (Adult) [2015] EWCA Civ 411, paras 80–81.

Available options and care home placement. The Court of Protection had to make a best interests decision about whether a woman should return from a care home to her husband of over 50 years. The local authority refused to raise her personal budget amount – sufficient for the care home costs but insufficient to meet her needs in her own home – to enable this to happen. The judge explained he was unable, under the Mental Capacity Act, to override this.[1]

Available options: hospital unit care or care at home. A man suffered serious injuries when he fell off a roof and, at the time of the court hearing, was judged to lack the relevant mental capacity. The local authority was funding his annual care in a special unit within a hospital at a cost of £156,000. He wanted to be cared for in the community: this would cost £468,000. The local authority was not prepared to offer the latter. It could therefore not be considered by the Court of Protection as a best interests option. A challenge would need to be made by way of judicial review (under the Care Act).[2]

Mental Health Act 1983
(MHA, section 117 after-care)

The MHA stands alone from the Care Act 2014 and NHS Act 2006. Therefore, section 117 of the 1983 Act, covering mental health after-care, is not part of the Care Act and not subject to its rules. Nonetheless, section 117 contains provisions relevant to social care (and health care) about the provision of after-care for certain patients who have been detained under the MHA. The duty is a joint one on local social services authorities and the NHS (clinical commissioning groups). Selected points from section 117 are as follows:

- **Duty to provide after-care services**. The duty is to provide after-care services until they are no longer required for patients detained under sections 3, 37, 45A, 48 and 49 but who have now been discharged from hospital. The duty

---

1   *Bedford Borough Council v C* [2015] EWCOP 25, para 26.

2   *A Local Authority v X* [2016] EWCOP 44, paras 15–16, 26.

is strong, requiring best or reasonable endeavours to meet the person's needs.[1] Neither a local authority nor CCG could simply plead lack of resources but could point to genuine difficulty in finding the required services and consider cost-effectiveness in terms of how the need is met. Section 117 is not a 'gateway': services are provided under it and not under other legislation such as the Care Act 2014 or NHS Act 2006.[2]

- **After-care services free of charge**. There is no allowance under section 117 for making a financial charge for services. This means that all services – residential or non-residential – must be arranged and provided free of charge. To the extent that, even if the person under section 117 has a personal injury award (which might be sufficient for or had been envisaged to cover care needs), neither the local authority nor the NHS has the power to refuse to provide services free of charge.[3] If it does refuse, it may lay itself open to a subsequent claim for repayment in restitution.[4]

- **Purpose of after-care services**. First, the services must meet a need arising from or related to the person's mental disorder. Second, they must also reduce the risk of a deterioration of the person's mental condition, thereby reducing the risk of the person requiring admission to a hospital again for treatment for mental disorder. For instance, when a person in the community and under section 117 entered a care home for reasons (unrelated to the mental health issue requiring detention), it was not maladministration to consider that the care home provision fell outside section 117 and would therefore be financially chargeable under adult social care legislation. The needs precipitating the care home admission were mobility, daily living skills and the onset of dementia.[5]

---

1   See e.g. *R(W) v Doncaster Metropolitan Borough Council* [2004] EWCA Civ 378. And *R v Ealing District Health Authority, ex p Fox* [1993] WLR 373, High Court. And *R(IH) v Secretary of State* [2003] UKHL 59, House of Lords.

2   *R(Stennett) v Manchester City Council* [2002] UKHL 34, para 10.

3   *Tinsley v Manchester City Council and South Manchester Clinical Commissioning Group* [2016] EWHC 2855 (Admin), para 38.

4   *Richards v Worcestershire County Council and South Worcestershire Clinical Commissioning Group* [2016] EWHC 1954 (Ch), paras 16, 17, 50.

5   *LGO, Dorset County Council*, 2016 (15 010 419), para 24.

- **Range of after-care services**. The Mental Health Act Code of Practice makes clear that a wide range of provision can be made under section 117.[1]

- **Ordinary accommodation**. The courts have held that section 117 after-care services are not legally capable of including ordinary or 'bare' accommodation (simply a roof over a person's head). It would need to be 'accommodation plus' (care), such as a care home or supported living accommodation.[2]

- **Stability and withdrawal of after-care services**. The defined purpose of after-care services supports previous case law that section 117 cannot be terminated simply because a person is stable in the community.[3] The reason for stability might be precisely because of the services being provided. (The incentive for local authorities to remove section 117 provision and provide instead under the Care Act is that under the latter they can make a financial charge.)

- **Reviewing section 117 services**. Section 117 services should be subject to regular review. For example, a failure to review for two years meant the woman concerned missed out on support she needed; this was maladministration.[4] In another case, it was maladministration when a woman was not reviewed for sixteen years. During this time, she had been charged transport costs for attending a day centre; this now had to be reimbursed.[5]

- **Withdrawal grounds**. The most obvious ground for withdrawal of after-care services is if the person's mental health has sufficiently improved so as not to need them.

The following are in themselves not sufficient to justify withdrawal – namely, if the patient has been discharged from the care of specialist mental health services, is deprived of their liberty under the MCA, has returned to hospital informally or under section 2 of the Act, or is no longer on a community

---

1   Department of Health *Mental Health Act 1983: Code of practice*. London: DH, 2015, para 33.4.

2   *R(Afework) v London Borough of Camden* [2013] EWHC 1637 (Admin), paras 14, 16.

3   *R v Manchester City Council, ex p Stennett* (1999) 2 CCLR 402, High Court, p.18. And *LGO, Clwyd County Council*, 1997 (97/0177, 97/0755). And Local Government Ombudsman *Investigation into a complaint against Bath and North East Somerset Council*, 2007 (06/B/16774), para 18.

4   *LGO, Darlington Borough Council*, 2016 (15 007 909), para 11.

5   *LGO, Dorset County Council*, 2016 (15 010 419), para 52.

treatment order or section 17 leave. Also, if an arbitrary period has passed, section 117 cannot then automatically be withdrawn.[1]

- **Change in care plan and withdrawal**. A change in care plan – for example, from support in a person's own home (because of a family carer's illness) to a care home placement – is not of itself a reason to withdraw section 117 services.[2]

- **Withdrawal process: involvement of person and carer**. Involvement of the patient and, where appropriate, their carer and/or advocate in the decision-making process will play an important part in the successful ending of after-care.[3] One local authority took the maladministrative decision to discharge a woman from section 117 two years after she had been forced to start to pay for services, without review and consultation at the time.[4] Another local authority tried to recoup money from a woman's estate after she had died, claiming it had discharged her from section 117 a long time before her death, even though neither she nor her carer had been consulted at the time of the purported discharge.[5]

- **Evidence of discharge from section 117**. There does need to be evidence of the discharge process, and the justification for it. But, the documents showing this (e.g. meeting notes, letter to GP) might be produced in a busy environment, and the courts would not bring to bear the same scrutiny as statutory provisions or a commercial contract.[6]

- **Unacceptable legal shortcuts**. Sometimes local authorities are driven to take extreme shortcuts. In one case, the local authority attempted to persuade a woman to waive her rights to free placement in a care home, suggesting there would be a 12-month delay if she didn't.[7]

---

1   Department of Health *Mental Health Act 1983: Code of practice*. London: TSO, 2015, paras 33.20–33.21.

2   *LGO, Poole Borough Council*, 2007 (06/B/07542), para 27.

3   Department of Health *Mental Health Act 1983: Code of practice*. London: TSO, 2015, para 33.20.

4   *LGO, Wiltshire County Council*, 1999 (98/B/0341).

5   *LGO, Leicestershire County Council*, 2001 (00/B/08307).

6   *R(Mwanza) v London Borough of Greenwich* [2010] EWHC 1462 (Admin), paras 86–87.

7   *LGO, York City Council*, 2006 (04/B/01280).

- **Responsible local authority: ordinary residence**. Section 117, as amended by the Care Act, now states that the local authority responsible for after-care services is the local authority where the person was ordinarily resident immediately before they were detained. This might or might not refer to where the person was ordinarily resident under the Care Act.

  The uncertainty is that if the reference to ordinary residence refers to the common law meaning (the *Shah* test)[1] – as opposed to the specific Care Act rules – then the Care Act 'deeming rule' would not apply. One reason for supposing that it is the common law rule is that there is no reference to the Care Act, and no particular reason to imply the words 'under the Care Act' into section 117. Another reason could be that the ordinary residence condition in section 117 applies to the NHS as well, which is not generally subject to such a deeming rule about ordinary residence.

  (If it is the Care Act meaning of ordinary residence, then if a local authority places a person in a care home in local authority B under the Care Act, the person remains ordinarily resident in local authority A. In which case, if they are then detained under the MHA, it would be local authority A that is responsible for after-care services under section 117. If correct, this would overturn previous legal case law.)[2]

- **Section 117 and Care Act: ordinary residence**. A person being provided with accommodation under section 117 is treated – under the Care Act, for other services they might need – as ordinarily resident in the local authority that has the section 117 responsibility.[3]

- **Responsible local authority: no ordinary residence**. If the person was not ordinarily resident in any local authority immediately before being detained – or this cannot be ascertained – then it is the local authority where the person 'is' resident, or to where they are discharged by the hospital.

- **Responsible NHS body**. The responsible NHS body is the clinical commissioning group (CCG) for the area in which the person was ordinarily resident before being detained. Failing that, it is the CCG for the area where they are now resident or where they are discharged to.

---

1 *R v Barnet London Borough Council, ex p Shah* (1983) 2 AC 309, House of Lords.

2 *R(JM) v London Borough of Hammersmith and Fulham* [2011] EWCA Civ 77.

3 Care Act 2014, s.39.

- **Disputes about ordinary residence**. If a dispute about section 117 responsibility is between two local authorities, then the process for disputes about ordinary residence under the Care Act – in section 40 of that Act – applies (see **Ordinary residence**).

- **Choice of accommodation**. The principle of choice of accommodation (care home, supported living or shared lives) and 'topping up' in some circumstances (for more expensive accommodation) applies to section 117. The rules are similar to those applying to the rules under the Care Act (see **Choice of accommodation**).

  However, there are two key differences. First, in the case of more expensive accommodation, it is not just a third party (such as family) who can pay the difference (a top-up) between what the local authority will pay and what the accommodation charge is. The person themselves can. Second, what the local authority should pay in the case of a top-up arrangement is determined not by the value of a person's personal budget (this doesn't apply in the case of section 117) but by the 'usual cost' that a local authority would expect to pay for the type of accommodation in question.[1]

Minor adaptations, see Home adaptations

---

1   See Mental Health Act 1983, section 117A, and SI 2014/2670. Care and Support and After-care (Choice of Accommodation) Regulations 2014.

N

National Health Service (NHS)

The NHS operates under legislation very different to the Care Act 2014. The NHS Act 2006 is large and complex and beyond the scope of this book to set out in detail.

NHS: COMPREHENSIVE HEALTH SERVICE. Under section 1 of the Act, the Secretary of State must continue the promotion of a comprehensive health service designed to secure improvement in the physical and mental health of the people of England and the prevention, diagnosis and treatment of physical and mental illness. This duty is difficult to pin down. It is general, since it is not expressed toward any individual patient, and it is about promoting a comprehensive health service, not necessarily achieving one.[1]

NHS: SERVICES FREE OF CHARGE. Section 1 of the NHS Act states that, unless otherwise legally specified, services must be free of charge. Certain charges are accordingly specified – for example, prescription items from general practitioners (listed in the Drug Tariff) and also certain outpatient appliances, such as wigs, spinal supports, abdominal supports and surgical brassieres.[2]

NHS bodies sometimes unlawfully, or with maladministration, charge people for items that should have been free.

---

1 *R(Coughlan) v North and East Devon Health Authority* [2001] Q.B. 213, para 25.

2 NHS Act 2006, ss.1, 172. And SI 2015/570. NHS (Charges for Drugs and Appliances) Regulations 2015.

Wrongly charging people with learning disabilities. A man with learning disabilities – who had NHS continuing health care status in a care home – was wrongly charged for lunches, toiletries, clothes, paint, room furnishings, holidays and incontinence pads.[1]

Orthopaedic shoes. A man was routinely charged for the repair of orthopaedic shoes – even though this would have been lawful only if he necessitated the repair by a particular act or omission.[2]

Children's chiropody appliances. Charging for a child's chiropody appliances was not within the legal rules and was therefore maladministration.[3]

NHS: NHS ENGLAND. A body called NHS England acts under a mandate from the Secretary of State for Health. The mandate sets out broad policy and priorities. NHS England is referred to in the NHS Act as the NHS Commissioning Board.[4]

NHS: CLINICAL COMMISSIONING GROUPS. Health services are commissioned at local level by clinical commissioning groups (CCGs). A CCG must arrange, under section 3 of the NHS Act, for the provision of certain services to such extent as it considers necessary to meet the reasonable requirements of the persons for whom it has responsibility. The services are:

- **hospitals**: hospital accommodation

- **medical, nursing, dental services, etc.**: other accommodation for the purpose of any service provided under this Act, medical, dental, ophthalmic, nursing and ambulance services

1   Health Service Ombudsman and Local Government Ombudsman *Investigations into complaints against Buckinghamshire County Council and against Oxfordshire & Buckinghamshire Mental Health Partnership*, 2008, paras 36–37.

2   Health Service Ombudsman *Investigation into a complaint against North Bristol NHS Trust*, 2000 (E.2041/98–99).

3   Health Service Ombudsman *Investigation into charging for chiropody appliances*, 1992 (W.226/91–92).

4   NHS Act 2006, ss.1H, 13A.

- **childbirth, etc.**: such other services or facilities for the care of pregnant women, women who are breastfeeding and young children as the group considers are appropriate as part of the health service

- **illness**: such other services or facilities for the prevention of illness, the care of persons suffering from illness and the after-care of persons who have suffered from illness as the group considers are appropriate as part of the health service

- **diagnosis and treatment**: such other services or facilities as are required for the diagnosis and treatment of illness.

The duty is vague and difficult to enforce. It is not expressed to be toward any one individual. The courts have noted the latitude involved in that the CCG has only to arrange services it considers necessary to meet reasonable requirements. For example, a lack of appropriate secure hospital accommodation in Wales, for women with a particular type of mental disorder, was not unlawful.[1] In the case of services for illness, care and after-care, the duty is qualified still further by reference to what the CCG considers appropriate as part of the health service.[2]

The courts have stated that the nature of the duty is such that the phrase 'within the resources available' should be read into section 3 – that is, implied, even though this is not stated.[3] Nonetheless, CCGs must have arrangements in place for complying with relevant recommendations by the National Institute for Clinical and Care Excellence (NICE) and at least consider funding for health treatments not covered by NICE recommendations.[4]

NHS: CLOSURE OF AND CHANGE TO SERVICES. Legal challenges are sometimes made about the adequacy of consultation in relation to closures or major changes to NHS services. Section 242 of the NHS Act 2006 requires involvement (which could mean consultation or just information provision) of service users (either directly or through representatives) in relation to

---

1   *Dyer v Welsh Ministers* [2015] EWHC 3712 (Admin), para 105.

2   *R(Coughlan) v North and East Devon Health Authority* [2001] Q.B. 213, para 24.

3   *R v Secretary of State for Social Services, ex p Hincks* [1980] 1 BMLR 93.

4   SI 2012/2996. NHS Commissioning Board and Clinical Commissioning Groups (Responsibilities and Standing Rules) Regulations 2012, rr.33–34.

plans which would, in summary, have a significant effect on local services. The extent of consultation required, or just information provision, will depend on the circumstances.

> **Too late to turn back the clock: independent treatment centre**. Even when the courts decide that an NHS body has acted unlawfully, they may not strike the decision down because of the difficulty in turning the clock back – for example, when there was no consultation about an independent sector treatment centre.[1]
>
> **Unlawful decision declared but no remedy for closure of rehabilitation beds**. The courts might hold that failure to consult, and provision of apparently disingenuous and misleading information, was unlawful but supply no remedy.[2]
>
> **Blocking community hospital disclosure until proper consultation takes place**. The courts sometimes interfere more robustly. When there was no consultation on closure of a community hospital on the grounds of supposed urgency, the judge ordered a halt until consultation had taken place.[3]
>
> **Quashing a GP contract award to a private health company**. When the NHS failed to consult publicly about awarding local general practitioner services to a private health company, the Court of Appeal intervened and quashed the decision to award the contract.[4]

NHS: RESPONSIBLE COMMISSIONER. The responsible CCG for a patient is identified by where the person is registered with a general practitioner. If the person is not so registered, then it is the CCG for the area in which the person is physically present.[5] This rule is varied in the case of NHS

---

1   *R(Fudge) v South West Strategic Health Authority* [2007] EWCA Civ 803.

2   *R(Morris) v Trafford Healthcare NHS* [2006] EWHC Admin 2334.

3   *R v North and East Devon Health Authority, ex p Pow* (1998) 39 BMLR 77.

4   *Smith v North Eastern Derbyshire Primary Care Trust and Secretary of State* [2006] EWCA Civ 1291.

5   NHS Act 2006, s.3(1A).

continuing health care: a person placed out of area remains the responsibility of the original CCG.[1]

NHS: PERSONAL HEALTH BUDGETS. Clinical commissioning groups have a duty in some circumstances to provide people with personal budgets. The rules in outline are as follows:[2]

- **Duty to arrange personal health budget.** A CCG must ensure that it is able to arrange a personal health budget to meet NHS continuing health care (CHC) needs for an adult (or continuing care for a child) when the CCG has accepted that CHC is necessary.

- **Direct payment or managed budget.** The personal health budget must be managed either in the form of giving a direct payment or managed in some other way.

- **Request.** If a request is made for a personal health budget for CHC, the CCG must grant the request unless it is not appropriate to do so in the individual's case. If the request is denied, written reasons must be given.

- **Definition of personal health budget.** The budget is an amount of money identified by the CCG 'as appropriate' for securing CHC.

NHS: DIRECT PAYMENTS. Under section 12A of the NHS Act 2006 more generally, CCGs have a power to make direct payments. Regulations spell out the detail. Some, but not all, of the rules are similar to those for direct payments under the Care Act. In summary:[3]

- **Power but no duty.** The CCG has a power but no duty to make a direct payment.

---

1   SI 2012/2996. NHS Commissioning Board and Clinical Commissioning Groups (Responsibilities and Standing Rules) Regulations 2012, schedule 1, para 3. And Department of Health *Who pays? Determining responsibility for payments to providers.* London: DH, 2013, para 60.

2   SI 2012/2996. NHS Commissioning Board and Clinical Commissioning Groups (Responsibilities and Standing Rules) Regulations 2012, rr.32A, 32B.

3   SI 2013/1617. National Health Service (Direct Payments) Regulations 2013.

- **Factors to consider**. The CCG must have regard to (a) whether it is appropriate for a person with that person's condition, (b) the impact of that condition on that person's life, and (c) whether a direct payment represents value for money.

- **Mental capacity**. A direct payment can be made to a representative or a nominee of a person who lacks capacity themselves to consent to it – subject to various rules.

- **Care plan, etc**. There must be a care plan (which must be followed and in respect of which the direct payment must be sufficient), a care coordinator and a discussion of risks.

- **Exclusions**. Direct payments cannot be used for certain services (e.g. general practitioner services) or for alcohol, tobacco or gambling.

- **Review**. Review must take place within the first three months, and then annually at a minimum.

- **Repayment and termination**. In certain circumstances, the payment can be terminated – and/or repayment demanded.

NHS: PUTTING SERVICES OUT TO TENDER. Section 75 of the Health and Social Care Act 2012, with regulations made under it, refers to patient choice and prohibits (subject to specific exceptions) CCGs from acting anti-competitively.[1] CCGs are under strong legal pressure to put services out to tender on the open market.

NHS continuing health care, see Continuing health care (CHC)

NHS England, see National Health Service (NHS)

---

1   SI 2013/500. National Health Service (Procurement, Patient Choice and Competition) (No. 2) Regulations 2013, rr.3, 5, 10.

Needs

The Care Act operates on the basis of 'need' – in the case of adults a need for care and support; in the case of carers a need for support (see **Eligibility**). Needs are distinct from wants, wishes or preferences; the latter must be taken account of but not necessarily catered for by a local authority. A need denotes more than a 'want' but is not so extreme as 'cannot survive without'.[1]

Neglect and abuse

Abuse or neglect (reasonably suspected) are at the heart of a local authority's duty to make enquiries under section 42 of the Care Act (see **Enquiries into abuse or neglect**). However, protecting people from neglect or abuse is referred to in a number of other sections of the Act relating, for instance, to well-being, cooperation, assessment and eligibility decisions (by considering well-being). The Act itself states only, curiously and selectively, that abuse includes financial abuse, and that financial abuse in turn includes:

- having money or other property stolen

- being defrauded

- being put under pressure in relation to money or other property, and

- having money or other property misused.

It is silent about neglect. Guidance is more expansive, giving illustrations, whilst urging local authorities not to limit their view of abuse and neglect:

- **Abuse**: includes physical abuse, domestic violence, sexual abuse, psychological abuse, financial or material abuse, modern slavery (encompassing slavery, human trafficking, forced labour and domestic servitude), discriminatory abuse (including forms of harassment, slurs or similar treatment because of race, gender and gender identity, age, disability, sexual orientation or religion) and organisational abuse

- **Neglect**: includes ignoring medical, emotional or physical care needs; failure to provide access to appropriate health, care and support or educational

---

1   *R(Davey) v Oxfordshire County Council* [2017] EWHC 354 (Admin), paras 49, 57.

services; and the withholding of the necessities of life, such as medication, adequate nutrition and heating

- **Self-neglect**: covers a wide range of behaviour – neglecting to care for one's personal hygiene, health or surroundings – and includes behaviour such as hoarding.[1]

It has been suggested that self-neglect includes the notion of self-harm.[2] It is not clear if this is so, since the word 'neglect' implies omission, not an act.

NEGLECT AND ABUSE: LINK TO CRIMINAL OFFENCES. Neglect and abuse under the Care Act 2014 should be distinguished from the criminal offences of wilful neglect and ill treatment. These two offences require a criminal mind (in terms of intent or recklessness), as well as a criminal standard of proof, and are to be found in three pieces of legislation – the Mental Health Act 1983, the Mental Capacity Act 2005 and the Criminal Justice and Courts Act 2015.

NEGLECT AND ABUSE: INTENTIONALITY. Guidance states that neglect might be unintentional, for example, by an informal carer trying to look after a family member, and indeed doing their best. And that although something would need to be done, the first port of call would be to assess the carer's needs and consider what support might be required. Reference to neglect could be upsetting for the carer and indeed other members of the family who might regard the label of 'safeguarding' and 'neglect' as unjustified and pejorative. The ombudsman has, however, found that the local authority is justified in treating such situations as neglect, involving safeguarding, since intentionality is not required.[3]

No recourse to public funds, see Immigration

---

1   Statutory guidance, 2016, paras 14, 17.

2   Spencer-Lane, T. *Care Act manual.* 2nd edition. London: Sweet and Maxwell, 2015, p.308.

3   *LGO, London Borough of Bromley*, 2016 (15 013 228), para 31.

Northern Ireland

Social and health care legislation in Northern Ireland differs to that in England:

- the **Health and Personal Social Services (Northern Ireland) Order 1972** covers both health services and social care services

- the **Chronically Sick and Disabled Persons (Northern Ireland) Act 1978** applies to social care for both adults and children

- the **Housing (Northern Ireland) Order 2003** includes disabled facilities grants for home adaptations

- the **Children (Northern Ireland) Order 1995** covers children's social care and child protection.

Nursing care

Section 3 of the NHS Act 2006 places a duty on clinical commissioning groups to arrange for the provision of nursing services. There are prohibitions on a local authority providing registered nursing care under the Care Act (see **Divide between social care and health care**).

O

Occupational therapy

Occupational therapy – and occupational therapists – are not mentioned in the Care Act. However, statutory guidance states that occupational therapists 'may be involved' in more complex assessments and, along with social workers, are a key profession.[1]

Ordinary residence

'Ordinary residence' is a term used under the Care Act 2014 to determine which area a person is living in, legally. It generally determines which local authority is responsible for meeting a person's needs.

ORDINARY RESIDENCE: DEFINITION AND *SHAH* TEST. Ordinary residence was defined in a legal case known as the *Shah* case. It is about a person being in a 'particular place or country which he has adopted voluntarily and for settled purposes as part of the regular order of his life for the time being, whether of long or short duration'.[2] Guidance spells out the implications of this definition:

- Ordinary residence can be acquired as soon as a person moves to an area

- If their move is voluntary and for settled purposes

---

1   Statutory guidance, 2016, paras 6.7, 6.82, 10.63.

2   *R v Barnet London Borough Council, ex p Shah* (1983) 2 AC 309, House of Lords.

- Irrespective of whether they own or have an interest in a property in another local authority area

- There is no minimum period in which a person has to be living in a particular place for them to be considered ordinarily resident there, because it depends on the nature and quality of the connection with the new place.[1]

ORDINARY RESIDENCE: PERSON LACKING CAPACITY. The *Shah* test is not obviously applicable in the case of a person lacking mental capacity to decide on a 'voluntary' basis where to live.[2] Guidance states that local authorities should apply the *Shah* test, but ignore the fact that the adult, by reason of lack of capacity, will not be living in a particular place voluntarily. This will involve considering all the facts, such as where the person is physically present, their purpose for living there, the person's connection with the area, their duration of residence there and the person's views, wishes and feelings (if ascertainable and relevant) to establish whether the purpose of the residence has a sufficient degree of continuity to be described as settled, whether of long or short duration.[3]

ORDINARY RESIDENCE: DEEMING RULE. There is a special rule about ordinary residence which applies, irrespective of mental capacity, to an adult living in certain types of accommodation. These are care homes, supported living and shared lives (defined under their respective headings in this book).

If a local authority has assessed that a person has care and support needs which can be met only in a care home, supported or a shared lives placement, then a so-called 'deeming rule' applies under section 39 of the Care Act. This rule states that the adult is to be regarded as legally ordinarily resident in the area he or she was ordinarily resident in immediately before beginning to live in the relevant accommodation (even if in a different local authority area). Or, if the adult had no ordinary residence before entering one of these three

---

1   Statutory guidance, 2016, para 19.21.

2   *R(Cornwall Council) v Secretary of State for Health* [2015] UKSC 46, para 46.

3   Statutory Guidance, 2016, para 19.32.

types of accommodation – and so had no settled residence – the responsible local authority is determined by where the person was present at the time.[1]

This rule does not explicitly state that the local authority must have then arranged (i.e. contracted for) the care home provision. (So, for example, if direct payments are being used for short-term – or maybe in the future long-term – stays in a care home, the rule would still apply, even though the contract is between the person and the home.)

ORDINARY RESIDENCE: DEEMING RULE AND SELF-FUNDING. If a self-funding resident in one area makes their own contractual arrangements with a care home in another area, then he or she becomes ordinarily resident in that other local authority area.[2] The other, the second, local authority then becomes responsible if the person's funds are subsequently depleted.[3] However, if the person had already been assessed by the first authority – as requiring to have their needs met only in a care home – then the Care Act wording might suggest that the first local authority remains responsible even if it is not arranging the accommodation. This appears to be suggested by the Department of Health, but the position seems unclear.[4]

ORDINARY RESIDENCE: THE CARE ACT AND MENTAL HEALTH ACT. If a person is being provided with accommodation, by way of after-care services under section 117 of the Mental Health Act, but needs other services under the Care Act, they are treated as ordinarily resident in the local authority which is responsible for provision under section 117.[5]

ORDINARY RESIDENCE: THE CARE ACT AND THE NATIONAL HEALTH SERVICE. A person provided with NHS accommodation is treated as

---

1   Care Act 2014, s.39.

2   *R(London Borough of Greenwich) v Secretary of State for Health* [2006] EWHC 2576, para 85.

3   Statutory guidance, 2016, para 19.54.

4   Department of Health. *Update on the final orders under the Care Act 2014*. London: DH, 2015, para 22.

5   Care Act 2014, s.39.

ordinarily resident, under the Care Act, in the area where they were ordinarily resident immediately before the NHS accommodation was provided. Alternatively, if the adult had no settled residence immediately before the NHS accommodation was provided, then their ordinary residence is the area in which they were present at that time.[1]

ORDINARY RESIDENCE: THE CARE ACT AND PRISONS. Guidance states that the same approach should be taken to prisons as to NHS accommodation. The assumption would be that, on release, the prisoner is still ordinarily resident in their original local authority. However, this presumption could be displaced – for example, by an intention to settle in another local authority area.[2]

ORDINARY RESIDENCE: PLACED OUT OF AREA AS A CHILD BUT NOW AN ADULT. If a child is placed out of area under the Children Act 1989, the question arises as to where they are ordinarily resident when they reach 18 and require a further placement but now under the Care Act. The courts have held that the original local authority retains responsibility, even if the child was out of area for many years and well settled with foster carers on the principle that local authorities should not export (thereby shedding) their responsibilities.[3]

ORDINARY RESIDENCE: DISPUTES. Regulations set out how disputes should be conducted about where somebody is ordinarily resident, including, importantly, meeting a person's needs during the dispute.[4]

- **Lead authority**. The 'lead authority' must coordinate the dispute and meet the person's needs during the dispute.

---

1   Care Act 2014, s.39.

2   Statutory guidance, 2016, para 17.48.

3   *R(Cornwall Council) v Secretary of State for Health* [2015] UKSC 46, paras 54–55.

4   SI 2014/2829. Care and Support (Disputes Between Local Authorities) Regulations 2014.

- **Identifying the lead authority**. The lead authority is the authority currently (at the time the dispute begins) meeting the person's needs. Or, if no local authority is currently meeting the needs, then it is the authority for the area where the person is currently living or present.

- **Meeting needs during the dispute**. The local authorities involved 'must not allow the existence of the dispute to prevent, delay, interrupt or otherwise adversely affect the meeting of the needs of the adult or carer to whom the dispute relates'.

- **Constructive engagement**. The local authorities involved must engage constructively with one another with a view to speedy resolution, comply without delay with requests for information by the lead authority, and keep the other authorities informed of developments.

- **Referral of dispute for determination**. If the dispute is not resolved within four months, it must be referred by the lead authority to the appropriate person (appointed by the Secretary of State).

- **Same rules for section 117 of the Mental Health Act 1983**. These dispute rules apply also to disputes relating to section 117 of the Mental Health Act.[1]

If local authorities allow the dispute to result in the person's needs not being met, the courts might penalise both.[2] It is maladministration if they fail to refer the dispute to the Secretary of State within four months, and if the lead authority fails to meet the person's eligible needs during the dispute.[3]

ORDINARY RESIDENCE: REIMBURSEMENT BETWEEN LOCAL AU-THORITIES. Section 41 of the Care Act states that if a local authority has been meeting a person's need, but it turns out that the person was ordinarily resident in another area, then the first local authority can recover the cost it has incurred from the second authority.

---

1   Mental Health Act 1983, s.117(4)(a).

2   *R v Hackney London Borough Council, ex p J* (1999) unreported, High Court.

3   *LGO, Surrey County Council*, 2016 (16 003 682), paras 35–39.

Ordinary residence for the NHS, see *National Health Service (NHS)*

Outcomes

As well as the language of well-being, the Care Act talks about outcomes.

OUTCOMES: ASSESSMENT. When assessing adults or carers, the local authority must assess outcomes the person wishes to achieve in everyday life and consider whether care and support could contribute to achieving those outcomes[1] (see **Assessment**).

OUTCOMES: ELIGIBILITY. More specifically, when determining whether a person is legally eligible for (and therefore entitled to) care and support, the local authority must consider whether the person is able to achieve specific outcomes prescribed in regulations. Inability to achieve two or more will indicate eligibility if, in addition, there is a significant impact on a person's well-being[2] (see **Eligibility**).

OUTCOMES: ACHIEVING THEM. First, in terms of people's own expressed outcomes they wish to achieve, there is no duty necessarily to ensure these are met.[3] For example, care and support plans must refer to which of the person's own expressed outcomes the provision of care and support 'could' be relevant.[4] This is not at all the same as a duty to ensure these are achieved – for example, enabling the person to attend regularly church, mosque, synagogue or local football club – or ride again their Penny Farthing bicycle.

---

1   Care Act 2014, ss.9, 10.

2   Care and Support (Eligibility Criteria) Regulations 2015.

3   *R(Davey) v Oxfordshire County Council* [2017] EWHC 354 (Admin), para 21.

4   Care Act 2014, s.25.

OUTCOMES: DISTINGUISHING NEEDS, OUTCOMES AND ASPIRATIONS.
Legally, it is therefore important to distinguish needs, outcomes and aspirations. The duty is to meet a person's eligible need. This might, up to a point, mean aiming at achieving outcomes a person wishes to achieve but not absolutely.[1] There is no duty to achieve aspirations, referred to in statutory guidance.[2] Aspirations do not feature in the legislation. As a case under the Children and Families Act 2014 – also about aspirations and outcomes – has emphasised, it is axiomatic that guidance cannot override legislation.[3]

Overseas visitors (NHS)

The rules affecting the NHS, under the NHS Act 2006 in relation to immigration and asylum, differ from those affecting local authorities under the Care Act. The rules are contained in the NHS (Overseas Visitors) Regulations 2015, supported by accompanying guidance.[4] They currently apply to hospital-based services only, and not to primary care services, such as general medical, dental or ophthalmic services.[5]

There is therefore no legal requirement that a patient proves immigration status when registering with a general practitioner. There are practical reasons why a GP practice might need to know who somebody is and where they live. But in that case, if they do request proof of identity or immigration status, they should do the same for all patients. And, in any case, GPs must provide clinically required emergency or immediately necessary treatment, irrespective of nationality or immigration status (and 14 days of further cover).[6]

---

1   *R(Davey) v Oxfordshire County Council* [2017] EWHC 354 (Admin), para 21.

2   Statutory guidance, 2016, paras 10.5, 10.31.

3   *Devon CC v OH* (SEN) [2016] UKUT 0292 (AAC), para 45.

4   Department of Health *Guidance on implementing the Overseas Visitor Hospital Charging Regulations 2015.* London: DH, 2015.

5   SI 2015/238. NHS (Overseas Visitors) Regulations 2015, r.2.

6   NHS England *Patient registration standard operating principles for primary medical care (general practice).* London: NHSE, 2015, paras 2.1, 4.

OVERSEAS VISITORS (NHS): DEFINITION. An overseas visitor means a person not ordinarily resident in the UK.[1]

OVERSEAS VISITORS (NHS): ORDINARY RESIDENCE. Guidance explains that a person is not ordinarily resident in the United Kingdom simply because they:

- have British nationality

- hold a British passport

- are registered with a GP

- have an NHS number

- own property in the UK, or

- have paid (or are currently paying) National Insurance contributions and taxes in the UK.

When assessing the ordinary residence status of a person seeking free NHS services, a relevant NHS body will need to consider whether they are living lawfully in the United Kingdom voluntarily and for settled purposes as part of the regular order of their life for the time being.

There must be an identifiable purpose for their residence here, one purpose or several, and it may be for a limited period. The purpose of living in the United Kingdom must have a sufficient degree of continuity to be properly described as 'settled'. Ordinary residence can be of long or short duration. A person can be ordinarily resident in more than one country at once. Non-EEA nationals subject to immigration control are not considered to be ordinarily resident in the UK, unless they also have the immigration status of 'indefinite leave to remain' (ILR) at the time of treatment; or, in other words, have the right to live here permanently.[2]

---

1   SI 2015/238. NHS (Overseas Visitors) Regulations 2015, r.2.

2   Department of Health *Guidance on implementing the Overseas Visitor Hospital Charging Regulations 2015*. London: DH, 2015, paras 3.5–3.10.

OVERSEAS VISITORS (NHS): SERVICES FREE OF CHARGE TO ALL. Certain services cannot be charged for, whatever a person's immigration status, and so are available on the same basis as to people ordinarily resident in the United Kingdom.

- **Accident and emergency**: accident and emergency (A&E) services provided at an NHS hospital (whether provided at an A&E department or elsewhere in the NHS hospital) but not services provided subsequently as an inpatient (even if it is emergency care) or at a follow-up outpatient appointment

- **Walk-in centres**: walk-in centres that provide primary health care services rather than A&E-type services

- **Not hospital-based services**: services not provided in an NHS hospital – or not provided by a person employed to work for, or on behalf of, an NHS hospital (so community services would only be chargeable if provided on behalf of a hospital)

- **Family planning**: family planning services, including contraceptive products and devices to prevent pregnancy, but termination of a pregnancy is not a method of contraception or family planning

- **Infectious diseases**: diagnosis and treatment of specified infectious diseases

- **Sexually transmitted infections**: diagnosis and treatment of sexually transmitted infections

- **Specific treatment**: treatment required for a physical or mental condition caused by torture, female genital mutilation, domestic violence or sexual violence, unless the overseas visitor has travelled to the UK for the purpose of seeking that treatment.[1]

OVERSEAS VISITORS (NHS): GROUPS OF PEOPLE EXEMPT FROM CHARGES. Some exemptions from charging are based on a person's status as opposed to the treatment they need.

---

1   Department of Health *Guidance on implementing the Overseas Visitor Hospital Charging Regulations 2015*. London: DH, 2015, para 1.2.

- **Refugees**: those granted asylum, humanitarian protection or temporary protection by the UK

- **Asylum seekers**: those applying for asylum, humanitarian protection or temporary protection whose claims, including appeals, have not yet been determined

- **Section 95 support**: individuals receiving support under section 95 of the Immigration and Asylum Act 1999 from the Home Office

- **Failed asylum seekers**: those receiving support under section 4(2) of the 1999 Act from the Home Office or under the Care Act 2014 from a local authority

- **Children**: who are looked after by a local authority

- **Human trafficking**: victims, and suspected victims, of human trafficking, as determined by the UK Human Trafficking Centre or the Home Office, plus their spouse/civil partner and any children under 18 provided they are lawfully present in the UK

- **Exceptional humanitarian reasons**: anyone in whose case the Secretary of State for Health determines there to be exceptional humanitarian reasons to provide a free course of treatment

- **Compulsory treatment or detention**: anyone receiving compulsory treatment under a court order or who is detained in an NHS hospital or deprived of their liberty (e.g. under the Mental Health Act 1983 or the Mental Capacity Act 2005) who is exempt from charge for all treatment provided, in accordance with the court order or for the duration of the detention

- **Detainees**: prisoners and immigration detainees

- **EU**: people with an enforceable right to health care under EU arrangements or other reciprocal health care agreements

- **Health surcharge**: non-EEA and Swiss nationals who have paid the health surcharge under section 38 of the Immigration Act 2014.[1]

---

1   Department of Health *Guidance on implementing the Overseas Visitor Hospital Charging Regulations 2015*. London: DH, 2015, para 1.2.

OVERSEAS VISITORS (NHS): IMMEDIATELY NECESSARY, URGENT OR NON-URGENT TREATMENT. If an overseas visitor should be charged, because they are not exempt from paying, then the guidance states that hospitals must distinguish between immediately necessary, urgent and non-urgent treatment and that only clinicians can make this assessment. Clinicians might first need to make initial assessments based on the patient's symptoms and other factors, and conduct investigations to make a diagnosis. These assessments and investigations will be included in any charges.[1]

OVERSEAS VISITORS (NHS): IMMEDIATELY NECESSARY TREATMENT. Guidance states:

- **Saving life, etc.** Immediately necessary treatment is what a patient needs to save their life; or to prevent a condition from becoming immediately life-threatening; or promptly, to prevent permanent serious damage from occurring.

- **Immediate provision.** Hospitals must always provide treatment classed as immediately necessary by the treating clinician, irrespective of whether the patient has been informed of, or agreed to pay, charges. It must not be delayed or withheld to establish the patient's chargeable status or seek payment. It must be provided even when the patient has indicated that they cannot afford to pay.

- **Maternity services.** Due to the severe health risks associated with conditions such as eclampsia and pre-eclampsia, and to protect the lives of both mother and unborn baby, all maternity services, including routine antenatal treatment, must be treated as being immediately necessary. No woman must ever be denied, or have delayed, maternity services due to charging issues.[2]

OVERSEAS VISITORS (NHS): URGENT TREATMENT. Guidance states:

1　Department of Health *Guidance on implementing the Overseas Visitor Hospital Charging Regulations 2015*. London: DH, 2015, para 8.4.

2　Department of Health *Guidance on implementing the Overseas Visitor Hospital Charging Regulations 2015*. London: DH, 2015, paras 8.4–8.6.

- **Not immediately necessary**. Urgent treatment is that which clinicians do not consider immediately necessary, but which nevertheless cannot wait until the person can be reasonably expected to return home.

- **Trying to secure payment before, but not delaying, treatment**. For urgent treatment, hospitals are strongly advised to make every effort, taking account of the individual's circumstances, to secure payment in the time before treatment is scheduled. However, if that proves unsuccessful, the treatment should not be delayed or withheld for the purposes of securing payment.[1]

OVERSEAS VISITORS (NHS): NON-URGENT TREATMENT. Guidance states:

- **Routine elective treatment: advance payment**. Non-urgent treatment is routine elective treatment that could wait until the patient can return home. Relevant NHS bodies do not have to provide non-urgent treatment if the patient does not pay in advance and should not do so until the estimated full cost of treatment has been received.

- **Estimated return date**. In determining if treatment should proceed even if payment is not obtained in advance, or if it can safely wait until the patient can return home (i.e. it is urgent or non-urgent), clinicians will need to know the patient's estimated return date.[2]

The courts have in the past approved this sort of approach – that is, providing sufficient treatment based on urgency but then demanding payment in advance for any further treatment, and otherwise suggesting the person should return to their country of origin for further treatment.[3]

---

1   Department of Health *Guidance on implementing the Overseas Visitor Hospital Charging Regulations 2015*. London: DH, 2015, paras 8.7–8.8.

2   Department of Health *Guidance on implementing the Overseas Visitor Hospital Charging Regulations 2015*. London: DH, 2015, paras 8.10–8.11.

3   *R v Hammersmith Hospitals NHS Trust, ex p Reffell* (2000) Lloyd's Rep Med 350, Court of Appeal, para 35.

Panels

Many local authorities use panels of managers or other senior staff to approve recommendations for care and support packages.

PANELS: ROLE. Guidance states that panels should not be used purely for financial purposes, to micro-manage or to amend care planning decisions. Panel members should be appropriately skilled and trained and consider larger (rather than smaller, everyday) proposed plans, as an appropriate governance mechanism. Timeliness and avoidance of bureaucracy should be kept in mind.[1] The following are examples of decisions involving panels, either unlawful or taken with maladministration:

- **Panel denying it is a panel but at fault all the same**. Panels sometimes deny they are panels and masquerade under other names. Their functioning, however, is to all intents often indistinguishable and a different name – for example, 'Practice Review Group' – will not save the local authority from a finding of maladministration, if its functioning – under whatever name – introduces fault into the decision-making process.[2]

- **Panel process delaying carer's services**. A carer was assessed by a voluntary organisation in April 2015 on behalf of the council, but its recommendations were not considered and ultimately approved by the panel until December. The support under consideration included

---

1   Statutory guidance, 2016, para 10.85.

2   *LGO, London Borough of Bromley*, 2016 (15 020 384), paras 23, 40.

a chair, handyperson scheme for the garden and taxi fares. The delay was maladministration.[1]

- **Panel overruling care manager on spurious ground of the person's 'resilience'.** A woman had a debilitating condition, affecting her ability to carry out daily activities. A care manager recommended that she receive a direct payment for support three times a week with showering, washing her hair and dressing afterwards. The woman explained that the impact of her condition had worsened over time and that she had more difficulty in winter months. The panel overruled the care manager on grounds of 'Care Act compliance' in terms of promoting independence and resilience; she could have advice on keeping warm.

  The ombudsman found maladministration, doubting that the panel was purely concerned with Care Act compliance. Had that been its remit, it had failed. Possibly, her needs could have been met in other ways, but only through proper care and support planning in consultation with the woman, not through a decision, in direct contravention of the care manager's recommendations, by a panel which was not involved in the assessment.[2]

- **Assessors failing to make recommendations to panel.** When professionals submit reports to panels, they should include not just evidence but also recommendations as to the care and support (or support for a carer) to be provided. The ombudsman is of the view that in the majority of cases assessors should therefore be capable of applying their own professional judgement from their personal knowledge of the family to make the necessary decisions. It is maladministration for the assessor not to do this, and for the panel then to take an uninformed decision because the assessor's recommendations are lacking.[3]

- **Twenty-two-month delay by panel.** In terms of timeliness and bureaucracy, the machinations of a panel led to a 22-month delay in

1   *LGO, London Borough of Southwark*, 2016 (15 020 031), paras 15–16.

2   *LGO, Brighton & Hove City Council*, 2016 (15 017 591), paras 11, 20.

3   *LGO, London Borough of Bromley*, 2016 (15 020 384), paras 35–38.

approval of a care plan for a man with learning disabilities. This was maladministration.[1]

- **Fourteen-month delay by panel**. When a woman applied for an increase in direct payment in March, the application waited until October to go to panel, was referred for further investigation, was reconsidered in December and finally approved in May of the following year. This length of time was maladministration.[2]

- **Seventeen-week delay by panel**. When a man was waiting for local authority funding for his care home placement, the panel's bureaucratic process meant a delay of 17 weeks, ten weeks of which were unjustifiable and maladministration.[3]

- **Unlawful overruling of a senior social worker's assessment**. A panel overruled a senior social worker, about the care of an elderly woman with dementia, without, crucially, giving reasons and instead relying on the view of a medical doctor who had never seen the woman. The Court of Appeal found both breach of community care legislation and human rights.[4]

- **Panel reducing care package contrary to assessed need**. When a chairman of a panel reduced a care package, with no record of the decision being made and contrary to the person's assessed needs, the ombudsman found maladministration.[5]

- **Panel unlawfully backtracking on decision already made**. If a panel, or a manager, backtracks on a decision – once that decision has been formally taken and communicated to the service user and family – this could be unlawful.[6]

1   *LGO, Essex County Council*, 2012 (10 013 477), para 25.

2   *LGO, London Borough of Ealing*, 2008 (07/A/08746), paras 9–21, 26.

3   *LGO, Staffordshire County Council*, 2000 (99/C/4295), para 25.

4   *R(Goldsmith) v Wandsworth London Borough Council* [2004] EWCA Civ, 1170, paras 68, 87.

5   *LGO, Thurrock Council*, 2013 (12 012 268 and 12 005 756), para 34.

6   *R v Wigan Metropolitan Borough Council, ex p Tammadge* [1998] 1 CCLR 581, High Court.

Personal budgets

A personal budget is defined in section 26 of the Care Act 2014 as a statement of:

- the cost to the local authority of meeting the needs of a person which it is required to meet or has decided to meet

- the amount which, on the basis of the financial assessment, the adult must pay towards that cost, and

- if on that basis the local authority must itself pay towards that cost, the amount which it must pay.

The Act states that care and support plans and support plans (for carers) must include the personal budget for the person.[1] Statutory guidance states that 'everyone whose needs are met by the local authority, whether those needs are eligible, or if the authority has chosen to meet other needs, must receive a personal budget as part of the care and support plan, or support plan'.[2] The personal budget is about meeting needs, not a wish list of wants, as the courts pointed out in a dispute about whether a personal budget should be finalised at £85,000 or £120,000 (or higher).[3]

PERSONAL BUDGETS: EXCLUSIONS. Regulations state that if a local authority is providing intermediate care or reablement, then the costs of that cannot be included within the personal budget – if the intermediate care or reablement is being provided without financial charge (which it must be, at least for the first six weeks) (see **Reablement**).[4]

PERSONAL BUDGETS: CARE AND SUPPORT PLANS (OR SUPPORT PLANS). Guidance states that the budget should precede the plan but should

---

1   Care Act 2014, s.25.

2   Statutory guidance, 2016, para 11.7.

3   *R(KM) v Cambridgeshire County Council* [2012] UKSC 23, para 34.

4   SI 2014/2840. Care and Support (Personal Budget: Exclusion of Costs) Regulations 2014.

only be indicative or an estimate because once the plan has been finalised, the budget may need to be adjusted.[1]

PERSONAL BUDGETS: RISK OF MARGINALISING NEEDS. The courts have in the past warned that indicative budgets need to be scrutinised before being finalised in each individual case since, at the indicative stage, they are just the 'starting point', and the local authority must never lose sight of its 'absolute duty' to meet the person's needs.[2] The legal risk is clear. Pressure on local authority finances might mean the indicative allocation carries too much sway. Some needs will still be met, but others risk being spirited away out of both the care plan and personal budget.

> **Needs compressed to fit personal budget.** Not explaining why costs of an assistance dog or swimming were not included within the personal budget was maladministration.[3]
>
> **Insufficient personal budget to meet need.** Assessing a person as needing 56 hours of care a week plus 20 hours a week for social activity but making a direct payment covering only 48 hours of assistance was also maladministration.[4]

PERSONAL BUDGETS: IDENTIFYING UNMET NEEDS. The courts have stated that if a personal budget is given as a general global sum (typically, a direct payment), it might be difficult to establish whether eligible needs are being met, whereas if the personal budget is used to provide 'services in kind' (typically by way of a managed budget), it will be easier. This means increased 'close scrutiny of the lawfulness of a general, monetary offer' will be required.[5] In other words, the vaguer the care and support plan underpinning

---

1   Statutory guidance, 2016, paras 11.3, 11.4, 11.24.

2   *R(Savva) v Royal Borough of Kensington of Chelsea* [2010] EWCA Civ 1209, para 18.

3   *LGO, Central Bedfordshire Council,* 2016 (13 014 946), paras 59–60.

4   *LGO, Royal Borough of Kingston upon Thames Council,* 2014 (11 022 473), paras 63–64.

5   *R(KM) v Cambridgeshire County Council* [2012] UKSC 23, para 36.

the direct payment, the more difficult it will be to pin down the duty that is owed.

PERSONAL BUDGETS: DIRECT PAYMENTS. If a person takes the personal budget as a direct payment, there is a risk that the amount allocated will be inadequate. This is because it will sometimes be more expensive for the person to buy the service than it would for the local authority. Guidance recognises this risk and suggests that local authorities base the personal budget amount on the cost of good quality local provision.[1] This seems to be an incoherent statement in the context of this particular problem: it would imply that the person could then afford to buy poor quality care using an amount of money with which the local authority, however, could have bought good quality care. A strange point for statutory guidance to be making.

PERSONAL BUDGETS: RESOURCE ALLOCATION SYSTEMS. Local authorities sometimes use a 'resource allocation system' (RAS) to determine the amount of a personal budget. Assessed needs are converted into points, and points into money. Guidance refers to an RAS as being complex, algorithmic based and not always suitable for people with more complex needs.[2] In any event, use of an RAS is not unlawful, as long as the indicative calculation is checked and the final amount reflects, realistically, the person's eligible needs and the duty to meet them.[3] A failure to do this – for example, resulting in a person being allocated £21.00 per day for a day centre that cost £47.00 – would be unlawful.[4]

---

1   Statutory guidance, 2016, para 11.25.

2   Statutory guidance, 2016, para 11.23.

3   *R(Savva) v Royal Borough of Kensington of Chelsea* [2010] EWCA Civ 1209, para 18. And *R(KM) v Cambridgeshire County Council* [2012] UKSC 23, paras 25–26.

4   *DM's Application* [2012] NIQB 98, para 27 (Northern Ireland).

Personal care

Under the Care Act 2014, personal care is referred to and defined only in the context of rules about choice of care home, of supported living, of shared lives accommodation and of rules about a person's ordinary residence. It is defined as follows:

- **Physical assistance**. Physical assistance given to a person in connection with:

    » eating or drinking (including the administration of parenteral nutrition)

    » toileting (including in relation to the process of menstruation)

    » washing or bathing

    » dressing

    » oral care

    » the care of skin, hair and nails (with the exception of nail care provided by a chiropodist or podiatrist), or

- **Prompting**. The prompting, together with supervision, of a person in relation to the performance of any of the above activities, where that person is unable to make a decision for themselves in relation to performing the activity without such prompting or supervision.[1]

Powers of entry

The Care Act 2014 contains no legal power of entry to a person's home. At one point, the Care Bill in its passage through Parliament did in fact contain such a power. As a last resort, a local authority would have been able to gain a court order. This would have granted the local authority power of entry to talk to and to assess the person about whom safeguarding concerns had arisen.[2] This part of the Bill was eventually discarded. This means that the position in England now differs from that in both Scotland and Wales, where

---

1   SI 2014/2828. Care and Support (Ordinary Residence) (Specified Accommodation) Regulations 2014. And SI 2014/2670. Care and Support and After-care (Choice of Accommodation) Regulations 2014.

2   Care Bill. *Hansard*, 10 March 2014, column 47.

just such a power of entry exists.[1] In England, therefore, a legal power to enter has to be sought under other legislation – and therefore, by definition – for purposes other than Care Act purposes.[2]

Prevention

Section 2 of the Act imposes a general duty on the local authority in relation to prevention, delay and reduction of need. It must provide or arrange services, facilities and resources, or take other steps, which it thinks will:

- contribute towards preventing or delaying the development by adults in its area of needs for care and support

- contribute towards preventing or delaying the development by carers in its area of needs for support

- reduce the needs for care and support of adults in its area

- reduce the needs for support of carers in its area.

PREVENTION: IDENTIFYING OTHER AVAILABLE SERVICES. It is not just about the local authority doing all the providing or arranging. Section 2 goes on to say that, in performing the prevention duty, the local authority must have regard to the importance of identifying services, facilities and resources already available – and to what extent the local authority could involve or make use of them in performing its duty. Sometimes such options are referred to as 'universal services' – that is, services in the community with relatively open access, for local people to use. They represent an enticing option for local authorities desperate to contain expenditure.

PREVENTION: IDENTIFYING ADULTS AND CARERS. Section 2 states also that local authorities must have regard to the importance of identifying

---

1 Social Services and Well-Being (Wales) Act 2014, s.127. And Adult Support and Protection (Scotland) Act 2007, s.37.

2 See e.g. Social Care Institute for Excellence *Gaining access to an adult suspected to be at risk of neglect or abuse: A guide for social workers and their managers in England.* London: SCIE, pp.8–15.

adults and carers in the area whose needs are not being met (either by the local authority or anybody else).

PREVENTION: SERVICES. The Act does not define or specify preventative services – or services to reduce or delay need. However, regulations prohibit financial charging for equipment, minor adaptations and reablement, which implies that the Department of Health regards these as important, preventative services. Statutory guidance reinforces this by referring at some length to these three forms of provision.[1] Statutory guidance makes clear that the ambit of section 2 is wide and could cover, for example, befriending schemes, handyman services, falls prevention classes, short-term provision of wheelchairs and telecare services.[2]

PREVENTION: ENFORCEABILITY OF PROVISION. Section 2 is a duty but a general one only, owed to 'adults in the authority's area' but not to any one individual person. It is almost certainly unenforceable by an individual, as long as the local authority is doing something in the area by way of prevention at least for some people – and has not, as it were, 'stopped production' of section 2 activity altogether.[3] In terms of identifying other local services, etc., the duty is vaguer still – referring only to the importance of having regard to such identification.

PREVENTION: AND ELIGIBILITY. Legislation stipulates that assessment must consider whether the person would benefit from preventative services. Guidance states that, during assessment, consideration should be given to whether the person would benefit from anything in the community, by way of preventative services or information and advice, under sections 2 and 4 of the Act.

Slightly confusingly, guidance seems to entertain two options – either access to such services precluding a finding of eligibility, or access to such

---

1   Statutory guidance, 2016, para 2.9.

2   Statutory guidance, 2016, para 2.7.

3   *Meade v Haringey London Borough Council* [1979] 1 WLR 637 (on enforcement of target duties).

services being a way of meeting eligible needs.[1] One middle way suggested by statutory guidance is for the local authority to pause an assessment, for the person to access preventative services for a period, and only then conclude the assessment and make a final determination of eligibility.[2] Either way, it may mean no financial cost to the local authority. But if the preventative or 'universal' service is to be used to meet an eligible need, then the local authority must beware of wishful thinking.

Reliability of universal service. A local authority decided that a local voluntary organisation could meet some of a person's eligible needs – even though there was no evidence that the organisation could reliably supply volunteers. This was maladministration.[3]

Offering universal services to a carer. With the implementation of the Care Act in 2015, a local authority stopped a short breaks service it had previously offered. The particular carer was belatedly assessed under the new eligibility criteria. It was decided that universal services could meet his needs, at no cost to the local authority, and that therefore he did not need a personal budget. The services were: access to emotional and cognitive support via GP and/or online; information about his health and well-being from the local authority's well-being officer; the opportunity for support to maintain and access links to the community through a voluntary organisation. The ombudsman did not find fault with this decision.[4]

PREVENTION: REFUSAL. Guidance states that a person, adult or carer, must agree to take up a preventative service. If they refuse, but still appear to have a need, then the local authority must still offer an assessment (under sections 9 and 10 of the Act).[5]

---

1 Statutory guidance, 2016, paras 2.48, 2.17.

2 Statutory guidance, 2016, para 6.62.

3 *LGO, London Borough of Southwark*, 2001 (99/A/00988).

4 *LGO, Herefordshire Council*, 2016 (15 019 035), paras 25–26, 36.

5 Statutory guidance, 2016, para 2.76.

Prevention: financial charging for services, see *Charging*

Principles in the Care Act

Section 1 of the Care Act defines well-being (see **Well-being**). It also contains eight principles, which local authorities must have regard to in particular when doing something under the Act in respect of an individual:

- **Judging well-being**: the importance of beginning with the assumption that the individual is best placed to judge their own well-being

- **Wishes, etc.**: the views, wishes, feelings and beliefs of the individual

- **Prevention**: the importance of preventing, delaying or reducing needs for care and support (or for support, by carers)

- **Individual circumstances and not making assumptions**: ensuring that decisions take account of all the individual's circumstances and are not based solely on the individual's age, appearance, other condition or behaviour, which might lead to unjustified assumptions about the individual's well-being

- **Participation**: the importance of the individual participating as fully as possible in decisions, and being given the necessary information and support to be able to do this

- **Balance**: the importance of the balance between the well-being of the individual and any friends or relatives involved in caring

- **Abuse and neglect**: the need to protect people from abuse and neglect

- **Restrictions to a minimum**: the need to ensure that restriction of the individual's rights or freedom of action is kept to the minimum necessary.

PRINCIPLES IN THE CARE ACT: IMPLICATIONS. Section 1 bites only when the local authority is performing functions under other sections of the Act. When it does, there might sometimes be tension between certain of the principles, which might pull in different directions. For instance, one of the purposes of the last principle – minimum restriction – might be to rein in disproportionately intrusive safeguarding interventions. Yet sometimes, imposing a restriction might be justifiable.

Protection from abuse or neglect as against minimum of restriction on people. A local authority wanted to replace a direct payment support provider suspected of fraud, but against the wishes of some service users. The latter challenged the decision. For the service users, the judge acknowledged the local authority's duty to have regard to the importance of beginning with the assumption that service users were best placed to judge their own well-being, and to have regard to the need to keep restriction of rights and freedom of action to a minimum. The judge held that, in the particular case, these principles were outweighed by the reference to protecting service users from abuse and neglect.[1]

Furthermore, the duty is on the local authority to have regard to this list of principles, not necessarily to follow them blindly.

Wishes, views and feelings. Having regard to a person's wishes means that those wishes may be a primary influence on the local authority's decision, but they are not overriding and do not mean that the service user has the final say.[2]

Individual circumstances. In one case this included having regard to the risk, of a revised care and support plan, of breaking up a stable team of personal assistants who had been with the service user for 17 years. However, the local authority did give consideration to this, did not believe that continuation of the existing team was absolutely essential to the meeting of the needs, did not anyway have evidence that the team would break up and was not under a duty to make judgements about future possibilities.[3]

---

1   *R(Collins) v Nottinghamshire County Council, Direct Payments Service* [2016] EWHC 996 (Admin), paras 18–20.

2   *R(Davey) v Oxfordshire County Council* [2017] EWHC 354 (Admin), paras 49, 121.

3   *R(Davey) v Oxfordshire County Council* [2017] EWHC 354 (Admin), paras 169–173.

Prisons

The Care Act, for the most part, applies to prisons, bail hostels and probation hostels.[1] In summary:

- **Prisons, bail hostels, probation hostels**. Section 76 of the Care Act states that the Act applies to prisons, bail hostels and probation hostels.

- **Responsible local authority**. The responsible local authority is the authority for the area in which the prison is situated.

- **Excluded parts of the Care Act**. Certain provisions of the Care Act do not apply. These are: choice of accommodation, direct payments, continuity of care rules, making safeguarding enquiries under section 42 of the Act, protecting people's property under section 47, safeguarding adults boards' help and protection activities under section 43, and safeguarding adults reviews under section 44. However, duties that do apply include, for example, prevention, advice, information, assessment, eligibility, care and support provision, and support provision.

- **Carer assessments**. In principle, the duty of carer assessment applies to prisons. But statutory guidance states that it is not intended, for Care Act purposes, that any prisoner or staff should take on the role of carer. Therefore, nobody would 'in general be entitled to a carer's assessment'.[2] Notwithstanding this guidance, were a prisoner in fact providing care, then he or she would arguably be entitled to an assessment and possible help.

- **Prisons: equipment and adaptations**. Apart from mental health problems in prisons,[3] an ageing prison population means also increased levels of physical disability.[4] It is no accident therefore that Department of Health guidance covers the need for equipment and adaptations in prison. Fixtures

---

1   Care Act 2014, s.76.

2   Statutory guidance, 2016, para 17.29.

3   For example, Prison Reform Trust *Too little, too late: An independent review of unmet mental health need in prison*. London: PRT, 2009. And Her Majesty's Inspector of Prisons *'No problems – old and quiet': Older prisoners in England and Wales. A thematic review by HM Chief Inspector of Prisons*. London: HMIP, 2004.

4   For example, Her Majesty's Inspectorate of Prisons *'No problems – old and quiet': Older prisoners in England and Wales. A thematic review by HM Chief Inspector of Prisons*. London: HMIP, 2004, p.vii. And Prisons and Probation Ombudsman *Learning lessons bulletin, fatal incidents investigations, issue 11: Dementia*. London: PPO, 2016, p.1.

and fittings, such as a grab rail or ramp, would usually be the prison's responsibility, whereas for specialised and movable items, such as beds and hoists, the local authority may be responsible under the Care Act.[1] Guidance from the National Offender Management Service is to similar effect.[2]

- **Prisons: leaving prison, duty to assess**. The wording of section 9 of the Care Act is such that the duty to assess if there is an appearance of need is couched in the present tense (not, as with carers, in section 10 of the Act, in relation to future needs also). In the past, the courts have interpreted such wording to mean that the local authority would not have a duty to assess in cases where release is too speculative or conditional but that the duty would apply in those release cases, analogous to a present need or at least to a narrow class of future, conditional cases.[3]

Probation hostels, see *Prisons*

Protection of property

Under section 47 of the Care Act, local authorities have a duty to take reasonable steps to protect people's movable property when they are in hospital or have been placed in accommodation (such as a care home) to meet their assessed need. Department of Health guidance makes clear that movable property can include pets, as well as personal possessions and furniture. The rules are as follows:[4]

- **Hospital admission or other accommodation**. The adult must be having their needs for care and support under sections 18 and 19 of the Act met in a way that involves the provision of accommodation or have been admitted to hospital.

1   Statutory guidance, 2016, para 17.35.

2   National Offender Management Service *Adult social care* (PSI 15/2015). London: NOMS, 2014, para 12.4.27.

3   *R(NM) v London Borough of Islington* [2012] EWHC 414 (Admin), paras 85–86.

4   Statutory guidance, 2016, para 10.88.

- **Danger to property**. It must appear to the local authority that there is a danger of loss or damage to the adult's movable property, which is within the area of the authority.

- **Adult unable to protect the property**. This danger must be because the adult is unable, permanently or temporarily, to protect or deal with the property and no suitable arrangements have been made.

- **Preventing loss or damage**. The local authority must take reasonable steps to prevent or mitigate loss of or damage to the property.

- **Entry of premises**. The local authority can at all reasonable times and on reasonable notice enter any premises in which the adult was living immediately before being provided with accommodation or admitted to hospital. It can also deal with any of the adult's movable property in any way which is reasonably necessary for preventing or mitigating loss or damage.

- **Entry with consent**. However, the local authority can only enter the premises and deal with the property if the adult has consented.

- **Lack of mental capacity**. If the adult lacks mental capacity to consent, then consent must be obtained from somebody authorised under the Mental Capacity Act 2005 to give such consent on behalf of the adult. (This would be somebody with a lasting power of attorney, deputyship or enduring power of attorney.) If there is no authorised person, then the local authority can still act in the person's best interests.

- **Valid documentation**. If the local authority decides it should enter and deal with the property, then the person doing this must – if requested – show valid documentation setting out the authorisation to do so.

- **Obstruction**. It is a criminal offence to obstruct, without reasonable excuse, the local authority from entering the premises.

- **Financial charging**. The local authority has discretion to charge reasonable expenses for any costs incurred.

Not securing property. A reclusive man in failing health was admitted to hospital. His house then appeared to be ransacked and valuable property stolen. The ombudsman found maladministration, on grounds that the local authority had failed to make an inventory, to remove valuable items and to secure the property.[1]

House clearance: communication with person. A house clearance that took place after a permanent admission to a care home was held to be maladministration. The clearance was an important and emotional issue. The woman concerned needed a sign language interpreter but was not given access to one; consequently, she was unable to specify adequately what items were to be kept.[2]

Provider failure, see *Business failure*

Public health

Following amendment to the NHS Act 2006, public health responsibilities were transferred away from the NHS to local authorities in England, each of which now has a duty to take such steps as it considers appropriate for improving the health of the people in its area.[3]

---

1   Local Government Ombudsman *Focus report: Learning the lessons from complaints about adult social care providers registered with the Care Quality Commission*. London: LGO, 2012, p.10.

2   *LGO, Coventry City Council*, 2016 (15 016 131) paras 20, 27.

3   NHS Act 2006, s.2A.

Reablement

Intermediate care, including reablement support, is defined, for the purpose of section 2 of the Care Act (prevention, etc.), as services, facilities or resources provided to an adult by a local authority under section 2(1) of the Act which:

- consist of a programme of services, facilities or resources

- are for a specified period of time, and

- have as their purpose the provision of assistance to the adult to enable the adult to maintain or regain the skills needed to live independently in their own home.[1]

The definition for the purpose of section 14 of the Act – about financial charging rules for meeting assessed need – is almost the same. However, the first line of the definition refers instead to a 'programme of care and support, or support', as opposed to 'services, facilities and resources'.[2]

REABLEMENT: LENGTH OF TIME AND CHARGING. For up to six weeks, intermediate care, including reablement, cannot be financially charged for.[3] Key points to note are:

- **Length of provision**. The rules are about financial charging only, not about how long reablement should be provided. In principle, the length of time is

---

1   SI 2014/2673. Care and Support (Preventing Needs for Care and Support) Regulations 2014.

2   SI 2014/2672. Care and Support (Charging and Assessment of Resources) Regulations 2014, r.3.

3   SI 2014/2673. Care and Support (Preventing Needs for Care and Support) Regulations 2014. And SI 2014/2672. Care and Support (Charging and Assessment of Resources) Regulations 2014, r.3.

governed by how long somebody would benefit, whether under, or in excess of, six weeks. Guidance states there should be no strict time limit.

- **Charging in excess of six weeks**. The local authority could exercise its power to charge after six weeks. Nonetheless, guidance states: 'local authorities should consider continuing to provide it free of charge beyond 6 weeks in view of the clear preventative benefits to the individual and, in many cases, the reduced risk of hospital admissions'.[1]

Discharge from hospital, reablement wrongly not considered. A woman was being discharged from hospital. She received 11 days care at home for which she was charged £300. However, she was not considered for reablement services during this period, which would have been free of charge. The local authority accepted the error and waived the charge.[2]

Reducing care on grounds of reablement input without explanation. A woman's care package was reduced – and in her view was now inadequate – on the grounds that reablement input would enable a reduction in the care package. But this was not communicated to the woman, depriving her of the opportunity to understand and agree to the change, and was maladministration.[3]

Reablement: distinguishing lack of cooperation from inability to benefit from it. Local authorities understandably look to reablement as a way of reducing a person's care needs, but when assessing a person's ongoing care needs, must be careful to distinguish between a person's inability to cooperate with a reablement team and their unwillingness.[4]

Reassessment, see *Reviewing need*

Refugees, see *Immigration*

1   Statutory guidance, 2016, paras 2.60–2.63.

2   *LGO, London Borough of Bromley*, 2016 (15 010 652).

3   *LGO, London Borough of Enfield*, 2016 (15 019 717), paras 31–36.

4   *LGO, Milton Keynes Council*, 2016 (16 004 600), paras 18–19.

Refusal of assessment, see *Assessment*

Refusal of service

A person with mental capacity is clearly at liberty to refuse the offer of a service by the local authority. However, there are circumstances in which a local authority might need to consider more closely, seek to continue to engage, and make further efforts or offers, as in the following cases:

- **Refusal by a mentally ill person**: a psychiatrically ill woman refusing residential accommodation[1]

- **Refusal of accommodation by a mentally ill man at risk of suicide**: a mentally ill man refusing the offer of accommodation (which would not meet his assessed social care needs) when his refusal was not unreasonable or 'willy nilly'[2]

- **Refusal of assistance**: a man with learning disabilities and autism refusing assistance[3]

- **Refusing one type of assistance but not another**: a local authority needing to offer at least some non-residential services to a woman who had refused a care home placement, even though the former would not fully meet her needs[4]

- **Unreasonable behaviour linked to depression and ill treatment**: in the face of unreasonable or even threatening behaviour, 'the duty of the local authority is not absolute in the sense that it has a duty willy-nilly to provide such accommodation regardless of the applicant's willingness to take advantage of it'. But it would have to bear in mind whether the behaviour was linked to the depression, in turn arising from the ill treatment he had been subject to before seeking asylum.[5]

---

1 *R(Patrick) v Newham London Borough Council* (2001) 4 CCLR 48.

2 *R(Batantu) v Islington London Borough Council* (2001) 4 CCLR 445, High Court.

3 *LGO, Sheffield City Council*, 2004 (02/C/08690).

4 *R(Khana) v Southwark London Borough Council* [2001] EWCA Civ 999.

5 *R v Kensington and Chelsea RB, ex p Kujtim* (1999) 2 CCLR 340, Court of Appeal, paras 30, 35.

REFUSAL OF SERVICE: REFUSAL TO PAY A CHARGE. There is a distinction between a person refusing a service and a person refusing to pay the financial contribution or charge. If a person refuses (with mental capacity) a service, the service will generally stop, whereas refusing to pay for it does not affect directly the duty to provide the service, although the local authority may choose to pursue the debt. If this distinction is not explained to people, the local ombudsman might find maladministration.[1]

Registers

A local authority has both a duty and power to keep registers.

- **Register: sight impairment, duty**. Under section 77 of the Care Act, a local authority must keep a register of sight-impaired and severely sight-impaired adults ordinarily resident in its area. Regulations state that a person is to be treated as sight impaired, or severely sight impaired, if a consultant ophthalmologist has certified this.[2]

- **Registers: disability, power**. The local authority also has a power, but not a duty, under section 77 to keep registers of three other categories of people for the purposes of planning services and monitoring levels of need. These are: disabled people; people with a physical or mental impairment but who are not disabled; and any other group of people who do, or who might at some point, have care and support needs.

Regulatory Reform (Housing Assistance) (England and Wales) Order 2002 (RRO)

The RRO gives local housing authorities a power to provide housing assistance to people. The assistance can include acquiring living accommodation but also adapting or improving it. Assistance may be provided in any form; it may be unconditional or subject to conditions, including repayment of, or contribution to, the assistance. The housing authority could take security,

---

1   *LGO, Durham County Council*, 2000 (99/C/1983).

2   SI 2014/2854. Care and Support (Sight-impaired and Severely Sight-impaired Adults) Regulations 2014.

including a charge over the property. Housing authorities must, under the Order, have a local, published policy, explaining what assistance is on offer. Local authorities have wide discretion. However, guidance points out that blanket policies – precluding consideration in individual cases of certain types of assistance (even if not in the local policy) – would risk unlawfully fettering the local authority's discretion.[1]

RRO: HOME ADAPTATIONS. The RRO could be used to assist with the following, for example:

- choice of means-tested mandatory disabled facilities grant (DFG) or the option of a non-means-tested loan

- relocation (if, for instance, the existing dwelling was in a severe state of disrepair making adaptation unsuitable)

- small-scale adaptations to avoid the complexity of a DFG

- topping up a DFG where the disabled person cannot afford a contribution or some of the works needed are not within the mandatory DFG purposes

- a safe play area for a child

- a 'complete solution' for the disabled person's needs.[2]

Rehabilitation

Rehabilitation is mentioned once in the Care Act 2014 (in the context of the NHS and hospital discharge rules) and once in the NHS Act 2006 (as part of the definition of a hospital). In neither Act is it defined. The term is often used to refer to services provided by NHS physiotherapists, occupational therapists, and speech and language therapists. As such, it is provided under

---

1 Office of the Deputy Prime Minister Circular ODPM 5/2003. *Housing renewal.* London: ODPM, 2003, para 4.5.

2 Department of Transport, Local Government and the Regions *Private sector housing renewal: A consultation paper,* 2001, para 9.7. And Department of Transport, Local Government and the Regions *Regulatory Reform (Housing Assistance) (England and Wales) Order 2002: Explanatory document,* 2001, pp.11, 27–29.

section 3 of the NHS Act 2006. It can be distinguished from the terms 'intermediate care' and 'reablement', which are given a specific legal meaning in relation to social care under the Care Act 2014 (see **Reablement**).

Remedies, see *Challenging decisions*

Removing people from their homes

A previous and controversial power under section 47 of the National Assistance Act 1948 to remove people from their own homes to care homes was repealed by, and is not replicated in, the Care Act 2014.[1]

Replacement care, see *Respite care*

Resources

Limited resources mean that local authorities inevitably explore the legal implications of restricting expenditure. In short, once a local authority has identified eligible needs under the Care Act, it has a duty to ensure that those needs are met (unless a carer is able and willing to meet them). This will normally involve expenditure. A local authority cannot avoid non-performance of the duty by arguing a lack of resources. However, local authorities can look to the most cost-effective – or cheapest – way of meeting the need as long as that cheaper option is capable of meeting the assessed, eligible need.[2]

---

1   Care Act 2014, s.46.

2   *R(McDonald) v Royal Borough of Kensington and Chelsea* [2011] UKSC 33, para 8.

Respite care

Carers sometimes need a break from caring. For this to happen, respite or replacement care will be needed for the adult. Under the Care Act, respite care will serve the function of meeting a carer's needs, and if the carer is eligible, the local authority will have a duty to arrange it. However, the service is provided for the adult. He or she will need to consent to it, the respite care will be part of the adult's care and support plan (if he or she has one), and it is the adult who would fall to be means tested and financially charged for the service.[1]

Reviewing need

A local authority must 'keep under review generally care and support plans, and support plans'. If the adult or a carer makes a reasonable request for a review, the local authority must provide one.[2] The local authority can revise a plan following review, but if circumstances have changed it must assess – in effect reassess – before the revision.

REVIEWING NEED: FREQUENCY. Guidance states that the 'expectation' is for 12-monthly reviews at a minimum, and that a 'light touch' review should be considered six to eight weeks after a care and support plan (or support plan) has been signed off.[3] This is somewhat vague: the words 'expectation' and 'should be considered' do not equate to the word 'must'.

REVIEWING NEED: REVISING A PLAN FOR ADULT OR CARER. The local authority can revise a care and support plan. In deciding whether and how to, it must consider issues of well-being and outcomes. It must involve the adult, any carer the adult has and anybody the adult requests or, if the adult lacks capacity to make that request, then anybody appearing to the local authority to be interested in their welfare. Likewise, the local authority can

---

1   Care Act 2014, s.20. And see Statutory guidance, 2016, para 11.38.

2   Care Act 2014, s.27.

3   Statutory guidance, 2016, para 13.32.

revise a support plan for a carer. In deciding whether and how to, it must involve the carer, the adult being cared for if the carer requests this and anybody else the carer requests. For example, a failure to involve the parents, in the annual review of their son with learning disabilities, in a care home, was maladministration.[1]

REVIEWING NEED: REASSESSMENT. If circumstances have changed so as to affect a plan, the local authority must carry out an assessment to the extent it considers appropriate and then proceed to revise the plan.[2] This suggests that even smaller changes of circumstance will trigger the duty to reassess and revise but that this could be done proportionately in a 'light touch' manner.[3] Even if the person's needs have not changed, circumstances might have. Review and reassessment must therefore precede any significant change or reduction in service.[4] On the other hand, in one previous case, and rather confusingly, it was held that reduction and then removal of direct payments – and their replacement with a managed service – did not result in any substantial change to the services being received. So, the duty to reassess before this change was made was not triggered.[5]

REVIEWING NEED: REFUSAL OF REASSESSMENT. Sometimes people refuse reviews and reassessments for fear of losing their services. A reassessment is in effect an assessment, so the rules about it (and refusal) in sections 9 and 11 of the Care Act would apply. For first-time assessment – and in the absence of lack of capacity or experience (or risk) of abuse or neglect – the local authority would not be obliged to assess and, in turn, would not then have a duty to provide services.

The logic of this would apply to a review as well, meaning that, at least in some circumstances, the local authority might contemplate, carefully,

---

1   *LGO, Buckinghamshire County Council,* 2016 (15 019 423), para 16.

2   Care Act 2014, s.27.

3   Statutory guidance, 2016, para 13.7.

4   *R(McDonald) v Royal Borough of Kensington and Chelsea* [2011] UKSC 33, para 4.

5   *R(G) v North Somerset Council* [2011] EWHC 2232 (Admin), para 11.

whether to consider withdrawing services in case of refusal. However, since it would have been already providing services, care would be needed. Yet, obviously, it cannot be – in the generality of cases – that simply because a person refuses a review and/or reassessment, the local authority is obliged to continue with services in perpetuity.

REVIEWING NEED: CHANGING OR CUTTING PROVISION. A revised plan must still be capable of meeting the person's eligible needs (which may or may not have changed). Following a review, it is permissible for the local authority to explore other, and sometimes cheaper, ways of meeting the need – for example, in one case substituting incontinence pads for a night-time carer.[1] Before changing the way in which it meets needs, the local authority must take all reasonable steps to reach agreement with the person.[2] However, such a change to the plan would need to reflect changed eligible needs, or at least another way of meeting them, or both. Absent both of these, and the decision might be held to be unlawful if the decision appears to be purely financially led.[3] As guidance points out, reviews must not be used arbitrarily to reduce a care and support package.[4]

In summary, review, reassessment, clear reasons and a revised care and support plan are basic requirements, before care and support are reduced.[5] The duty is not to reach agreement but to make a substantial effort to do so. For example, drawing out an assessment over six months, in order fully to engage, hold meetings and exchange views, was evidence of such effort.[6] Up to a point, the cooperation of the person will also be relevant to the local authority's ability to discharge this duty.

---

1   *R(McDonald) v Royal Borough of Kensington and Chelsea* [2011] UKSC 33.

2   Care Act 2014, s.27.

3   *R v Birmingham City Council, ex parte Killigrew* [1999] EWHC Admin 611, paras 34, 54. And *R v Staffordshire County Council, ex parte Farley* [1997] 7 CL 572, High Court.

4   Statutory guidance, 2016, para 13.33.

5   e.g. *OH v London Borough of Bexley* [2015] EWHC 1843 (Admin), paras 59–60.

6   *R(Davey) v Oxfordshire County Council* [2017] EWHC 354 (Admin), paras 158–162.

Cutting other services on review, without explanation, because of increase manual handling needs. Recognising the need for manual handling to be carried out by two carers (and thus at greater expense) cannot justify a revised care and support plan omitting the meeting of other needs (such as housework and gardening) – without explaining how those other needs were going to be met.[1]

Unjustified forced change of care provider under Care Act review, leading to risk of neglect. A woman had multiple sclerosis affecting her from the neck down, and very high level of care needs. She received satisfactory care at home for a number of years. Her care package was made up of a 60-minute morning call and a 30-minute evening call daily; two days at a day centre; a 24-hour live-in carer and five additional hours care to cover breaks for the live-in carer. With the Care Act approaching, in late 2014, a local authority panel refused to pay a fee increase requested by her current care provider. It said she would have to change provider. By April 2015, the local authority conceded there was a safeguarding issue because she was at risk of neglect by the new care provider; this was maladministration, because the care provider was acting on behalf of the local authority.

The authority claimed the personal budget amount, which it had refused to increase, was based on 'detailed projected costs for such services based on the local market'. But the local authority could not provide the ombudsman with details setting out the woman's needs against costs based on the local market. Furthermore, the local authority could not provide the ombudsman with a copy of the care and support plan for April 2015, nor explain its deficiencies or how it had acted to remedy these. This was further maladministration.[2]

Unjustifiable care cut on review despite deteriorating health needs. A woman's care and support personal budget was cut on review, under the Care Act, from 24 to 20 hours per week, although the reassessment had recommended an increase to 38 hours. Evidence of her deteriorating health, from both medical professionals and a charity, was submitted to the local authority. The local authority could not show the basis for the

---

1   *LGO, Essex County Council*, 2016 (14 016 856), para 70.

2   *LGO, London Borough of Bexley*, 2016 (15 020 770), paras 7–13.

reduction, something it needed to do, given its duty to meet eligible needs; this was maladministration.[1]

Review, reduced personal budget, but ignoring transport needs. A man's needs were reviewed under the Care Act. The assessment concluded that his needs were the same as previously, but his personal budget was reduced by £4000. This equated to the cost of the transport he arranged to attend a day centre five days a week (in order that his needs be met). Without the transport element, he could not attend and his needs would be unmet, so the transport was part of the assessed need. The ombudsman found maladministration.[2]

Review and reduction of personal budget without explanation. A man was assessed for help in April 2015, under the Care Act. He was described as elderly, diabetic, with osteoporosis and poor mobility. In November 2015, a review determined that this personal budget should reduce by nearly ten hours a week. As a result, he complained that he had had five falls and could no longer walk with confidence. His son had now to stay overnight three or four times a week. He was effectively housebound and struggled to manage the stairs in his home and to use the bathroom. He no longer cooked as he was worried about falling. He also needed help to get in and out of the bath. He sent a letter from his GP. This said a reduction in hours of care would be detrimental to his health.

The local authority stood by its decision: the local ombudsman found maladministration, on the ground that it was not clear either how the man's needs had reduced, or how those needs could be met with the reduced care and support package.[3]

Reduction of care justified, following reassessment and lack of information and cooperation. A woman had a diagnosis of bipolar disorder, had not had a manic episode for many years, but suffered from low mood. At the beginning of 2015, she was diagnosed with cancer and underwent a major operation. She also had diabetes and recently changed from tablets to insulin injections. Her main carer was her son. A social worker did a reassessment. The care package was reduced from 49 to 21 hours.

---

1   *LGO, Norfolk County Council*, 2016 (15 016 495), paras 7–18.

2   *LGO, London Borough of Barking & Dagenham*, 2016 (16 000 679), paras 9–12.

3   *LGO, Royal Borough of Greenwich*, 2016 (16 002 988), paras 13–16, 27.

The assessment – 'as comprehensive as possible' – had considered the relevant outcomes under the Care Act, including managing and maintaining nutrition, being appropriately clothed and personal hygiene. But the woman and her son would not discuss her care with local authority staff and, as a result, they could not gain information, do a proper assessment or make observations. The local authority had also offered access to occupational health, an out-of-hours emergency service and reablement carers, all of which were declined. The reduction was therefore justified and there was no maladministration.[1]

Drastic reduction of care, justified, following lack of cooperation. A woman with a variety of medical conditions refused to allow the local authority access to the necessary information, including her GP. On the basis of a therefore limited assessment, the local authority drastically reduced the amount of help it was prepared to provide. The ombudsman found no fault.[2]

REVIEWING NEED: WHO SHOULD DO IT? Guidance states that local authorities should consider authorising others to do the review – for example, the person themselves, the carer, a care provider, another professional – with the local authority adopting an assurance and sign-off approach.[3] Local authorities need to be confident, with some sort of rationale for that confidence, that the method of review chosen for each person is likely to be reliable. Failure to review (at all or adequately) can result in people's needs not being met:

- **Twenty-month gap and deterioration of health**. A 20-month gap in reviewing a care home resident – during which time his health deteriorated – was maladministration, whether or not the deterioration was anyway inevitable.[4]

- **Absence of six-monthly reviews for vulnerable resident**. Not reviewing at least six-monthly a care home resident – reported as sitting in

1   LGO, *Blackpool Borough Council*, 2016 (16 000 560), paras 33–35.

2   LGO, *Lincolnshire County Council*, 2016 (15 015 348).

3   Statutory guidance, 2016, para 13.3.

4   LGO, *London Borough of Bromley*, 2011 (08 019 214), para 48.

urine-soaked clothing, needing assistance with feeding (she lost over four stone in weight) and receiving inappropriate medication – was maladministration.[1]

- **Making reasonable efforts to review: letters insufficient**. Writing letters to vulnerable people and offering a review if they replied, but otherwise threatening to remove or reduce services in the event of non-reply, would risk unlawfulness.[2]

- **Individual review, not a blanket decision**. Review and reassessment must be on an individual basis; a blanket decision cannot be made about the outcome and what would happen to people's services.[3]

- **Balanced approach to reviews and saving money**. A general reviewing process, designed to save money, included individual reviews. It concluded that seven service users remained with the more expensive provider, but six were switched to a cheaper provider. The reviewing exercise was held to be balanced and lawful.[4]

- **Two-year gap in review: impact on carer**. The failure to review a man's care package for two years did not mean that the man's needs went unmet, but it placed a great burden on his carer (his wife) who was not offered a carer's assessment or support for her role. This was maladministration.[5]

1   *LGO, Wigan Metropolitan Borough Council*, 2001 (99/C/05493).

2   *R v Gloucestershire County Council, ex parte RADAR* [1996] COD 253, High Court.

3   *R v Gloucestershire County Council, ex parte Mahfood* (1997–98) 1 C.C.L. Rep. 7.

4   *R v Essex County Council, ex p Bucke* [1997] COD 66, High Court.

5   *LGO, Surrey County Council*, 2016 (15 009 321), paras 24–25.

S

Safeguarding

The Care Act itself talks mostly about protecting people – adults and carers – from abuse or neglect rather than about 'safeguarding' them. Protection from abuse and neglect are contained in sections of the Act dealing with well-being (and therefore part of assessment and eligibility decisions), cooperation and making enquiries into abuse and neglect (the latter not applying to carers).[1] In any event, the convenient term 'safeguarding' means protecting people from abuse and neglect – not simply protecting them from harm. Because of course whilst abuse or neglect may well result in harm, it is self-evidently not the case that all harm is caused or linked to abuse or neglect (see **Enquiries into abuse or neglect** and **Neglect and abuse**).

Safeguarding adults boards

Each local authority must establish a safeguarding adults board (SAB). The objective of a board is to 'help and protect adults in its area' – that is, adults about whom the duty to make enquiries arises under section 42 of the Act. The SAB 'must seek to achieve its objective by coordinating and ensuring the effectiveness of what each of its members does'. It can do anything 'which appears to it to be necessary or desirable for the purpose of achieving its objective'. In particular, it has a duty and power to arrange safeguarding adults reviews (SARs; see below).

---

1   See e.g. Care Act 2014, ss.1, 6, 7, 42.

SAFEGUARDING ADULTS BOARDS: CHALLENGES TO. The local ombudsman has expressed the view that a SAB is, under the Care Act, in effect an administrative function of the local authority,[1] meaning that a complaint about a SAB could be made against the local authority and investigated by the ombudsman.[2] An information tribunal effectively took the same view, holding – in the particular circumstances – that information relating to a serious case review conducted by the SAB was effectively held by the local authority in its own right (not just on behalf of the SAB). The SAB is not listed as a legal body covered by the Freedom of Information Act (FOIA), but the local authority is. So the latter was amenable to the FOIA request, which was within the tribunal's jurisdiction.[3]

SAFEGUARDING ADULTS BOARDS: MEMBERSHIP. The Care Act stipulates that the three core members of a local board must be the local social services authority, the NHS clinical commissioning group and the police. The membership of a SAB may also include anybody else the local authority considers appropriate, having first consulted the core members. A chair must be a person whom the local authority considers has the required skills and experience. There is no requirement that the chair be independent. Statutory guidance states only that the local authority should consider appointing an independent chair.[4] Members of the board must have regard to guidance issued by the Department of Health.[5]

---

1 Local Government Ombudsman *Casework guidance statement: Safeguarding adults boards.* London: LGO, undated, pp.3–4.

2 *LGO, Nottinghamshire County Council,* 2016 (16 002 691). A complaint (not upheld) against a local authority about whether recommendations made by the SAB had been acted on by various agencies.

3 *McClatchey v Information Commissioner.* First-Tier Tribunal, General Regulatory Chamber (Information Rights), Ea/2014/0252, February 2016, paras 16, 29. And see McClatchey, T. 'Was action taken over Mental Health Act misuse at Winterbourne View?' *Community Care.* Accessed on 30 September 2016 at www.communitycare.co.uk/2016/09/19/action-taken-mental-health-act-misuse-winterbourne-view.

4 Care Act 2014, s.43 and schedule 2. And Statutory guidance, 2016, para 14.150.

5 Care Act 2014, schedule 2.

SAFEGUARDING ADULTS BOARDS: OBTAINING INFORMATION. If a SAB requests information from somebody, the latter must comply with the request in the following circumstances. The SAB can ask for the information to be supplied to it, the SAB, or to somebody else.

- **Relevant to a SAB's functions**. The purpose of the request must be to do with enabling or assisting the SAB to exercise its functions.

- **Relevant functions of person requested**. In addition, the request must have been made to somebody 'whose functions or activities' are such that the SAB thinks they are likely to have information that is relevant to the SAB's functions.

- **One of two further conditions must be met**.

  » Either the information that has been requested must relate to (a) the person to whom the request has been made or to a function or activity of that person, or (b) it must relate to another person 'in respect of whom' the requested person exercises a function or activity.

  » Or the information is requested from somebody 'to whom information was supplied in compliance with another request under this section' and the information requested 'is the same as, or is derived from, information so supplied'.

- **Use of the information**. Having obtained the information, the SAB – or other person to whom it has been supplied – can use the information only for enabling or assisting the SAB to exercise its functions.

The duty on the requested organisation or person to comply is blunt and, on its face, absolute. However, this duty must presumably be subject to compliance with rules about sensitive personal data under the Data Protection Act 1998 about the right to respect for private life under article 8 of the European Convention on Human Rights and about the common law of confidentiality.

Safeguarding adults reviews

A safeguarding adults board (SAB) has both a duty and power to arrange a safeguarding adults review (SAR) in certain circumstances under section 44 of the Care Act. The overall purpose of such a review is to learn lessons and apply them in the future. Each member of the SAB must cooperate in relation to a review and contribute to carrying it out.

SAFEGUARDING ADULTS REVIEWS: DUTY. The duty to carry out a SAR under section 44 of the Act arises as follows:

- **Adult in area**. It must involve an adult in its area with needs for care and support (whether or not the local authority has been meeting any of those needs).

- **Cause for concern**. There also must be 'reasonable cause for concern' about how the SAB, members of it or anybody else 'with relevant functions' worked together to safeguard the adult.

- **Death resulting from abuse or neglect**. The adult has died and the SAB 'knows or suspects that the death resulted from abuse or neglect'. It is irrelevant whether, before the adult died, the SAB knew about, or suspected, the abuse or neglect.

- **Serious abuse or neglect but not death**. The adult is still alive and the SAB 'knows or suspects that the adult has experienced serious abuse or neglect'.

- **Purpose of review**. Members of the SAB must cooperate in, and contribute to, the review for the purpose of identifying lessons and applying them in the future.

- **Speed**. Guidance states that reviews should be completed within a reasonable period of time and, in any event, within six months.[1]

- **Publication**. Guidance states that in the interests of transparency and learning lessons, reports should be published within the parameters of confidentiality.[2]

Several points, and questions, arise from these rules.

- **Eligibility and ordinary residence not required**. The adult need not have eligible needs, nor be ordinarily resident in the local authority's area. Any needs for care and support, and simply being in the area, are sufficient.

---

1   Statutory guidance, 2016, para 14.173.

2   Statutory guidance, 2016, para 14.179.

- **Concern about working together**. Abuse or neglect alone is not enough to trigger the duty because there must be reasonable cause for concern about how members of the safeguarding adults board – or other relevant organisations – worked together to safeguard the adult. Were they to argue that they had worked well together, and that the abuse or neglect was unavoidable, there would be no duty to conduct a review.

  Under similar, though not identical, rules in children's legislation,[1] the courts have ruled that alleged abuse or neglect – in terms of actions or inactions – by a local authority itself would not legally trigger a review unless the child had been directly in the care of the local authority.[2] Were a similar approach to be adopted in relation to adults, it would mean that local authorities would, at least to some extent, be protected from reviews into their own actions or omissions, which arguably might have been abusive or neglectful, unless the SAB decided anyway to exercise its power, rather than duty, to conduct a review (see below).

- **Death and causation**. In case of death, the abuse or neglect does not have to be 'serious' (although of course it could be). However, there must be reasonable cause to suspect that the abuse or neglect caused the death. If it is clear from the outset that it did not cause death, the duty would not be triggered, no matter how serious the abuse or neglect.

- **Still living**. For an adult still alive, the duty is triggered by 'serious' abuse or neglect only, which raises the logical question as to the distinction between serious and 'non-serious' abuse or neglect.

  Guidance states that abuse or neglect is serious if the person 'would have been likely to have died but for an intervention, or has suffered permanent harm or has reduced capacity or quality of life (whether because of physical or psychological effects) as a result of the abuse or neglect'.[3]

SAFEGUARDING ADULTS REVIEWS: POWER. The SAB has a power, but no duty, to arrange a review in any other case involving an adult in its area with needs for care and support (whether or not the local authority has been

---

1   SI 2006/90. Local Safeguarding Children Boards Regulations 2006, r.5.

2   *R(Mohammed) v Local Safeguarding Children's Board for Islington (London Borough of Islington)* [2014] EWHC 3966 (Admin), paras 43–46.

3   Statutory guidance, 2016, para 14.163.

meeting any of those needs).[1] This power could therefore be exercised, for example, in a case involving abuse or neglect which does not fall within the circumstances triggering the duty to arrange a review.

Scotland

Social and health care legislation in Scotland differs to that in England. In summary, equivalent legislation is:

- **Social Work (Scotland) Act 1968** (adult social care)

- **Chronically Sick and Disabled Persons (Scotland) Act 1972** (applying the Chronically Sick and Disabled Persons Act 1970 to social care for both adults and children)

- **Children (Scotland) Act 1995** (children's social care)

- **NHS (Scotland) Act 1978** (health care)

- **Housing (Scotland) Act 2006** (housing grants).

Self-assessment, see Assessment

Self-neglect, see Neglect and abuse

Services

There is no formal list of services for meeting needs set out in the Care Act. Instead, a few general examples are given in section 8 of the Act as to ways in which the care and support needs of adults and carers can be met (see **Care and support (or support)**).

---

1   Care Act 2014, s.43.

Shared lives accommodation

Shared lives accommodation is defined under the Care Act for two different purposes: the rules about ordinary residence and the rules about choosing, and sometimes paying extra for (or 'topping up'), accommodation. Shared lives scheme accommodation means accommodation which is provided for an adult by a shared lives carer. Such a carer is an individual who provides personal care for adults – and, where necessary, accommodation in the carer's home, all under the terms of an agreement between the carer and the local authority.[1]

Social work

Social work is mentioned in section 8 as one of the ways in which an adult's or carer's needs could be met under the Act. Statutory guidance states that social workers 'may be involved' in more complex assessments, and along with occupational therapists are a key profession. It also states that mental capacity assessments should be carried out by a social worker or other suitably qualified professional.[2]

Statutory guidance, see Guidance

Support

Support is the term used throughout the Care Act to refer to the help that a carer might need, in contrast with the term 'care and support' which refers to what an adult in need might require (see **Care and support (or support)**).

---

1   SI 2014/2828. Care and Support (Ordinary Residence) (Specified Accommodation) Regulations 2014. And SI 2014/2670. Care and Support and After-care (Choice of Accommodation) Regulations 2014.

2   Statutory guidance, 2016, paras 6.7, 6.82, 10.63.

Supported living

Supported living accommodation is defined under the Care Act for two different purposes: the rules about ordinary residence and the rules about choosing, and sometimes paying extra for (or 'topping up'), the accommodation. (Application of the definition may prove problematic in some circumstances.) The definition for both purposes is the same, except in one respect. The italicised words are included as part of the definition in relation to choice of accommodation but not for the purpose of ordinary residence.[1] It is either:

- **Designed or adapted premises**. This is accommodation in premises which are specifically designed or adapted for occupation by adults with needs for care and support to enable them to live as independently as possible. *However, this does not include adapted premises in which the adult was living prior to the adaptations being made.*

Or:

- **Intention for use of premises, with personal care available**. It is accommodation which is provided (i) in premises which are intended for occupation by adults with needs for care and support (whether or not the premises are specifically designed or adapted for that purpose); and (ii) in circumstances in which personal care is available if required. The personal care may be provided by somebody other than the provider of the accommodation.

Supported living is also defined similarly (without the italicised part of the definition) for the purpose of deferred payments but with an additional two conditions – first, that the person is not entitled to sell the property, and second that he or she is not a licensee or tenant.[2]

---

1   SI 2014/2828. Care and Support (Ordinary Residence) (Specified Accommodation) Regulations 2014. And SI 2014/2670. Care and Support and After-care (Choice of Accommodation) Regulations 2014.

2   SI 2014/2671. Care and Support (Deferred Payment) Regulations 2014, r.3.

U

United Nations Convention on the Rights of Persons with Disabilities (UNCRPD)

The courts have held that the UNCRPD, as far as domestic law is concerned, has no direct application in the United Kingdom. However, there would be a presumption that domestic legislation, passed after the Convention was ratified (2009), would be consistent with it. Thus, the UNCRPD could be used to interpret a provision of legislation such as the Care Act, in case of ambiguity or uncertainty, but not otherwise.[1]

Universal services, see *Prevention*

Urgent need

Under section 19 of the Care Act, a local authority has a power to meet an adult's needs for care and support if they appear to be urgent – whether or not the adult is ordinarily resident in the area – even if it has not yet carried out an assessment of need or made an eligibility decision. Urgency can include somebody who is terminally ill.

---

1   *R(Davey) v Oxfordshire County Council* [2017] EWHC 354 (Admin), para 46.

Urgent need: local authority delay. A local authority's delay in identifying a suitable placement meant that it might have to do a new assessment. However, the delay had given rise to urgency, and an interim temporary placement – ahead of any new assessment – could be made on the grounds of urgency.[1]

Urgent need: destitution. A destitute, failed asylum seeker suffering from Hepatitis B was in urgent need. The court held that the local authority had the power, under urgency provisions in section 47 of the NHS and Community Care Act 1990, to provide accommodation.[2]

Urgent need: deprivation of liberty. A local authority had made an interim care home placement for a person lacking capacity under the urgency provisions of the community care legislation. The court pointed out that the fact it was made as a matter of urgency in no way changed the legal position of deprivation of liberty and the need to comply with the Human Rights Act 1998 and Mental Capacity Act 2005.[3]

1   *R(Alloway) v London Borough of Bromley* [2004] EWHC 2108 (Admin), paras 77–81.

2   *R(AA) v London Borough of Lambeth* [2001] EWHC Admin 741, para 17.

3   *AJ v A Local Authority* [2015] EWCOP 5, para 50.

Wales

Social and health care legislation in Wales differs to that in England. In summary, equivalent legislation is:

- **Social Services and Well-Being (Wales) Act 2014** (adult and children's social care)

- **NHS (Wales) Act 2006** (health care)

- (The **Housing Grants, Construction and Regeneration Act 1996** applies to both England and Wales. However, the maximum mandatory grant, determined by regulations, is higher in Wales: £36,000 compared to £30,000 in England.)

Well-being

Section 1 of the Care Act states that whatever a local authority does under the Care Act in respect of an individual person, it has a general duty to promote the well-being of that individual. This duty is all encompassing but at the same time vague.[1] It nonetheless needs to be considered, by default, by local authorities.

First, for example, parts of the definition – such as emotional well-being and personal dignity – can be highly subjective and difficult to judge. Second, section 1 sits in relative isolation, and takes its practical hue and application from other sections of the Act. Whatever a local authority does under other sections of the Act – such as prevention, advice provision, assessment, care and support planning, safeguarding, etc. – only then does the duty to promote

---

1   *R(SG) v Haringey LBC* [2015] EWHC 2579 (Admin).

well-being kick in. Nonetheless, once it does, then it constitutes a statutory duty in its own right and a ground of challenge.[1] Third, the word 'general' tends to weaken a duty (for example, as in section 17 of the Children Act 1989).[2] And the word 'promote' is not, for example, as strong as 'achieve'.

All that said, the definition of well-being has more specific application when eligibility decisions are made under the Act. This is because the third and final eligibility question is whether there is a significant impact on the person's well-being.

WELL-BEING: DEFINITION. Well-being is defined to include nine components, and could be viewed as a 'holistic' approach:

- personal dignity
- physical and mental health and emotional well-being
- protection from abuse and neglect
- control by the individual over day-to-day life (including over the care and support provided to the adult and the way in which it is provided)
- participation in work, education, training or recreation
- social and economic well-being
- domestic, family and personal relationships
- suitability of living accommodation
- the adult's contribution to society.

WELL-BEING: WHO IS BEST PLACED TO JUDGE IT? Under section 1 of the Care Act, local authorities must have regard to the importance of beginning with the assumption that the person themselves is best placed to judge their own well-being. The rather contorted wording means that local authorities have discretion to take a different view as to a person's well-being in some cases – or to take into account countervailing considerations.

---

1   *R(Davey) v Oxfordshire County Council* [2017] EWHC 354 (Admin), para 19.

2   *R(G) v Barnet London Borough Council* [2003] UKHL 57, House of Lords.

> **Going against the person's judgement of their own well-being**. In one case, the court took account of this principle, which some service users put forward as a reason for the local authority not taking certain protective action. But the court held that the principle was outweighed by the need to protect them from abuse or neglect.[1]

Wheelchairs

The NHS Act 2006 states that clinical commissioning groups may make arrangements for the provision of vehicles, including wheelchairs, for people who appear to have a physical impairment which has a substantial and long-term adverse effect on their ability to carry out normal day-to-day activities.[2] This is a power, not a duty, and would appear, in any case, to preclude provision of wheelchairs for clearly short-term need.

In practice, local NHS wheelchair services operate criteria as to who is eligible for a wheelchair and what sort of wheelchair might be provided. A Department of Health report suggested that wheelchairs could sometimes be provided by local authorities as part of social care – for example, when the NHS would not provide, and the wheelchair would be a cost-effective way of meeting a person's assessed, eligible, social care needs.[3]

Wilful neglect and ill treatment

Wilful neglect and ill treatment are criminal offences.[4] They should be distinguished from the words 'neglect' and 'abuse' used in the Care Act.

---

1   *R(Collins) v Nottinghamshire County Council, Direct Payments Service* [2016] EWHC 996 (Admin).

2   National Health Service Act 2006, schedule 1, para 9.

3   Department of Health *Out and about: Wheelchairs as part of a whole-systems approach to independence.* London: DH, p.15.

4   They are to be found in s.127 of the Mental Act 1983, s.44 of the Mental Capacity Act 2005 and most recently in ss.20–21 of the Criminal Justice and Courts Act 2015.

Y

Young carers, see *Children*